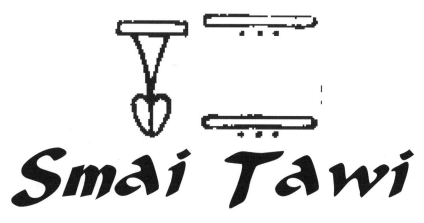

Smai Tawi

"Egyptian Yoga"
(The Philosophy of Enlightenment)

Volume 1 - 10th Edition
By
Dr. Muata Abhaya Ashby

EGYPTIAN YOGA VOLUME 1
ABOUT THE COVER:

Osiris is shown sitting, enthroned in a shrine surmounted by a winged sundisk. The winged sundisk represents Horus (Heru), the hawk, the all encompassing all pervading divinity.

Osiris, who in this teaching assumes the role of the physical manifestation of NETER (The God), represents, like Horus, *"that which is up there"*, the Supreme Divinity.

In this aspect, the green Osiris' mummified form represents neither existence nor non-existence, neither life nor death but that which lies beyond, the Life Force (green) which vivifies all things. In the realm of Osiris there is only eternal life.

Osiris holds the Flail and Crook staffs in his hands symbolizing that he holds the power of leading one to absolute reality (Shepherd's Crook), and the power to separate the mortal human body from the soul just as the winnowing whip or Flail separates the chaff from seed.

From the feet of Osiris arises the World Lotus, symbol of creation which is supporting an Egyptian female in a yoga Wheel pose with an Ankh rising out of her naval center, symbolizing that the Ankh, representing the union of opposites which leads to eternal life, rises out of the body perfected by yoga practices.

The sundisk emanating rays unto her body symbolizes the eternal spirit.

The seven rays represent the Seven Powers of creation as well as the seven energy centers (Chakras) which are fully awakened and transcended upon the attainment of the state of spiritual enlightenment.

The inscription on the columns and across the first step reads as follows: Woman and man live in bondage and duality, but through love and devotion to spirituality, the harmonious union of one's male and female aspects, raising one's spiritual life force through inner purification, climbing the pyramid of immortality by the practice of yoga, with balance, order, good judgment and wisdom, one is transformed, one gains life eternal, this is the most beautiful attainment, the transcendental vision of eternity, supreme peace, birth into Godhood, one's original, true nature. This is the ultimate union of all opposites within oneself, the state of YOGA.

The cover theme was developed and designed by Karen Asha Clarke-Ashby. It was composed by Karen and Muata. The graphics and artwork were designed by Muata.

Cover mechanical composition, Color matching, Color separations by Creative Color Copies, Miami, Fl. (305) 253-8388

☥ SEMA INSTITUTE OF YOGA ☥

Sema or Smai (☥) is the Ancient Egyptian word and symbol meaning *union* of the Higher and Lower Self which leads to spiritual enlightenment in a human being. The Sema Institute is dedicated to the propagation of the universal teachings of spiritual evolution. It is a non-denominational, non-profit organization which recognizes the unifying principles in all spiritual and religious systems of evolution throughout the world. Our primary goals are to provide the wisdom of ancient spiritual teachings in books, courses and other forms of communication. Secondly, to provide expert instruction and training in the various yogic disciplines including Ancient Egyptian Philosophy, Christian Gnosticism, Indian Philosophy and modern science. Thirdly, to promote world peace and Universal Love.

SPIRITUAL COUNSELING

The primary goal of the of the organization is to assist in the dissemination and correct understanding of the teachings of universal spirituality. The Sema Institute provides Spiritual Counseling to all those who make contact either by phone or by correspondence. In order for us to provide this service we accept donations from those who make contact the institute or who would like to contribute to this service.

SEMINARS AND WORKSHOPS IN YOUR AREA

Seminars and workshops can be arranged for a minimum of 15 people beginning at a cost of $50 per person. Call for details.

DONATIONS

Please note that the Sema Institute of Yoga is a non-profit organization recognized by the Internal Revenue Service and all contributions are tax deductible. All contributions will be used for the dissemination of the teachings of universal spirituality, world peace and spiritual enlightenment and the creation of the SEMA Institute Yoga Center. The proposed center will be a place for ongoing lectures, counseling, exercise sessions and Egyptian Yoga retreats and training of teachers.

SEMA UNIVERSITY

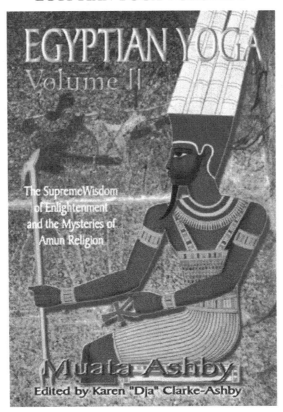

EGYPTIAN YOGA II
The Supreme Wisdom of Enlightenment

by Dr. Muata Ashby
ISBN 1-884564-01-1 8.5" X 11" $18.95 U.S.
C.M. Books 305-378-6253 P.O. Box 570457 Miami Fl. 33157

In this long awaited sequel to *Egyptian Yoga: The Philosophy of Enlightenment* you will discover the teachings which constituted the epitome of Ancient Egyptian spiritual wisdom. What are the disciplines which lead to blessedness and fulfillment of all desires? What is the supreme knowledge knowing which nothing is left unknown? The teachings of the city of Waset (Thebes) were the crowning achievement of the Sages and Saints of Ancient Egypt because they summarize and comprehensively explain the mysteries of the entire symbolism of the Ancient Egyptian pantheon of gods and goddesses that emanate from a Supreme Being who forms Creation while emerging as a Trinity. Theban Theology sheds light on the Trinity system of Christianity as well as that of Hinduism in India and establishes the standard mystical keys for understanding the profound mystical symbolism of the Triad of Human consciousness which leads to spiritual enlightenment, supreme peace and immortality.

- Discover the mystical Hymns of Amun.
- Discover the mystical wisdom of the Trinity symbol and the secret of the realms of existence and the three states of consciousness.
- Discover the mystic wisdom which leads to discovering the transcendental Self beyond all the three states.

EGYPTIAN YOGA VOLUME 1

Cruzian Mystic Books
P.O.Box 570459
Miami, Florida, 33257
(305) 378-5432 Fax: (305) 378-6253

The author is available for group lectures and individual counseling. For further information contact the publisher.

Ashby, R. Muata
Egyptian Yoga ISBN: 1-884564-01-1

Library of Congress Cataloging in Publication Data

1 Egyptian Philosophy, 2 Yoga, 3 Asia, 4 Egyptian Mythology, 5 African Philosophy, 6 Eastern Philosophy, 7 Esoterism, 8 Symbolism, 9 Egypt, 10 Meditation, 11 Self Help.

SEMA INSTITUTE OF YOGA

Check out the latest books, audio and video presentations on Egyptian Yoga and seminars, classes and courses now on the World Wide Web!

INTERNET ADDRESS:
http://www.Egyptianyoga.com

Dedication

To the Divine BA in All!

To Horus who is the soul of everything!

To the Neters who inspired this book!

To Swami Jyotirmayananda.

To the Alkebulan Study Group.

To Karen Clarke-Ashby, Editor
whose editorial management and critical analysis made this work possible.

...and to all others whose support, editorial and critical skills assisted in this project, without whose valuable help and guidance it would not have been possible: Carmen Ashby, Reginald T. Ashby, Faraha Kennerly, Esther Clarke, Ted Eason, Betty Nicholas, Galina Clarke, Gamba Arun (Rudy) Walker and Nzinga Sudha (Jozette) Walker.

"The word which appeared as a pillar of flame out of the darkness is the Son of God, born of the mystery of the Mind. The name of the Word is Reason. Reason is the offspring of Thought and Reason shall divide the light from the darkness and establish Truth in the midst of the waters."

Egyptian Proverb

"On this path, no effort is ever rendered void, nor is there a risk of negative result. Even a small measure of this righteousness protects a person from the great fear of the world process, life, death and reincarnation"

Bhagavad Gita

*"Knowing ignorance is strength.
Ignoring knowledge is sickness."*

Tao Te Ching

ABOUT THE AUTHOR

About the Author

Who is Sebai Muata Abhaya Ashby D.D. Ph. D.?

Priest, Author, lecturer, poet, philosopher, musician, publisher, counselor and spiritual preceptor and founder of the Sema Institute-Temple of Aset, Muata Ashby was born in Brooklyn, New York City, and grew up in the Caribbean. His family is from Puerto Rico and Barbados. Displaying an interest in ancient civilizations and the Humanities, Sebai Maa began studies in the area of religion and philosophy and achieved doctorates in these areas while at the same time he began to collect his research into what would later become several books on the subject of the origins of Yoga Philosophy and practice in ancient Africa (Ancient Egypt) and also the origins of Christian Mysticism in Ancient Egypt.

Sebai Maa (Muata Abhaya Ashby) holds a Doctor of Philosophy Degree in Religion, and a Doctor of Divinity Degree in Holistic Health. He is also a Pastoral Counselor and Teacher of Yoga Philosophy and Discipline. Dr. Ashby received his Doctor of Divinity Degree from and is an adjunct faculty member of the American Institute of Holistic Theology. Dr. Ashby is a certified as a PREP Relationship Counselor. Dr. Ashby has been an independent researcher and practitioner of Egyptian Yoga, Indian Yoga, Chinese Yoga, Buddhism and mystical psychology as well as Christian Mysticism. Dr. Ashby has engaged in Post Graduate research in advanced Jnana, Bhakti and Kundalini Yogas at the Yoga Research Foundation. He has extensively studied mystical religious traditions from around the world and is an accomplished lecturer, musician, artist, poet, screenwriter, playwright and author of over 25 books on Kamitan yoga and spiritual philosophy. He is an Ordained Minister and Spiritual Counselor and also the founder the Sema Institute, a non-profit organization dedicated to spreading the wisdom of Yoga and the Ancient Egyptian mystical traditions. Further, he is the spiritual leader and head priest of the Per Aset or Temple of Aset, based in Miami, Florida. Thus, as a scholar, Dr. Muata Ashby is a teacher, lecturer and researcher. However, as a spiritual leader, his title is *Sebai,* which means Spiritual Preceptor. Sebai Dr. Ashby began his research into the spiritual philosophy of Ancient Africa (Egypt) and India and noticed correlations in the culture and arts of the two countries. This was the catalyst for a successful book series on the subject called "Egyptian Yoga". Now he has created a series of musical compositions which explore this unique area of music from ancient Egypt and its connection to world music.

Who is Hemt Neter Dr. Karen Dja Clarke-Ashby?

Karen Clarke-Ashby (Seba Dja) is a Kamitan (Kamitan) priestess, and an independent researcher, practitioner and teacher of Sema (Smai) Tawi (Kamitan) and Indian Integral Yoga Systems, a Doctor of Veterinary Medicine, a Pastoral Spiritual Counselor, a Pastoral Health and Nutrition Counselor, and a Sema (Smai) Tawi Life-style Consultant." Dr. Ashby has engaged in post-graduate research in advanced Jnana, Bhakti, Karma, Raja and Kundalini Yogas at the Sema Institute of Yoga and Yoga Research Foundation, and has also worked extensively with her husband and spiritual partner, Dr. Muata Ashby, author of the Egyptian Yoga Book Series, editing many of these books, as well as studying, writing and lecturing in the area of Kamitan Yoga and Spirituality. She is a certified Tjef Neteru Sema Paut (Kamitan Yoga Exercise system) and Indian Hatha Yoga Exercise instructor, the Coordinator and Instructor for the Level 1 Teacher Certification Tjef Neteru Sema Training programs, and a teacher of health and stress management applications of the Yoga / Sema Tawi systems for modern society, based on the Kamitan and/or Indian yogic principles. Also, she is the co-author of "The Egyptian Yoga Exercise Workout Book," a contributing author for "The Kamitan Diet, Food for Body, Mind and Soul," author of the soon to be released, "Yoga Mystic Metaphors for Enlightenment."

Hotep -Peace be with you! Seba Muata Ashby & Karen Ashby

FOREWORD TO THE SECOND EDITION

Pet Ta Smai (Heaven and Earth Unite)
Pet Ta Smai (Heaven and Earth Unite)
Pet Ta Smai (Heaven and Earth Unite)
Pet Ta Smai (Heaven and Earth Unite)

So says the Kheri Heb four times...
(Hekau from the mystery teachings of
The Ausarian resurrection)

I would like to express my deepest appreciation for all who have called and written to me in reference to the teachings of Egyptian Yoga. Since its first printing in 1995 the book *Egyptian Yoga: The Philosophy of Enlightenment* has grown in popularity and it is now available all over the world and is soon to be published in Russian. Also it has spawned many other books (currently 17 titles). This explosion in writing came as a result of the many calls requesting more details and insights into the teachings presented in this volume. Thus, almost every chapter in this book as been expounded in separate volumes. Still, *Egyptian Yoga: The Philosophy of Enlightenment* remains a landmark in the study of Ancient Egyptian mystical religion and Yoga Spirituality.

Having studied "Egyptology" previously from the traditional perspective, the teachings, while intriguing, still remained as dry knowledge, unfathomable in their depths like a thought that escapes the minds understanding or a memory that defies remembrance. It is possible to know all of the facts about Ancient Egyptian Dynastic history. You certainly can visit the temples and other sites in Egypt but what can this do for you? Can the awe inspiring tours lead you to inner peace and contentment? Can the intellectual knowledge lead you to discover how to go deep into the mysteries of the soul or to discover the nature of Creation?

The great success of Egyptian Yoga is not that it has come as a new creation out of thin air but that through the application of traditional spiritual principles known as Yoga Philosophy a new light has been shed on the teachings which allows deeper comprehension of not only what the teachings mean but how to practice them. In the light of Yoga the Ancient Egyptian spiritual teachings take on an entirely new light and as the teachings are studied from the perspective of Yoga it becomes clear that Yoga Mystical Philosophy was first applied in ancient Africa and later emerged in India, and from there it developed in other parts of the world as well. This new way of looking at *Shetaut Neter* or *Smai Taui* (Egyptian Yoga - Ancient Egyptian Religion and Mystical Philosophy) allows a person to go beyond the study of Ancient Egyptian religion from the standpoint of stories and monuments reflecting primitive and pagan beliefs or fables without any rhyme or reason or reality.

With the correct understanding of the universal principles upon which all mystical spirituality is constructed Ancient Egyptian mystical religion emerges as a shining beacon of spiritual enlightenment because what emerges is the earliest known system of religion which incorporates all of the steps which allow a person to develop from spiritual ignorance to self-knowledge (mythology, ritual, and mystical experience). Ancient Egyptian mystical religion and yoga also emerges as the common source of modern day world spirituality since in ancient times (over a period of several thousands of years) these principles were taught to the emerging civilizations of the ancient world and since that time the principles have been carried on in various forms throughout history.

This is one of the great strengths of Egyptian Yoga. Its teachings are universal and its legacy can be traced to the major spiritual traditions of the present. However, when the Ancient Egyptian teachings are studied with this new perspective they shed new light upon all spiritual traditions since the Ancient Egyptian perspective reflects a unique vision of spiritual life and the mystical essence of Creation. The success of Ancient Egyptian society came from the ideal of incorporating spiritual wisdom into every aspect of life, personal, professional, business, government, education, health, etc. When this no longer became possible, Ancient Egyptian culture succumbed to the ravages of greed, egoism, ignorance and the winds of time. Does this situation sound familiar?

Can there be anything more timely than a recapturing of that which gives life true meaning and leads to peace and prosperity? We should not desire to return to ancient times but we certainly can aspire to discover the truth which leads to supreme peace, contentment, abiding happiness and spiritual enlightenment which once supported the most magnificent civilization that there is any record of in history. If the mysteries of life were discovered and used in the past should it not be possible to discover and apply them today? The truth which allowed Ancient Egyptian civilization to exist for *thousands of years* and to create a philosophy and architecture which is unsurpassed even today can be learned, experienced and applied in modern times. This is only possible because the same principles which we are looking for today are the same ones which have existed since the beginning of time and are the same ones which the Ancient Egyptian Sages and Saints discovered and wrote about. Therefore, there is no need to create new systems of philosophy which will lead to confusion and misunderstanding. However, correct understanding is the key of the spiritual principles by which the ancients lives is the key to comprehending the teachings.

> *43. Thou art Temu, who didst create beings endowed with reason; thou makest the color of the skin of one race to be different from that of another, but, however many may be the varieties of mankind, it is thou that makest them all to live.*

Verse 43 from The Ancient Egyptian Hymns of Amun

All that is necessary to achieve true understanding is the study of religion and spirituality with an open mind and with those teachers who have discovered the universality of all life and of all Creation. This is the true legacy which the great teachers of ancient Africa, Asar (Osiris), Aset (Isis), Ptahotep, Imhotep and many others have bequeathed to humanity. If you have an honest desire to understand and practice the teachings of Egyptian Yoga they will become effective in your life. What you learned previously about Ancient Egyptian mythology, religion and all which might have seemed as mysterious mystical knowledge will fall into place as you grow in knowledge and experience. Also, your previous religious training will as well come into clear view when you see that it is part of the great plan of the ancient Sages who created myths and mystical philosophy to assist human beings in discovering the ultimate objective and greatest destiny.

May you discover the philosophy which leads to harmony, peace, prosperity and spiritual enlightenment.

—Dr. Muata Abhaya Ashby 1997

FOREWORD TO THE TENTH ANNIVERSARY EDITION

Udja (Greetings),

It gives me much pleasure to present the 10th anniversary edition of this book. When it came out in 1995 it stirred much interest in the Ancient Egyptian philosophy and religion and that it has survived 10 years signifies that it is continually finding new interest. Perhaps more important is that it spawned many other books which were actually started as expansions of most of the chapters of this book. They can be seen in the back section).

There are many books on Ancient Egyptian religion and philosophy. What makes this one (and its "children") different is that it not only seeks to bring forth Ancient Egyptian religion and philosophy as an authentic teaching that strongly influenced ancient cultures but also as a living tradition; A tradition that can be adopted as a spiritual path in life, as a religion, as a system of yoga or as a philosophical discipline of life on a par with any of the great religions and philosophies of the present.

Many have sought to adopt the Kemetic teaching (Ancient Egyptian religion and philosophy) in the last 10 years. Many more have allowed it to influence their current practice of religion and yoga. There can be no better tribute to a culture than to remember its religion and philosophy and no better way to do that than to practice it and live it day to day.

In the past 10 years I have received letters from all over the world, including India, Japan, Europe and Africa, the Caribbean and So. America and Canada. Most people are amazed to discover the teachings presented and more so perhaps the relationships to other religions and even the proofs that Neterian (Ancient Egyptian) religion was instrumental in the origin and/or development of the present day world religions, extending its influence as far as China and Europe and of course Sub-Saharan Africa.

If I were asked what I would like to see for the next 10 years I would say more following and more qualitative following of the teachings. In order to have better experience of the teachings there needs to be more followers who will accept the path and take it on as their vocation and career. Then it will be possible to expose more people to the teaching and develop better financial resources to produce better venues for the practice of the teachings. Then people will discover the true glory of the Neterian teachings and how their power can be discovered today, not as a long past tradition, but as a reality that remains with us, simply dormant, waiting for the true aspirants to accept the challenge of self improvement that leads to self knowledge and personal power.

To all who have tasted of these waters in the past and all who will taste in the future I greet you in the name of the Neteru (Ancient Egyptian Gods and Goddesses). May you walk in peace, may you discover the powers within and the wisdom of the soul. May you glorify the teaching and reap the fruit of enlightenment and immortality.

Preface: Why Yoga?

Yoga Is

The purpose of this book is to introduce to the reader the idea that what has been refered to as "YOGA" was practice in Ancient Egypt (Kemet) earlier than any other place in human history. Also, I wish to convey that the Ancient Egyptian Yoga is actually a discipline that is part of the overall system of spirituality of Ancient Egypt called Shetaut Neter." Further I wish to introduce the idea that Shetaut Neter is the basis of Kemetic Yoga and the major world religions also have their basis in Shetaut Neter. So this book is a comparative religious and philosophical work that will compare the basic teachings of Ancient Egyptian religion and other religions in the hope that the reader may gain a deeper understanding of Ancient Egyptian spirituality and the source of their own religions in Ancient Africa and thereby discover the common source of religion and its deeper teachings.

The literal meaning of the word YOGA is to *"YOLK"* or to *"LINK"* back. The implication is: to link back to the original source, the original essence, that which transcends all mental and intellectual attempts at comprehension, but which is the essential nature of everything in CREATION.

The Science of Yoga constitutes the teachings required to achieve perfection which is the original essence of every human spirit. Nature herself offers one path to perfection. The path of nature, learning through mistakes and suffering, the process of trial and error, is arduous and requires many reincarnations.

Through self discipline, the path of Yoga offers a "short cut" to ending the pains of human existence and to exalt the pleasure (bliss) of existence, by achieving self-mastery and self-realization, the realization of one's true nature: GOD. The process is to become a Horus, a Christ (literally means the anointed one), an Enlightened Being, while still alive. To attain this level of being, we must first control the forces of our own lower nature. In essence, we must learn how to give up our egotistical ideas and allow them to dissolve so that we may discover our deepest self, who is nameless, bodiless, immortal and eternal.

"Short cut" here should not be taken to mean easy for indeed what we are asking is that we be trained to meet the challenge of life. Training implies: the correct knowledge in order to perform right action and develop right thinking, but we need to put forth the effort and discipline to reach the goal. As Yoga is the highest goal of our human existence, the highest goal requires the highest dedication, desire and will. Yoga training allows for the development of these qualities so that we may reach the coveted goal of becoming Sages, Saints, Horus' and Christ's.

There are many forms of Yoga. In this volume, emphasis will be placed on the Yoga of Wisdom and the Yoga of Action, known in the Indian Vedanta philosophy as Jnana Yoga and Karma Yoga, respectively. However, all paths are integral to some degree, using elements of each other as needed, thus leading to the same destination. From an advanced standpoint, any activity which allows us to move into harmony with our true selves is YOGA.

The symbols and philosophies that will be presented should be reflected upon, with respect to the symbolic nature of the universal principals presented, as they apply in one's life. No philosophical or religious system can be expected to exactly correlate with any other given system, because of the nature of individual cultures, individual expressions of the ideas and individual experiences. Therefore, accepting any myth or story as wholly factual would be immature. A disciple must seek to answer the questions of the innermost heart, however, not always expecting answers in an intellectual form. At the level of deep introspection and study of philosophical systems, one will discover that there is a common basis to all. Faith turns into intuition through study, listening, reflection and meditation.

Yoga is a science by which humankind can find its *"ROOTS."* But more importantly, Yoga Philosophy and other Ancient Mystical Philosophies are concerned with the *"HERE AND NOW,"* the raising of consciousness in the very present.

The Science of Yoga teaches us how to promote correct thinking so that we may understand who we are, why we are here, and how to obtain the highest bliss.

EGYPTIAN YOGA VOLUME 1

Happiness

Correct thinking leads to correct actions. Correct actions lead to happiness while still alive. This is the highest goal: the attainment of the heights of self mastery while still alive. In this way life is *"LIVED"* to the fullest.

Yoga Philosophy helps us to have no illusions about true happiness . It can be ours, but on the condition that we work to purify our minds as well as our bodies. When we are disillusioned by all that is temporary and transient in this world, we will search for stability. Stability or steadfastness is the most important element of happiness.

Once true happiness is found, it will never be lost. Regardless of the situation, rich or poor, scorned or famous, we will be above human frailties.

To be truly happy, we must have a stable point to hold onto permanently so we will never lose our balance. That center is within ourselves and once we know it, we can always return to it.

If through ignorance we don't know how to think about things or how to act and feel, we will become uneasy, afraid, and at the mercy of every situation that arises. Happiness is a state of consciousness, a way of understanding, thinking, feeling and behaving. It is an attitude we can learn through study and knowledge of a science which we can put into practice right here and now. If we do, we will learn how to appreciate our existence every second, every hour, and every day on earth, and beyond. *Understanding things as they really are will help us act as we should. This in turn will make us happy.*

The One Truth

From the earliest times it was known in Egypt that there is only one GOD, the ONE Truth. This is why a deep study of the many religions, mystery systems and myths around the world reveals "similarities" in philosophy and symbolism; it is due to the one common source of them all. It is our duty to inquire deeply into the nature of that truth since knowing the exact truth is the basis of our well being.

The danger of studying the past lies in the "purpose." Are we studying it for personal achievement, that is, to get a degree, to attain stature and respect, for financial gain, for power and control of others through information, to prove that we are better than someone else, or to understand and assist ourselves and others in the journey of life, the highest goal of service? Surely, truth must be our goal, as nothing else can set us free.

The aim of this work is to show and explore a deeper historical background of Yoga and to provide a simplified guide for this discipline. The author hopes that those seekers who are interested in expanding their consciousness will have further information to draw on to attain a deeper understanding of themselves through a deeper understanding of the mystical discipline called YOGA from the Egyptian perspective. The better the understanding of a given thing, the better one is able to apply and use it. It is not the intention of this author to prove that Egyptian philosophy was the basis of the Judeo-Christian Religion. This was shown long ago by researchers such as Count Volney, Gerald Massey, Charles Finch, Albert Churchward and others.

The final answers to questions as to the origin of the mysteries and mystical systems pales in comparison to the more important point: the honest inquiry of every aspirant who is devoted to know the truth for him/her self. This truth can only be known in one's own heart. This truth leads to the highest freedom: Salvation, from a life of misery and the end of the Cycle of Birth and Death.

Egyptian Yoga

Yoga means "Union".

The philosophy of YOGA as espoused by the ancient Egyptians incorporated no less than four words whose exact meanings are equal to the Indian word *"YOGA"* which means *"spiritual union"*. The four hieroglyphic symbols used on the front cover of this book represent the four words in Egyptian Philosophy which mean *"YOGA"*. They are: *"Nefer"*, *"Sema"*, *"Ankh"* and *"Hetep"*. A more detailed examination of these symbols may be found in Chapter Seven: Symbols.

The name **"Egyptian Yoga"** comes from the Ancient Egyptian terms:

Shetaut Neter meaning: "The way of the hidden Supreme Being" and

Smai Taui meaning: "The union of the two lands."

Smai means union and the following determinative terms give it a spiritual significance, at once equating it with the term "Yoga" as it is used in India..

The "two lands" refer to Upper and Lower Egypt as well as Horus and Set who represent the Higher Self and the Lower Self of every human being respectively.

Thus, we also have the Ancient Egyptian term:

Smai Heru-Set.

The Egyptian language and symbols provide the first "historical" record of Yoga Philosophy and Religious literature. The Indian culture of the Indus Valley Dravidians and Harappans appear to have carried it on and expanded much of the intellectual expositions in the form of the Vedas, Upanishads, Puranas and Tantras, the ancient spiritual texts of India.

Ancient Egyptian scriptures show that the Egyptians understood the singularity of that which is called "GOD" and further, understood the timeless, formless, space-less, sexless nature of GOD from which time, form, space, and sex (duality) come.

Thus, a nameless "Supreme Being", *"Neter Neteru"*, *"GOD of Gods"*, was referred to as *"The Hidden One"* until later times when myths were constructed for the understanding of the common people and immature souls (humans with lesser number of incarnations). *"PA NETER"*, or "THE GOD" was thought of as a FATHER-MOTHER CREATOR GOD and must not be confused with the *"Neters"* or "Gods", which represented the cosmic forces of the Universe. The Creator is viewed as both female and male until creation is created, at which time creation becomes the female (receiving) principle and GOD, the mover-vivifier, becomes the male (giving) principle. From an advanced point of view however, GOD is neither male nor female, but GOD is the source from which the Gods (Neters), humans and all creation comes. Therefore, the concept of *"NETER"*, as will be seen in the following chapters, encompasses a concept that goes beyond ordinary human - mental understanding. For the "common folk", *"NETER"* was referred to as *Nebertcher* (*Neberdjer*), or *Amon - Ra - Ptah* (Holy Trinity), and was represented by a Sundisk or a single flag.

Mythology and Philosophy

Mythology and philosophy are ways to explain that which is difficult to explain in words, that which goes beyond the ordinary reasoning faculties of the average mind. Through stories and similes which convey the meaning of deep philosophical thought, myths carry the message to the heart of the listener.

Mythology and philosophy carry rich symbolism and wisdom within but the wisdom from mythology should not be understood as a story of an event which may have occurred "a long time ago, in the beginning" but as something that relates an idea, a theme that was true in the beginning, is true now and will always be true.

The value of ancient teachings lies in the application of their truths. What can we learn and benefit from Ancient Mystical Philosophy right now? Ancient civilizations have proven by their demise that they did not have or were unable to apply all of the truth, otherwise, they would be with us today. Therefore, it is wise to study them, and to benefit from their wisdom gained through their successes and their mistakes. In this task we are sometimes required to "unlearn what we have learned" in order to grow in wisdom and consciousness.

What does ancient wisdom and history mean in our lives at this date in time and history? What can we learn from civilizations that lasted for thousands of years (Ethiopia and Egypt) whose recorded history only chronicles the decline period and only hints at the grandeur that it once was? Should we attempt to recreate this long period in human history or should we perhaps consider using the example of their deeds to build something new, original and more divine? Whichever road we choose, the scriptures, texts and ancient papyri are not enough, but they are a possible first step in understanding the mysteries of life and living.

The Veil of Ignorance

As stated in the ancient Egyptian text, *"The Book of Coming Forth by Day"*, the eternal soul comes to earth to learn certain lessons and to become purified. In the process of evolution, virtues as wel as vices are experienced by us based on our own mental disposition. Our purity of heart determines the situations and outcomes of those situations. Through repeated embodiments (reincarnation), we are lead by our own soul to experience the act of living, attempting all the time to find that Ultimate-Absolute Bliss which will eliminate all pain.

It is because of the veil of ignorance as to the true nature of the soul and of GOD that we interact with the universe as if it "really exists", as if we were interacting with an entity other than ourselves. If we knew the truth, we would become enlightened Sages and Saints, thereby achieving ultimate freedom. This point is the main theme of Egyptian Yoga and will be elaborated on throughout this volume.

When the spirit, our innermost self, is ready to make the final "journey home", back to its source, GOD, it begins to inquire about the nature of its existence and thereby causes pressure on the mind, namely the ego-personality. Our BA, our individual GOD consciousness, begins to apply subtle pressure on our waking consciousness in the form of subtle suggestions. We begin to recognize the wisdom of ancient scriptures and develop an interest in books such as this one.

Becoming in tune with the pressure of the spirit is allowing ourselves to be guided by our intuition and the letting go of ideas and thoughts which we know to be untrue or fruitless. Mental purification requires the utmost patience with ourselves. Interest in the world as an Absolute reality (the notion there is nothing else beyond "this" physical reality) is left behind gradually and new psychological impressions and experiences are introduced until we become established in this "other" reality. At this point, we wake up from the consciousness we have been used to as if waking up from a dream. This is attaining "Horushood", "Christhood", or becoming "Buddha" or "Krishna."

"That which is the Fundamental Truth, the Substantial Reality, is beyond true naming, but the Wise men call it The All."

Egyptian Proverb

There are many paths of Liberation, but they all lead to the same destination, the "ONE", the "ALL" that is within us and all other things. This world of "apparent multiplicity" with many different objects and people is really a manifestation of one true reality. Complete understanding of this most important point leads to the "Realization" of the TRUTH. This is self-mastery, cosmic consciousness, liberation, enlightenment, salvation, etc.

Dispassion and detachment are indispensable sciences to be practiced once an understanding of the teachings has begun to take root in our hearts. Neither loving nor hating, neither wanting nor not wanting. All actions should be based on and guided by MAAT (truth, justice, righteousness, balance). No longer is there an action - reaction mentality of doing something to someone because someone did something to you, etc. One is more and more able to control one's emotions and behavior. No longer will it be necessary to act as an animal or to indulge in one's ego when one is ridiculed or praised. One will live above these ignorant concepts (praise or ridicule). One will live with one's divine essence and truth. One will recognize the ignorance of others and will be strong enough to exercise compassion and understanding for them. From this position, it will be possible to do the greatest good for others. Thus, a true transformation occurs. In ancient Egyptian mythology, the scarab is the symbol of transformation, from mortal to spiritual consciousness.

This is the nurturing of baby Horus (the divine soul) by mother ISIS (life giving force, love, foundation, nourishing support) in secret hiding until he was old enough to do battle with his Uncle Set (greed, ignorance). As a baby tree is fenced off to protect it, so too we must protect ourselves during the process of spiritual growth by limiting contact with negative people or circumstances and keeping company with people of raised consciousness (enlightened Sages preferably).

The Paths of Wisdom and Action have been emphasized in this volume, however, all paths must be integrated. Although one may focus on any one yogic path, one will find that aspects of the others are always involved. The essence of the journey is a personal search.

"Salvation is accomplished through the efforts of the individual. There is no mediator between man and his/her salvation."

Egyptian Proverb

Reliance or dependency on a particular path or method is useful to a point, but ultimately, when the nurturing by ISIS is accomplished through devoting oneself to the discovery of one's true self by listening, reflection and meditation on the scriptures, one must do battle and vanquish the enemies of the innermost self: ignorance, greed, hate, passion, etc. A dynamic balance of the opposites within one's own consciousness must be sought. Ultimately, all paths are transcended.

Ancient Egypt

The oral history suggests that the Pyramids may date from the time of the Sphinx (10,000-5,500 B.C.E.) and that they were used for initiation rites into the higher Mysteries of YOGA and as repositories of ancient knowledge to promote the spiritual evolution of humans who would assist in the development of humanity. Many western archaeologists promote the idea that the pyramids were used as burial tombs although at no time in history has there been evidence to suggest that mummies were found in any of them.

History oftentimes is presented in a biased manner, reflecting attitudes and views from the perspective of the conquering group, a new empire or "new world order" who wish to establish an historical basis for their existence. Thus, most of us are unable to get a true and accurate picture of history.

Egyptian Yoga, as it was presented to the masses of the Egyptian population, involved two major areas. First, the country as a whole was seen by outside observers such as Herodotus and Plutarch unanimously as *"The most religious of all the Lands."*
It may be difficult to imagine an entire country where the doctrines of eternal life and reincarnation are accepted by all in the manner which the modern world accepts television. The psychological makeup of every individual was tuned to "The Neters" (cosmic forces both within and out of the body). An afterlife existence was an unquestionable fact, whereas modern day students need to "convince themselves" through the elaborate system of Yoga discipline presented here and elsewhere.

The next most important element of the mass spiritual education program was the compilation of a philosophical system that explained the cause and purpose of existence through stories such as The Creation Mythology, The Osirian Resurrection Myth, The Story of HORUS and SET, and *"The Book of Coming Forth By*

Day", more commonly known as "The Egyptian Book of The Dead", which contains much of the essential wisdom of virtue (MAAT).

As previously discussed, there are two basic paths to spiritual evolution: The Path of Passion (nature) and the Direct Path. The path of passion requires many incarnations, births and deaths, and many painful and happy life experiences. The direct path is the path of Yoga. Through the science of Yoga (Ancient Mysteries), one is able to accelerate one's evolution towards perfection. For those who chose the direct path, the Temples were a training center, university, hospital and refuge.

The striking symbolism of the Ethiopian-Egyptian philosophies combined with the Egyptian understanding of GOD in a culture which saw religion in "everything" constituted a formidable system of Yoga which may partially explain the longevity of Egypt, a civilization in many ways surpassing modern day society and still confounding the Egyptologists and others who try to understand Egypt through a purely intellectual approach rather than as a Student of Life and Self-Improvement.

The world is not wholly intellectual, therefore not all answers are intellectual. At some point, it is necessary to use one's "gut feelings", one's higher intuitive nature, to "feel" the truth and not be afraid to discard an old truth in favor of a new one. This is the process of growth until we **"FULLY KNOW"** Absolute truth, the never ending expansion of thought which leads to wisdom and health. Contraction in our consciousness as opposed to expansion, represents ignorance, tension, and dis-ease (mental and physical). Recent linguistic and archeological evidence is compelling but the information that comes to us from contemporary historians is inescapable.

World History In Cosmic Infinity

Modern physics has proven through the theory of relativity that time is a relative factor, a mental concept, an idea which we have created in order to help us understand the changes that seem to be occurring around us in a sequential fashion. Time is a mental idea which exists to the extent that we adhere to and believe in it. As such, the ancients speak of several "time periods", eons, etc. which have existed. The earth, being a changing, dynamic, living entity is said to have undergone and up to this day continues to undergo various changes in its surface appearance due to volcanic and other normal weather patterns. The ancient writings speak of civilizations which far surpassed that of the present day with respect to technology and human achievement. Further, it is stated that several high cultures have existed in the past in a cycle of growth which lead to their ultimate demise. One such civilization was that of Atlantis.

The Greek, Solon, visited Egypt around the year 590 B.C.E. and was instructed about the existence of a land called Atlantis where a high civilization once existed, but which was destroyed due to the inability of its inhabitants to control the powerful forces of nature which they had been able to release. There existed an imbalance between their spiritual maturity and their technological-mental advancement.

In the year 395 B.C.E., the Egyptian priests under whom Plato had studied told him that there had been many "floods" which had devastated the earth and changed its appearance, and that the greatest one had totally devastated Atlantis. Atlantians were said to be capable of levitating large stones, weighing many tons, with the use of their mental powers, the same kind of power necessary to create the Great Pyramids, the Sphinx of Egypt and the City of Machu Pichu in Peru. Therefore, many ages have seen various high cultures.

It is interesting to note that the decline of all intellectually advanced civilizations has been related to the loss of balance between intellectual-mental advancement and that of the spiritual-moral nature.

It is evident from the writings of the Egyptian high priest Manetho (280 B.C.E.), the Egyptian Calendar and the dating of the Sphinx at Giza, that *"KMT"* (Egypt) had its origins prior to 20,000 B.C.E. This date is supported by Herodotus, a famous ancient Greek historian and other Greek and Roman writers of the time.

Kamitan Terms and Ancient Greek Terms

It is important to understand that the names of the Ancient Egyptian divinities which have been used widely in Western literature and by Western scholars are actually Greek interpretations of the Kamitan (Ancient Egyptian) names. In keeping with the spirit of the culture of Kamitan spirituality, in this volume we will use the Kamitan names for the divinities through which we will bring forth the Philosophy of Neterianism (Ancient Egyptian religion and myth). Therefore, the Greek name Osiris will be converted back to the Kamitan (Ancient Egyptian) Asar (Asar), the Greek Isis to Aset (Auset), the Greek Nephthys to Nebthet, Anubis to Anpu or Apuat, Hathor to Hetheru, Thoth or Hermes to Djehuti, etc. (see the table below) Further, the term Ancient Egypt will be used interchangeably with "Kamit," or "Ta-Meri," as these were the terms used by the Ancient Egyptians to refer to their land and culture. The table below provides a listing of the corresponding names of the main Kamitan divinities.

Kamitan Names of the main Gods and Goddesses of Ancient Egypt and the Greek translation in common use.

Kamitan (Ancient Egyptian) Names	Greek Names
Amun	Zeus
Ra	Helios
Ptah	Hephastos
Nut	Rhea
Geb	Kronos
Net	Athena
Khonsu	Heracles
Set	Ares or Typhon
Bast	Artemis
Uadjit	Leto
Asar (Asar)	Osiris or Hades
Aset (Auset)	Isis or Demeter
Nebthet	Nephthys
Anpu or Apuat	Anubis
Hetheru	Hathor (Aphrodite)
Heru	Horus or Apollo
Djehuti	Thoth or Hermes
Maat	Astraea or Themis
Sekhmit	Nemesis

ABOUT THE ANCIENT ETHIOPIANS, EGYPTIANS AND INDIANS:

"When therefore, though hearest the myths of the Egyptians concerning the Gods - wanderings and dismemberings and many such passions, think none of these things spoken as they really are in state and action. For they do not call Hermes "Dog" as a proper name, but they associate the watching and waking from sleep of the animal who by Knowing and not Knowing determines friend from foe with the most Logos-like of the Gods."

Plutarch

"The Egyptians and Nubians have thick lips, broad noses, wooly hair and burnt skin...
...And the Indian tribes I have mentioned, their skins are all of the same colour, much like the Ethiopians... their country is a long way from Persia towards the south..."

Herodotus

"The riches of Egypt are for the foreigners therein."

Anonymous Arabic proverb.

"Truly at weaving wiles the Egyptians are clever."

Anonymous

The Ethiopians and Egyptians are very black."

Aristotle

"Compared with the Egyptians, the Greeks are childish mathematicians."

Plato

"And upon his return to Greece, they gathered around and asked, "tell us about this great land of the Blacks called Ethiopia." And Herodotus said, "There are two great Ethiopian nations, one in Sind (India) and the other in Egypt."

Recorded by *Diodorus* **(Greek historian 100 B.C.)**

From the Tomb of Ramses III: The four branches of mankind, according to the Egyptians: A- Egyptian as seen by himself, B- Indo-European, C- Other Afrikans, D- Semites (Middle Easterners).
Photo: From Cheikh Anta Diop's *"Civilisation ou Barbarie",* Courtesy of Présence Africaine.

INTRODUCTION TO SEMA TAWI AND SHETAUT NETER

The Fundamental Principles of Ancient Egyptian Religion

NETERIANISM
(The Oldest Known Religion in History)

The term "Neterianism" is derived from the name "Shetaut Neter." Shetaut Neter means the "Hidden Divinity." It is the ancient philosophy and mythic spiritual culture that gave rise to the Ancient Egyptian civilization. Those who follow the spiritual path of Shetaut Neter are therefore referred to as "Neterians." The fundamental principles common to all denominations of Ancient Egyptian Religion may be summed up in four "Great Truths" that are common to all the traditions of Ancient Egyptian Religion.

Summary of Ancient Egyptian Religion

Maa Ur n Shetaut Neter
"Great Truths of The Shetaut Neter Religion"

I

Pa Neter ua ua Neberdjer m Neteru
"The Neter, the Supreme Being, is One and alone and as Neberdjer, manifesting everywhere and in all things in the form of Gods and Goddesses."

II

an-Maat swy Saui Set s-Khemn
"Lack of righteousness brings fetters to the personality and these fetters cause ignorance of the Divine."

III

s-Uashu s-Nafu n saiu Set
"Devotion to the Divine leads to freedom from the fetters of Set."

IIII

ari Shedy Rekh ab m Maakheru

"The practice of the Shedy disciplines leads to knowing oneself and the Divine. This is called being True of Speech"

Neterian Great Truths

1. *"Pa Neter ua ua Neberdjer m Neteru"* -"The Neter, the Supreme Being, is One and alone and as Neberdjer, manifesting everywhere and in all things in the form of Gods and Goddesses."

Neberdjer means "all-encompassing divinity," the all-inclusive, all-embracing Spirit which pervades all and who is the ultimate essence of all. This first truth unifies all the expressions of Kamitan religion.

2. **"an-Maat swy Saui Set s-Khemn"** – **"Lack of righteousness brings fetters to the personality and these fetters lead to ignorance of the Divine."**

When a human being acts in ways that contradict the natural order of nature, negative qualities of the mind will develop within that person's personality. These are the afflictions of Set. Set is the neteru of egoism and selfishness. The afflictions of Set include: anger, hatred, greed, lust, jealousy, envy, gluttony, dishonesty, hypocrisy, etc. So to be free from the fetters of set one must be free from the afflictions of Set.

3. **"s-Uashu s-Nafu n saiu Set"** -**"Devotion to the Divine leads to freedom from the fetters of Set."**

To be liberated (Nafu - freedom - to breath) from the afflictions of Set, one must be devoted to the Divine. Being devoted to the Divine means living by Maat. Maat is a way of life that is purifying to the heart and beneficial for society as it promotes virtue and order. Living by Maat means practicing Shedy (spiritual practices and disciplines).

Uashu means devotion and the classic pose of adoring the Divine is called "Dua," standing or sitting with upraised hands facing outwards towards the image of the divinity.

4. **"ari Shedy Rekh ab m Maakheru"** - **"The practice of the Shedy disciplines leads to knowing oneself and the Divine. This is called being True of Speech."**

Doing Shedy means to study profoundly, to penetrate the mysteries (Shetaut) and discover the nature of the Divine. There have been several practices designed by the sages of Ancient Kamit to facilitate the process of self-knowledge. These are the religious (Shetaut) traditions and the Sema (Smai) Tawi (yogic) disciplines related to them that augment the spiritual practices.

All the traditions relate the teachings of the sages by means of myths related to particular gods or goddesses. It is understood that all of these neteru are related, like brothers and sisters, having all emanated from the same source, the same Supremely Divine parent, who is neither male nor female, but encompasses the totality of the two.

The Spiritual Culture and the Purpose of Life: Shetaut Neter

> "Men and women are to become God-like through a life of virtue and the cultivation of the spirit through scientific knowledge, practice and bodily discipline."

> -Ancient Egyptian Proverb

The highest forms of Joy, Peace and Contentment are obtained when the meaning of life is discovered. When the human being is in harmony with life, then it is possible to reflect and meditate upon the human condition and realize the limitations of worldly pursuits. When there is peace and harmony in life, a human being can practice any of the varied disciplines designated as Shetaut Neter to promote {his/her} evolution towards the ultimate goal of life, which Spiritual Enlightenment. Spiritual Enlightenment is the awakening of a human being to the awareness of the Transcendental essence which binds the universe and which is eternal and immutable. In this discovery is also the sobering and ecstatic realization that the human being is one with that Transcendental essence. With this realization comes great joy, peace and power to experience the fullness of life and to realize the purpose of life during the time on earth. The lotus is a symbol of Shetaut Neter, meaning the turning towards the light of truth, peace and transcendental harmony.

Shetaut Neter

We have established that the Ancient Egyptians were African peoples who lived in the north-eastern quadrant of the continent of Africa. They were descendants of the Nubians, who had themselves originated from farther south into the heart of Africa at the Great Lakes region, the sources of the Nile River. They created a vast civilization and culture earlier than any other society in known history and organized a nation that was based on the concepts of balance and order as well as spiritual enlightenment. These ancient African people called their land Kamit, and soon after developing a well-ordered society, they began to realize that the world is full of wonders, but also that life is fleeting, and that there must be something more to human existence. They developed spiritual systems that were designed to allow human beings to understand the nature of this secret being who is the essence of all Creation. They called this spiritual system "Shtaut Ntr (Shetaut Neter)."

Shetaut means secret. ***Neter*** means Divinity.

Who is Neter in Kamitan Religion?

Ntr

The symbol of Neter was described by an Ancient Kamitan priest as:
"That which is placed in the coffin"

The term Ntr, or Ntjr, comes from the Ancient Egyptian hieroglyphic language which did not record its vowels. However, the term survives in the Coptic language as *"Nutar."* The same Coptic meaning (divine force or sustaining power) applies in the present as it did in ancient times. It is a symbol composed of a wooden staff that was wrapped with strips of fabric, like a mummy. The strips alternate in color with yellow, green and blue. The mummy in Kamitan spirituality is understood to be the dead but resurrected Divinity. So the Nutar (Ntr) is actually every human being who does not really die, but goes to live on in a different form. Further, the resurrected spirit of every human being is that same Divinity. Phonetically, the term Nutar is related to other terms having the same meaning, such as the latin "Natura," the Spanish Naturalesa, the English "Nature" and "Nutriment", etc. In a real sense, as we will see, Natur means power manifesting as Neteru and the Neteru are the objects of creation, i.e. "nature."

Neter and the Neteru

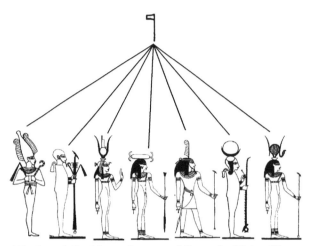

The Neteru (Gods and Goddesses) proceed from the Neter (Supreme Being)

As stated earlier, the concept of Neter and Neteru binds and ties all of the varied forms of Kamitan spirituality into one vision of the gods and goddesses all emerging from the same Supreme Being. Therefore, ultimately, Kamitan spirituality is not polytheistic, nor is it monotheistic, for it holds that the Supreme Being is more than a God or Goddess. The Supreme Being is an all-encompassing Absolute Divinity.

The Neteru

"Neteru"

The term "Neteru" means "gods and goddesses." This means that from the ultimate and transcendental Supreme Being, "Neter," come the Neteru. There are countless Neteru. So from the one come the many. These Neteru are cosmic forces that pervade the universe. They are the means by which Neter sustains Creation and manifests through it. So Neterianism is a monotheistic polytheism. The one Supreme Being expresses as many gods and goddesses. At the end of time, after their work of sustaining Creation is finished, these gods and goddesses are again absorbed back into the Supreme Being.

All of the spiritual systems of Ancient Egypt (Kamit) have one essential aspect that is common to all; they all hold that there is a Supreme Being (Neter) who manifests in a multiplicity of ways through nature, the Neteru. Like sunrays, the Neteru emanate from the Divine; they are its manifestations. So by studying the Neteru we learn about and are led to discover their source, the Neter, and with this discovery we are enlightened. The Neteru may be depicted anthropomorphically or zoomorphically in accordance with the teaching about Neter that is being conveyed through them.

Sacred Scriptures of Shetaut Neter

The following scriptures represent the foundational scriptures of Kamitan culture. They may be divided into three categories: *Mythic Scriptures*, *Mystical Philosophy* and *Ritual Scriptures*, and *Wisdom Scriptures* (Didactic Literature).

MYTHIC SCRIPTURES Literature	Mystical (Ritual) Philosophy Literature	Wisdom Texts Literature
SHETAUT ASAR-ASET-HERU The Myth of Asar, Aset and Heru (Asarian Resurrection Theology) - Predynastic **SHETAUT ATUM-RA** Anunian Theology Predynastic *Shetaut Net/Aset/Hetheru* Saitian Theology – Goddess Spirituality Predynastic **SHETAUT PTAH** Memphite Theology Predynastic *Shetaut Amun* Theban Theology Predynastic	**Coffin Texts** (C. 2040 B.C.E.-1786 B.C.E.) **Papyrus Texts** (C. 1580 B.C.E.- Roman Period)[1] Books of Coming Forth By Day Example of famous papyri: Papyrus of Any Papyrus of Hunefer Papyrus of Kenna Greenfield Papyrus, Etc.	*Wisdom Texts* (C. 3,000 B.C.E. – PTOLEMAIC PERIOD) Precepts of Ptahotep Instructions of Any Instructions of Amenemope Etc. **Maat Declarations** Literature (All Periods) Blind Harpers Songs

---

[1] After 1570 B.C.E they would evolve into a more unified text, the Egyptian Book of the Dead.

The Neteru and Their Temples

Diagram 1: The Ancient Egyptian Temple Network

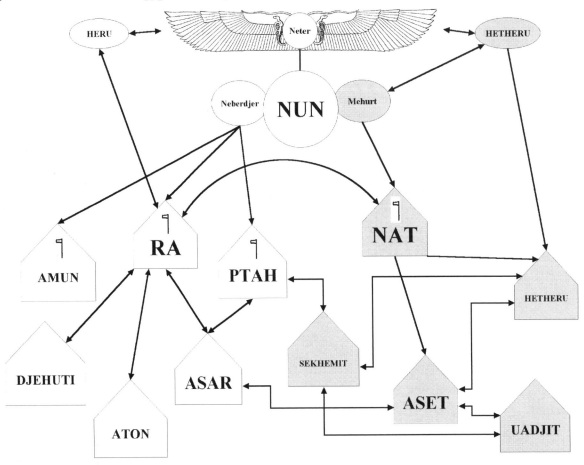

The sages of Kamit instituted a system by which the teachings of spirituality were espoused through a Temple organization. The major divinities were assigned to a particular city. That divinity or group of divinities became the "patron" divinity or divinities of that city. Also, the Priests and Priestesses of that Temple were in charge of seeing to the welfare of the people in that district as well as maintaining the traditions and disciplines of the traditions based on the particular divinity being worshipped. So the original concept of "Neter" became elaborated through the "theologies" of the various traditions. A dynamic expression of the teachings emerged, which though maintaining the integrity of the teachings, expressed nuances of variation in perspective on the teachings to suit the needs of varying kinds of personalities of the people of different locales.

In the diagram above, the primary or main divinities are denoted by the Neter symbol ( ). The house structure represents the Temple for that particular divinity. The interconnections with the other Temples are based on original scriptural statements espoused by the Temples that linked the divinities of their Temple with the other divinities. So this means that the divinities should be viewed not as separate entities operating independently, but rather as family members who are in the same "business" together, i.e. the enlightenment of society, albeit through variations in form of worship, name, form (expression of the Divinity), etc. Ultimately, all the divinities are referred to as Neteru and they are all said to be emanations from the ultimate and Supreme Being. Thus, the teaching from any of the Temples leads to an understanding of the others, and these all lead back to the source, the highest Divinity. Thus, the teaching within any of the Temple systems would lead to the attainment of spiritual enlightenment, the Great Awakening.

Sema Tawi means Egyptian Yoga

Most students of yoga are familiar with the yogic traditions of India consider that the Indian texts such as the Bhagavad Gita, Mahabharata, Patanjali Yoga Sutras, etc. are the primary and original source of Yogic philosophy and teaching. However, upon examination, the teachings currently espoused in all of the major forms of Indian Yoga can be found in Ancient Egyptian scriptures, inscribed in papyrus and on temple walls as well as steles, statues, obelisks and other sources.

What is Yoga?

Yoga is the practice of mental, physical and spiritual disciplines which lead to self-control and self-discovery by purifying the mind, body and spirit, so as to discover the deeper spiritual essence which lies within every human being and object in the universe. In essence, the goal of Yoga practice is to unite or *yoke* one's individual consciousness with Universal or Cosmic consciousness. Therefore, Ancient Egyptian religious practice, especially in terms of the rituals and other practices of the Ancient Egyptian Temple system known as *Shetaut Neter* (the way of the hidden Supreme Being), also known in Ancient times as *Smai Tawi* "Egyptian Yoga," should as well be considered as universal streams of self-knowledge philosophy which influenced and inspired the great religions and philosophers to this day. In this sense, religion, in its purest form, is also a Yoga system, as it seeks to reunite the soul with its true and original source, God. In broad terms, any spiritual movement or discipline that brings one closer to self-knowledge is a "Yogic" movement. The main recognized forms of Yoga disciplines are:

- *Yoga of Wisdom,*
- *Yoga of Devotional Love,*
- *Yoga of Meditation,*
  - *Physical Postures Yoga*
- *Yoga of Selfless Action,*
- *Tantric Yoga*
  - *Serpent Power Yoga*

The diagram below shows the relationship between the Yoga disciplines and the path of mystical religion (religion practiced in its three complete steps: 1st receiving the myth {knowledge}, 2nd practicing the rituals of the myth {following the teachings of the myth} and 3rd entering into a mystical experience {becoming one with the central figure of the myth}).

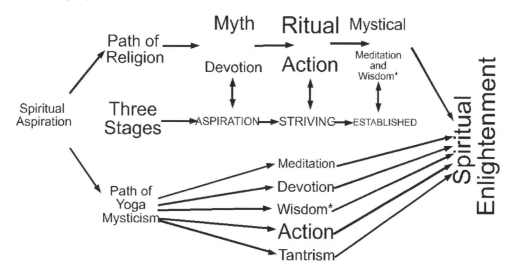

The disciplines of Yoga fall under five major categories. These are: *Yoga of Wisdom, Yoga of Devotional Love, Yoga of Meditation, Tantric Yoga* and *Yoga of Selfless Action.* When these disciplines are practiced in a harmonized manner this practice is called "Integral Yoga." Within these categories there are subsidiary forms which are part of the main disciplines. The emphasis in the Kamitan Asarian (Osirian) Myth is on the Yoga of Wisdom, Yoga of Devotional Love and Yoga of Selfless Action. The important point to remember is that all aspects of Yoga can and should be used in an integral fashion to effect an efficient and harmonized spiritual movement in the practitioner. Therefore, while there may be an area of special emphasis, other elements are bound to become part of the Yoga program as needed. For example, while a Yogin (practitioner of Yoga, aspirant, initiate) may place emphasis on the Yoga of Wisdom, they may also practice Devotional Yoga and Meditation Yoga along with the wisdom studies. So the practice of any discipline that leads to oneness with Supreme Consciousness can be called Yoga. If you study, rationalize and reflect upon the teachings, you are practicing *Yoga of Wisdom.* If you meditate upon the teachings and your Higher Self, you are practicing *Yoga of Meditation.*

Thus, whether or not you refer to it as such, if you practice rituals which identify you with your spiritual nature, you are practicing *Yoga of Ritual Identification* (which is part of the Yoga of Wisdom {Kamitan-Rekh, Indian-Jnana} and the Yoga of Devotional Love {Kamitan-Ushet, Indian-Bhakti} of the Divine). If you develop your physical nature and psychic energy centers, you are practicing *Serpent Power* (Kamitan-*Uraeus* or Indian-*Kundalini*) *Yoga* (which is part of Tantric Yoga). If you practice living according to the teachings of ethical behavior and selflessness, you are practicing *Yoga of Action* (Kamitan-Maat, Indian-Karma) in daily life. If you practice turning your attention towards the Divine by developing love for the Divine, then it is called *Devotional Yoga* or *Yoga of Divine Love.* The practitioner of Yoga is called a Yogin (male practitioner) or Yogini (female practitioner), or the term "Yogi" may be used to refer to either a female or male practitioner in general terms. One who has attained the culmination of Yoga (union with the Divine) is also called a Yogi. In this manner, Yoga has been developed into many disciplines which may be used in an integral fashion to achieve the same goal: Enlightenment. Therefore, the aspirant is to learn about all of the paths of Yoga and choose those elements which best suit {his/her} personality or practice them all in an integral, balanced way.

Enlightenment is the term used to describe the highest level of spiritual awakening. It means attaining such a level of spiritual awareness that one discovers the underlying unity of the entire universe as well as the fact that the source of all creation is the same source from which the innermost Self within every human heart arises.

What is Egyptian Yoga?

The Term "Egyptian Yoga" and The Philosophy Behind It

As previously discussed, Yoga in all of its forms were practiced in Egypt apparently earlier than anywhere else in our history. This point of view is supported by the fact that there is documented scriptural and iconographical evidence of the disciplines of virtuous living, dietary purification, study of the wisdom teachings and their practice in daily life, psychophysical and psycho-spiritual exercises and meditation being practiced in Ancient Egypt, long before the evidence of its existence is detected in India (including the Indus Valley Civilization) or any other early civilization (Sumer, Greece, China, etc.).

The teachings of Yoga are at the heart of *Prt m Hru.* As explained earlier, the word "Yoga" is a Sanskrit term meaning to unite the individual with the Cosmic. The term has been used in certain parts of this book for ease of communication since the word "Yoga" has received wide popularity especially in western countries in recent years. The Ancient Egyptian equivalent term to the Sanskrit word yoga is: *"Smai."* *Smai* means union, and the following determinative terms give it a spiritual significance, at once equating it with the term "Yoga" as it is used in India. When used in conjunction with the Ancient Egyptian symbol which means land, *"Ta,"* the term "union of the two lands" arises.

In Chapter 4 and Chapter 17 of the *Prt m Hru,* a term "Smai Tawi" is used. It means "Union of the two lands of Egypt," ergo "Egyptian Yoga." The two lands refer to the two main districts of the country (North and South). In ancient times, Egypt was divided into two sections or land areas. These were known as Lower and Upper Egypt. In Ancient Egyptian mystical philosophy, the land of Upper Egypt relates to the divinity Heru (Heru), who represents the Higher Self, and the land of Lower Egypt relates to Set, the divinity of the lower self. So *Smai Taui* means "the union of the two lands" or the "Union of the lower self with the Higher Self. The lower self relates to that which is negative and uncontrolled in the human mind including worldliness, egoism, ignorance, etc. (Set), while the Higher Self relates to that which is above temptations and is good in the human heart as well as in touch with transcendental consciousness (Heru). Thus, we also have the Ancient Egyptian term **Smai Heru-Set,** or the union of Heru and Set. So Smai Taui or Smai Heru-Set are the Ancient Egyptian words which are to be translated as **"Egyptian Yoga."**

Above: the main symbol of Egyptian Yoga: *Sma.* The Ancient Egyptian language and symbols provide the first "historical" record of Yoga Philosophy and Religious literature. The hieroglyph Sma, ⵎ "Sema," represented by the union of two lungs and the trachea, symbolizes that the union of the duality, that is, the Higher Self and lower self, leads to Non-duality, the One, singular consciousness.

The Ancient Egyptians called the disciplines of Yoga in Ancient Egypt by the term *"Smai Tawi."* So what does Smai Tawi mean?

Smai Tawi
(From Chapter 4 of the *Prt m Hru*)

The Ancient Egyptian Symbols of Yoga

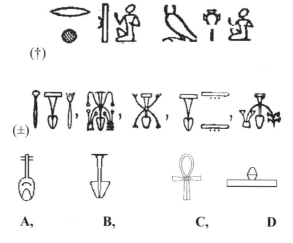

A,   B,   C,   D

The theme of the arrangement of the symbols above is based on the idea that in mythological and philosophic forms, Egyptian mythology and philosophy merge with world mythology, philosophy and religion. The hieroglyphic symbols at the very top (†) mean: ***"Know Thyself," "Self knowledge is the basis of all true knowledge"*** and (±) abbreviated forms of ***Smai taui,*** signifies "Egyptian Yoga." The next four below represent the four words in Egyptian Philosophy, which mean ***"YOGA."*** They are: (A) ***"Nefer"*** (B) ***"Sema"*** (C) ***"Ankh"*** and (D) ***"Hetep."***

The Term "Egyptian Yoga" and The Philosophy Behind It

As previously discussed, Yoga in all of its forms were practiced in Egypt apparently earlier than anywhere else in our history. This point of view is supported by the fact that there is documented scriptural and iconographical evidence of the disciplines of virtuous living, dietary purification, study of the wisdom teachings and their practice in daily life, psychophysical and psycho-spiritual exercises and meditation being practiced in

EGYPTIAN YOGA VOLUME 1

Ancient Egypt, long before the evidence of its existence is detected in India (including the Indus Valley Civilization) or any other early civilization (Sumer, Greece, China, etc.).

The teachings of Yoga are at the heart of *Prt m Hru.* As explained earlier, the word "Yoga" is a Sanskrit term meaning to unite the individual with the Cosmic. The term has been used in certain parts of this book for ease of communication since the word "Yoga" has received wide popularity especially in western countries in recent years. The Ancient Egyptian equivalent term to the Sanskrit word yoga is: *"Smai." Smai* means union, and the following determinative terms give it a spiritual significance, at once equating it with the term "Yoga" as it is used in India. When used in conjunction with the Ancient Egyptian symbol which means land, *"Ta,"* the term "union of the two lands" arises.

In Chapter 4 and Chapter 17 of the *Prt m Hru,* a term "Smai Tawi" is used. It means "Union of the two lands of Egypt," ergo "Egyptian Yoga." The two lands refer to the two main districts of the country (North and South). In ancient times, Egypt was divided into two sections or land areas. These were known as Lower and Upper Egypt. In Ancient Egyptian mystical philosophy, the land of Upper Egypt relates to the divinity Heru (Heru), who represents the Higher Self, and the land of Lower Egypt relates to Set, the divinity of the lower self. So *Smai Taui* means "the union of the two lands" or the "Union of the lower self with the Higher Self. The lower self relates to that which is negative and uncontrolled in the human mind including worldliness, egoism, ignorance, etc. (Set), while the Higher Self relates to that which is above temptations and is good in the human heart as well as in touch with transcendental consciousness (Heru). Thus, we also have the Ancient Egyptian term *Smai Heru-Set,* or the union of Heru and Set. So Smai Taui or Smai Heru-Set are the Ancient Egyptian words which are to be translated as **"Egyptian Yoga."**

Above: the main symbol of Egyptian Yoga: *Sma.* The Ancient Egyptian language and symbols provide the first "historical" record of Yoga Philosophy and Religious literature. The hieroglyph Sma, ⚍ "Sema," represented by the union of two lungs and the trachea, symbolizes that the union of the duality, that is, the Higher Self and lower self, leads to Non-duality, the One, singular consciousness.

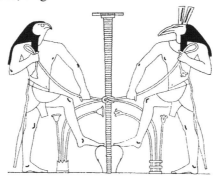

Above left: Smai Heru-Set, Heru and Set join forces to tie up the symbol of Union (Sema –see (B) above). The Sema symbol refers to the Union of Upper Egypt (Lotus) and Lower Egypt (Papyrus) under one ruler, but also at a more subtle level, it refers to the union of one's Higher Self and lower self (Heru and Set), as well as the control of one's breath (Life Force) through the union (control) of the lungs (breathing organs). The character of Heru and Set are an integral part of the **Pert Em Heru.**

The central and most popular character within Ancient Egyptian Religion of Asar is Heru, who is an incarnation of his father, Asar. Asar is killed by his brother Set who, out of greed and demoniac (Setian) tendency, craved to be the ruler of Egypt. With the help of Djehuti, the God of wisdom, Aset, the great mother and Hetheru, his consort, Heru prevailed in the battle against Set for the rulership of Kemit (Egypt). Heru's struggle symbolizes the struggle of every human being to regain rulership of the Higher Self and to subdue the lower self.

The most ancient writings in our historical period are from the Ancient Egyptians. These writings are referred to as hieroglyphics. The original name given to these writings by the Ancient Egyptians is *Metu Neter,* meaning "the writing of God" or *Neter Metu* or "Divine Speech." These writings were inscribed in temples, coffins and papyruses and contained the teachings in reference to the spiritual nature of the human being and the ways to promote spiritual emancipation, awakening or resurrection. The Ancient Egyptian proverbs presented in this text are translations from the original hieroglyphic scriptures. An example of hieroglyphic text was presented above in the form of the text of Smai Taui or "Egyptian Yoga."

Egyptian Philosophy may be summed up in the following proverbs, which clearly state that the soul is heavenly or divine and that the human being must awaken to the true reality, which is the Spirit, Self.

"Self knowledge is the basis of true knowledge."

"Soul to heaven, body to earth."

"Man is to become God-like through a life of virtue and the cultivation of the spirit through scientific knowledge, practice and bodily discipline."

"Salvation is accomplished through the efforts of the individual. There is no mediator between man and {his/her} salvation."

"Salvation is the freeing of the soul from its bodily fetters, becoming a God through knowledge and wisdom, controlling the forces of the cosmos instead of being a slave to them, subduing the lower nature and through awakening the Higher Self, ending the cycle of rebirth and dwelling with the Neters who direct and control the Great Plan."

Egyptian Yoga is a revolutionary new way to understand and practice Ancient Egyptian Mysticism, the Ancient Egyptian mystical religion (*Shetaut Neter*). Egyptian Yoga is what has been commonly referred to by Egyptologists as Egyptian "Religion" or "Mythology," but to think of it as just another set of stories or allegories about a long lost civilization is to completely miss the greatest secret of human existence. What is Yoga? The literal meaning of the word YOGA is to *"YOKE"* or to *"LINK"* back. The implication is to link back individual consciousness to its original source, the original essence: Universal Consciousness. In a broad sense Yoga is any process which helps one to achieve liberation or freedom from the bondage to human pain and spiritual ignorance. So whenever you engage in any activity with the goal of promoting the discovery of your true Self, be it studying the wisdom teachings, exercise, fasting, meditation, breath control, rituals, chanting, prayer, etc., you are practicing yoga. If the goal is to help you to discover your essential nature as one with God or the Supreme Being or Consciousness, then it is Yoga. Yoga, in all of its forms as the disciplines of spiritual development, as practiced in Ancient Egypt earlier than anywhere else in history. The ancient scriptures describe how Asar, the first mythical king of Ancient Egypt, traveled throughout Asia and Europe establishing civilization and the practice of religion. This partially explains why the teachings of mystical spirituality known as Yoga and Vedanta in India are so similar to the teachings of Shetaut Neter (Ancient Egyptian religion - Egyptian Yoga. This unique perspective from the highest philosophical system which developed in Africa over seven thousand years ago provides a new way to look at life, religion, psychology and the way to spiritual development leading to spiritual Enlightenment. So Egyptian Yoga is not merely a philosophy but a discipline for promoting spiritual evolution in a human being, allowing him or her to discover the ultimate truth, supreme peace and utmost joy which lies within the human heart. These are the true worthwhile goals of life. Anything else is settling for less. It would be like a personality who owns vast riches thinking that he is poor and homeless. Every human being has the potential to discover the greatest treasure of all existence if they apply themselves to the study and practice of the teachings of Yoga with the proper guidance. Sema (⌽) is the Ancient Egyptian word and symbol meaning *union or Yoga.* This is the vision of Egyptian Yoga.

The Study of Yoga

When we look out upon the world, we are often baffled by the multiplicity, which constitutes the human experience. What do we really know about this experience? Many scientific disciplines have developed over the last two hundred years for the purpose of discovering the mysteries of nature, but this search has only engendered new questions about the nature of existence. Yoga is a discipline or way of life designed to promote the physical, mental and spiritual development of the human being. It leads a person to discover the answers to the most important questions of life such as, Who am I? Why am I here? Where am I going?

As explained earlier, the literal meaning of the word *Yoga* is to *"Yoke"* or to *"Link"* back, the implication being to link the individual consciousness back to the original source, the original essence, that which transcends all mental and intellectual attempts at comprehension, but which is the essential nature of everything in Creation, termed "Universal Consciousness. While in the strict sense, Yoga may be seen as a separate discipline from religion, yoga and religion have been linked at many points throughout history and continue to be linked even today. In a manner of speaking, Yoga as a discipline may be seen as a non-sectarian transpersonal science or practice to promote spiritual development and harmony of mind and body thorough mental and physical disciplines including meditation, psycho-physical exercises, and performing action with the correct attitude.

The teachings which were practiced in the Ancient Egyptian temples were the same ones later intellectually defined into a literary form by the Indian Sages of Vedanta and Yoga. This was discussed in our book *Egyptian Yoga: The Philosophy of Enlightenment*. The Indian Mysteries of Yoga and Vedanta may therefore be understood as representing an unfolding exposition of the Egyptian Mysteries.

The question is how to accomplish these seemingly impossible tasks? How to transform yourself and realize the deepest mysteries of existence? How to discover "Who am I?" This is the mission of Yoga Philosophy and the purpose of yogic practices. Yoga does not seek to convert or impose religious beliefs on any one. Ancient Egypt was the source of civilization and the source of religion and Yoga. Therefore, all systems of mystical spirituality can coexist harmoniously within these teachings when they are correctly understood.

The goal of yoga is to promote integration of the mind-body-spirit complex in order to produce optimal health of the human being. This is accomplished through mental and physical exercises which promote the free flow of spiritual energy by reducing mental complexes caused by ignorance. There are two roads which human beings can follow, one of wisdom and the other of ignorance. The path of the masses is generally the path of ignorance which leads them into negative situations, thoughts and deeds. These in turn lead to ill health and sorrow in life. The other road is based on wisdom and it leads to health, true happiness and enlightenment.

The central and most popular character within ancient Egyptian Religion of Asar is Heru who is an incarnation of his father, Asar. Asar is killed by his brother Set who, out of greed and demoniac (Setian) tendency, craves to be the ruler of Egypt. With the help of Djehuti, the God of wisdom, Aset, the great mother and Hetheru, his consort, Heru prevails in the battle against Set for the rulership of Egypt. Heru' struggle symbolizes the struggle of every human being to regain rulership of the Higher Self and to subdue the lower self. With this understanding, the land of Egypt is equivalent to the Kingdom/Queendom concept of Christianity.

The most ancient writings in our historical period are from the ancient Egyptians. These writings are referred to as hieroglyphics. Also, the most ancient civilization known was the ancient Egyptian civilization. The proof of this lies in the ancient Sphinx which is over 12,000 years old. The original name given to these writings by the ancient Egyptians is *Metu Neter,* meaning "the writing of God" or *Neter Metu* or "Divine Speech." These writings were inscribed in temples, coffins and papyruses and contained the teachings in reference to the spiritual nature of the human being and the ways to promote spiritual emancipation, awakening or resurrection. The —Ancient Egyptian Proverbs presented in this text are translations from the original hieroglyphic scriptures. An example of hieroglyphic text is presented on the front cover.

Egyptian Philosophy may be summed up in the following proverbs which clearly state that the soul is heavenly or divine and that the human being must awaken to the true reality which is the spirit Self.

"Self knowledge is the basis of true knowledge."
"Soul to heaven, body to earth."

"Man is to become God-like through a life of virtue and the cultivation of the spirit through scientific knowledge, practice and bodily discipline."

"Salvation is accomplished through the efforts of the individual. There is no mediator between man and his / her salvation."

"Salvation is the freeing of the soul from its bodily fetters, becoming a God through knowledge and wisdom, controlling the forces of the cosmos instead of being a slave to them, subduing the lower nature and through awakening the Higher Self, ending the cycle of rebirth and dwelling with the Neters who direct and control the Great Plan."

CHAPTER 1: Ancient Origins

"Under, and back of, the Universe of Time and Space and Change, is ever to be found The Substantial Reality: the Fundamental Truth."

Egyptian Mystical Wisdom

EGYPTIAN YOGA VOLUME 1

Ancient Origins: The Ethiopian-Egyptian Origin of Yoga Philosophy

Since according to Manetho (High Priest of Egypt and other ancient writers, there have been many periods of "history" and "civilizations" which have come and gone, the current historical period is only one in a series of "historical" periods; there is no one beginning and there is no end. However, the ancient mystical wisdom is the same from age to age as it has the same origin. The current age begins in Afrika (Africa) - Ethiopia - Egypt.

Oral tradition claims that Asar was the first King of Egypt, and that he and Aset were actually a God and Goddess, divine beings, who came to earth to establish civilization. They are said to have arrived on the earth about 18,000 B.C., and to have left the earth around 10,000 B.C.

Diodorus Siculus (Greek Historian) writes in the time of Augustus (first century B.C.):

"Now the Ethiopians, as historians relate, were the first of all men and the proofs of this statement, they say, are manifest. For that they did not come into their land as immigrants from abroad but were the natives of it and so justly bear the name of autochthones **(sprung from the soil itself),** *is, they maintain, conceded by practically all men..."*

"They also say that the Egyptians are colonists sent out by the Ethiopians, Asar having been the leader of the colony. For, speaking generally, what is now Egypt, they maintain, was not land, but sea, when in the beginning the universe was being formed; afterwards, however, as the Nile during the times of its inundation carried down the mud from Ethiopia, land was gradually built up from the deposit...And the larger parts of the customs of the Egyptians are, they hold, Ethiopian, the colonists still preserving their ancient manners. For instance, the belief that their kings are Gods, the very special attention which they pay to their burials, and many other matters of a similar nature, are Ethiopian practices, while the shapes of their statues and the forms of their letters are Ethiopian; for of the two kinds of writing which the Egyptians have, that which is known as popular **(demotic)** *is learned by everyone, while that which is called sacred* **(hieratic)**, *is understood only by the priests of the Egyptians, who learnt it from their Fathers as one of the things which are not divulged, but among the Ethiopians, everyone uses these forms of letters. Furthermore, the orders of the priests, they maintain, have much the same position among both peoples; for all are clean who are engaged in the service of the gods, keeping themselves shaven, like the Ethiopian priests, and having the same dress and form of staff, which is shaped like a plough and is carried by their kings who wear high felt hats which end in a knob in the top and are circled by the serpents which they call asps; and this symbol appears to carry the thought that it will be the lot who shall dare to attack the king to encounter death-carrying stings. Many other things are told by them concerning their own antiquity and the colony which they sent out that became the Egyptians, but about this there is no special need of our writing anything."*

The ancient Egyptian texts state:

"KMT" "Egypt", "Burnt", "Land of Blackness", "Land of the Burnt People."

KMT (Egypt) is situated close to Lake Victoria in present day Africa. This is same location where the earliest human remains have been found, in the land currently known as Ethiopia-Tanzania. Recent genetic technology as reported in the new encyclopedias and leading news publications has revealed that all peoples of the world originated in Africa and migrated to other parts of the world prior to the last Ice Age 40,000 years ago. Therefore, as of this time, genetic testing has revealed that all humans are alike. The earliest bone fossils which have been found in many parts of the world were those of the African Grimaldi type. During the Ice Age, it was not possible to communicate or to migrate. Those trapped in specific locations were subject to the regional forces of weather and climate. Less warmer climates required less body pigment, thereby producing lighter pigmented people who now differed from their dark skinned ancestors. After the Ice Age when travel was possible, these light skinned people who had lived in the northern, colder regions of harsh weather during the Ice Age period moved back to the warmer climates of their ancestors, and mixed with the people there who had remained dark skinned, thereby producing the Semitic colored people. "Semite" means mixture of skin color shades.

Below: This predynastic symbol of the female - mother - Goddess, is also represented in other parts of Afrika and in the dynastic period of Egypt in the same pose. The wings are symbolic of the Egyptian Sky God Heru. Aset and Maat of Egypt are also female Godesses represented with wings.

Therefore, there is only one human race who, due to different climactic and regional exposure, changed to a point where there seemed to be different "types"of people. Differences were noted with respect to skin color, hair texture, customs, languages, and with respect to the essential nature (psychological and emotional makeup) due to the experiences each group had to face and overcome in order to survive.

From a philosophical standpoint, the question as to the origin of humanity is redundant when it is understood that _ALL_ come from one origin which some choose to call the "Big Bang" and others "The Supreme Being."

Historical evidence proves that Ethiopia-Nubia already had Kingdoms at least 300 years before the first Kingdom-Pharaoh of Egypt.

"Ancient Egypt was a colony of Nubia - Ethiopia. ...Asar having been the leader of the colony..."

"And upon his return to Greece, they gathered around and asked, "tell us about this great land of the Blacks called Ethiopia." And Herodotus said, "There are two great Ethiopian nations, one in Sind (India) and the other in Egypt."

Recorded by Egyptian high priest *Manetho* **(300 B.C.)**
also Recorded by *Diodorus* **(Greek historian 100 B.C.)**

The pyramids themselves however, cannot be dated, but indications are that they existed far back in antiquity. The Pyramid Texts (hieroglyphics inscribed on pyramid walls) and Coffin Texts (hieroglyphics inscribed on coffins) speak authoritatively on the constitution of the human spirit, the vital Life Force along the human spinal cord (known in India as *"Kundalini"*), the immortality of the soul, reincarnation and the law of Cause and Effect (known in India as the Law of Karma).

On The Meaning of The Hieroglyphs:

"We must now speak of the Ethiopian writing which is called hieroglyphic by the Egyptians, in order that we may omit nothing in our discussion of their antiquities. Now it is found that the forms of their letters take the shape of animals of every kind, and of the members of the human body, and of implements and especially carpenter's tools; for their writing does not express the intent concept by means of syllables joined one to another, but by its figurative meaning which has been impressed upon the memory by practice. For instance, they draw the picture of a hawk, a crocodile, a snake, and all of the members of the human body-an eye, a hand, a face, and the like. Now the hawk signifies to them everything which happens swiftly, since this animal is practically the swiftest of winged creatures...And the crocodile is a symbol of all that is evil, and the eye is the warder of justice and the guardian of the entire body. And as for the members of the body, the right hand with fingers extended signifies a procuring of livelihood, and the left with the fingers closed, a keeping and guarding of property. The same way of reasoning applies to the remaining characters, which represent parts of the body and implements and all other things; for by paying close attention to the significance which is inherent in each object and by training their minds through drills and exercise of the memory over a long period, they read from habit everything which has been written."

On the Relationship Between Egypt - Ethiopia and India:

"From Ethiopia, he (Asar) passed through Arabia, bordering upon the Red Sea to as far as India, and the remotest inhabited coasts; he built likewise many cities in India, one of which he called Nysa, willing to have remembrance of that (Nysa) in Egypt where he was brought up. At

this Nysa in India he planted Ivy, which continues to grow there, but nowhere else in India or around it. He left likewise many other marks of his being in those parts, by which the latter inhabitants are induced, and do affirm, that this God was born in India. He likewise addicted himself to the hunting of elephants, and took care to have statues of himself in every place, as lasting monuments of his expedition."

-Recorded by *Diodorus* **(Greek historian 100 B.C.)**

A Latin work written for Roman emperor Constantius states:

"India taken as a whole, beginning from the north and embracing what of it is subject to Persia, is a continuation of Egypt and the Ethiopians."

The Itinerarium Alexandri
A.C.E. 345

"There are Egyptian columns as far off as NYASA, Arabia...Aset and Asar led an army into India, to the source of the Ganges, and as far as the Indus Ocean."

Recorded by Egyptian High Priest *Manetho* **(300 B.C.) and** *Diodorus* **(Greek historian 100 B. C.)**

Other evidence of the connection between Egypt, the Middle East and East Asia include the inscriptions from the Egyptian Pharaoh Ramses III which state that he sent naval expeditions to the far reaches of the world. This is verified by the ancient inscriptions found in the Mesopotamian area which speak of a conqueror who used a standard composed of a **"Rams Head with a Snake Overlooking It."** This description matches the standard of Ramses III. Further, the practice of circumcision was believed by the ancients to have originated in Egypt. It was practiced by Palestinians, Jews, Colchians and other Asians, who claimed to have learned the practice from the Egyptians.

"Recent linguistic discovery tends to show that a Cushite or Ethiopian race did in the earliest times extend itself along the shores of the Southern ocean from Abyssinia to India. The whole peninsula of India was peopled by a race of this character before the influx of the Aryans; it extends from the Indus along the seacoast through the modern Beloochistan and Kerman, which was the proper country of Asiatic Ethiopians; the cities on the northern shores of the Persian Gulf are shown by the brick inscriptions found among their ruins to have belonged to this race; it was dormant in Susiana and Babylonia, until overpowered in the one country by Aryan, in the other by Semitic intrusion; it can be traced, both by dialect and tradition, throughout the whole south coast of the Arabian peninsula, and it still exists in Abyssinia, where the language of the principal tribe (the Galla) furnishes, it is thought, a clue to the cuneiform inscriptions (Mesopotamia) of Susiana and Elymais, which date from a period probably a thousand years before our era."

Commentary on History of Herodotus by Henry C. Rawlinson

Thus, the Indus Valley Culture (earliest know civilization of India), which were later known as the Dravidians and Harrapans, appears to have been culturally and economically connected to Ethiopia and Egypt.   After the destruction of the Indus Valley culture by the *Aryans,* a warrior group from Eurasia (Europe), the Indus Valley Culture merged culturally with the Aryan descendants and further developed the wisdom of the *Mysteries* into modern Indian Philosophy (Vedanta). Descendants of the Indus Valley culture live in India to this day.

"Some Hindus claim the Nile to be one of their sacred rivers; they also regard as sacred the Mountains of the Moon (in Uganda-Congo) and Mount Meru (in Tanzania). Both in India and in the Indianized Kingdoms, Southern Mount Meru was regarded as the mythical dwelling place of the Gods. Each of these statements reflect millennia old relationships between the blacks of Africa and South Asia. The Ethiopian Kebra Negast regarded Western India as a portion of the Ethiopian Empire. "Murugan, the God of mountains", the son of the mother Goddess is a prominent and typical deity of the Dravidian India. It is interesting to note that at least 25 tribes in East Africa worship "Murungu" as supreme God, and like the Dravidian God Murugan, the African Murungu resides in sacred mountains."

From: U.P. Upadhyaya

EGYPTIAN YOGA VOLUME 1

"Dravidian and Negro-African International Journal of Dravidian Linguistics" v.5, No 1 January 1976, p 39.

A Chronology of Ancient Egypt:

36,766 B.C.E
End of Atlantean Age. Antediluvian Egyptian civilization according to Manetho.

10,858 B.C.E.
End of last Great Year and beginning of current one in which we live.

11,000 - 9,000 B.C.E.
New conservative estimate of the construction of the Great Sphinx.

10,500 B.C.E.
Cayce dating of the beginning of the post-diluvian predynastic period.

10,500 - 5,700 B.C.E.
Post-diluvian predynastic period, early Asian invasions, the Great Pyramid, land occupied by various kingdoms made up of the decedents of the original Ethiopians and Egyptians, land finally was divided into north and south.

5,700 - 342 B.C.E.
Historical dynastic period.

500 B.C.E.
Invasion and occupation by the Persians.

340 B.C.E.
Invasion and occupation by the Greeks.

150 B.C.E. - 500 B.C.E.
Invasion and occupation by the Romans who instituted the systematic destruction of Egyptian temples and libraries to allow the rise of Christianity.

CONCLUSION: <u>THE INDUS - KAMIT - KUSH CONNECTION</u>

It is clear from the historical record that the early civilizations of India, Indus, and of Africa, Egypt (Kamit) - Ethiopia (Kush), shared an intimate social, cultural and genetic link. Both India and Egypt were invaded by violent groups from Eurasia, namely the Aryans and Asiatics, respectively, resulting in ethnic, social and cultural changes. The Indus and Kamitic peoples became lighter in skin pigmentation as a result of mixing with the lighter skinned foreigners. In addition, seemingly new philosophies and religions emerged.

From this study, clues emerge as to the origin of the teachings of current world philosophies and religions. We may now see our present day philosophies and religions as extensions of ancient wisdom as opposed to irrelevant ideas belonging to alien civilizations from long ago. Understanding this connection allows us to integrate our current knowledge of philosophy and religion with the ancient wisdom which gave birth to it.

The archeological record, linguistic and mythological correspondences show that in the early times of antiquity, the entire area from Ethiopia to southern Eurasia to China was populated by a single group who shared cultural, social and genetic relations. Even today, pictures of Ethiopians (Nubians - Kushites), Southern Indians (Dravidians), Northern Indians from Orisa, Malaysians and Southern Arabians show similarities in physical appearance and complexion. Inscriptions found in these areas support the idea that a mythological and philosophical unity existed throughout the area prior to the invasions from the north (Aryans, Eurasians and Asiatics).

INDUS - KAMIT - KUSH

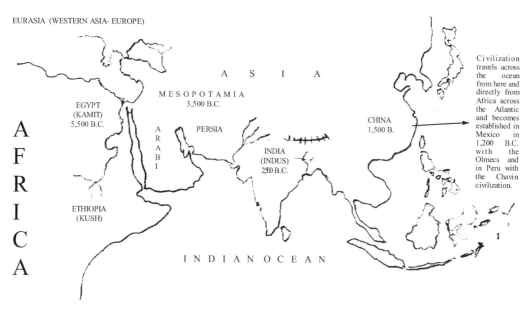

It would be a mistake to assume that everything is known about all of the historical periods in Egyptian history since at the very least, this would require the discovery of all its cities, monuments, and temples. It would be equally erroneous to assume that a definitive historical record of any period throughout human history is essential to the goal of enlightenment, since any and all histories and mythologies must ultimately be understood as relative realities. Even modern day society with its many secret organizations withholds vital historical information about the events that shape our lives. Therefore, the purpose of making sense of history as best we can is to help us to better understand and unravel our own involvement in time and space as individuals or as members of a particular group, in order that we may see through the illusoriness of our associations and experiences.

As occurred with several other mythological systems around the world, the influx of new philosophies, ideas and events served to test the strength of Egyptian mythology and to provide then, as current events do now, an opportunity for us, as divine beings, to have experience. From an initiatic perspective, the most important factor to consider is that in each successive new mythology, the attributes of NETER (The GOD), NETER NETERU (GOD of Gods), and Amun (Hidden One), were attributed to the new forms of the God / Goddess. Indeed, what appears to be "new" philosophies and mythologies are really only a new way of presenting the original teaching about the ultimate truth. Thus, these changes not only served to accommodate a new generation but also to preserve the essence of the teaching. That ultimate teaching, regardless of the name or form, refers to the underlying basis of each one of us which is immutable regardless of the passage of time or events in history, past, present or future. Therefore, any interest in the events of the past or future should be based on their impact on our understanding of our present situation, and on how they can help us to reach intuitional rather than intellectual enlightenment.

*The dates included represent the earliest known dates for the establishment of civilized cultures in the world. It would appear that all of the high cultures of the world are reflections of that which originated in Ancient Egypt, Africa.

NOTE: For more on the mythological of Ancient Egypt and the origins of Yoga philosophy see the book

THE AFRICAN ORIGINS OF CIVILIZATION,
RELIGION, MYSTICISM AND YOGA PHILOSOPHY
Coming Fall 2001

‖

CHAPTER 2: PHILOSOPHY

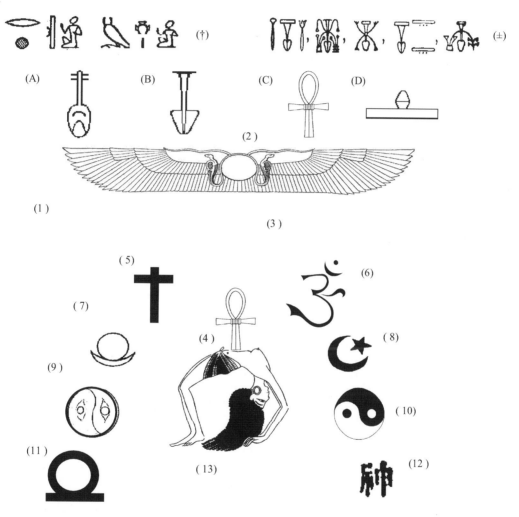

The theme of the arrangement of the symbols above is based on the idea that in mythological and philosophic forms, Egyptian mythology and philosophy merge with world mythology, philosophy and religion. The hieroglyphic symbols at the very top (†) mean: *"Know Thyself"*, *"Self knowledge is the basis of all true knowledge"* and (±) signifies *Smai taui* or "Egyptian Yoga." (see also page 99 (*Smai Heru-Set*). The next four below represent the four words in Egyptian Philosophy which mean *"YOGA"*. They are: (A) *"Nefer"*(B) *"Sema"* (C) *"Ankh"* and (D) *"Hetep".* The remaining symbols used are: (1) The Winged Sundisk, symbolizing Heru the hawk, the all encompassing, all pervading divinity, it incorporates the double Uraeuses (Cobras) and the Sundisk (2) The circle sometimes depicted with a dot in the center, also used in the Kabbalah and in Hinduism to symbolize the sun and the union of male and female, God and Creation. (3) The rays, symbolize the seven powers of creation and the pyramid. (4) In the center, the Egyptian and Indian Ankh (symbol of life), (5) The Christian and Egyptian Cross. (6) The Indian Sanskrit symbol AUM. (7) The Egyptian Moon and Sun, and (8) the Islamic Moon and Star. (9) The Egyptian and (10) Chinese symbol of the complementary opposites. (11) The Egyptian and (12) Chinese Shen, symbols of eternity. (13) An Egyptian female in the Wheel yoga pose. The Ankh (life) rises out of the body perfected by Yoga .

Ancient Mystical Philosophy is

Ancient Mystical Philosophy is the precursor of Religion and Yoga. It is the higher intellectual process which led Sages to question the nature and origin of their existence. Ancient Mystical Philosophy is a way to intellectually understand the process of existence, the reason for life, and the means to master it through wisdom. Intellectual wisdom and knowledge gradually become intuitive. This process leads to complete psychological liberation from worldly attachments.

Ancient Mystical Philosophy states that "Creation" has not been "Created", that "Creation" is in fact a mental manifestation, and that all mental manifestations are emanations of the Supreme Being. Further, it states that we (our souls) are not only manifestations of the "Creator", but that we are the "Creator"---as the Creator alone exists.

"GOD is everywhere and in all things."

From The Bible (c. 1,500 B.C.E.)

Our soul has experiences through the prism of the mind. Our bodies are manifestations of our mind. Further, a purified mind can attain the vision of "reality" as it really is.

In studying Ancient Mystical Philosophy, we will see that we are "one" with the Creator and that we are taking a journey through the world of time and space with a veil of ignorance so that we may "feel" the journey as if it is real. In short, anything that can have a name or form is an illusory representation of the true reality which is the spirit, GOD.

Further, the experiences of the "world" do not affect the soul or divine nature in any way. Therefore, nothing is really happening except in the mentations of each of us. In a war for example, no one is killing and no one is being killed. It may be stated that GOD is interacting with GOD. This can be more easily understood by imagining that all objects in creation including us, are like actors on a movie screen. Though someone may seemingly be born or die, the screen as well as the actors are unaffected in "real life." Similarly, we are appearing on the screen of pure consciousness, which is in fact what we call GOD. The idea that we are "really" doing something, that something is really occurring, constitutes "wrong thinking." Wrong thinking continues one's involvement and belief that this physical world is the only "reality"; this is egoism. Right thinking implies living in the world, seeing everything as part of GOD, one's very own SELF, therefore, living in peace and harmony with all things. There is no need to wage war. This is the state of highest mental sanity and purity achieved by those who are spiritually advanced.

The intellect required to grasp the above stated points is said to be that of advanced souls who are nearing the end of their journey through the world process of illusion. They are ready to attain "*SALVATION.*"

With a purified mind attained through the disciplines of meditation, hekau (mantra) repetition and correct thinking, it is possible to transcend the "physical reality" and attain the higher vision while still alive.

As the teachings become "intuitionally" understood, the unconscious is cleansed of the "wrong" thinking to such a degree that a "new" vision is experienced. Those who attain this higher vision will live on in it after the death of the body because they live within their "real" identity. Those who at the time of death persist in believing that they are a particular person, born in a particular place, to particular parents, loyal to a particular country or a particular race, will die with these ideas because these are perishable ideas that never existed: Illusions.

In the final years of his life, Albert Einstein regretted his participation in the creation of the nuclear bomb. He attempted to construct a mathematical representation of the universe as a unified whole, the "Unified Field Theory."

Einstein also admitted having experienced ecstatic psychological moments where all things including his body and mind were united in one whole; thus he experienced glimpses of cosmic consciousness. Present day scientists have continued his work and believe a unified theory will be possible.

The world and everything in it (including our bodies) as we see it with ordinary eyes is only a reflection of the true reality. "True reality" is mental, energy and spirit: PURE CONSCIOUSNESS. Therefore, the correct attitude toward physical life should be one which encompasses surrendering one's ego consciousness and accepting one's true identity, loving all impersonally, relinquishing possessiveness and accepting the true underlying reality: GOD.

This is the highest teaching of the Yoga of Wisdom. Once it is understood, even in part, feelings of "detachment" and "dispassion" for objects of the world begin to occur in the individual. One experiences a feeling of "participating" in the world but understanding that it is not the "Absolute" reality. The concept of the Absolute reality is embodied in the *NETER (NTR)* of Egypt, *Ntu* of the Yorubas, *Amma* of the Dogon, *Brahman* if Hinduism, the *Tao* of Taoism, the *Darmakaya* of Buddhism, *Kingdom of Heaven* of Christianity, *Kether* of the Kabbalah, the *Great Spirit and Quetzalcoatle* of Native Americans, and *Allah* of the Muslims.

One who understands the teaching will not be susceptible to sorrow at the loss of a "loved one" since he or she will realize that the loved one has only passed on in the journey, or rather, that they have gone nowhere except to a different plane of "reality" to which all things belong.

Detachment from small individual things allows one to perceive one's connection to everything.

At this stage, various levels of peace are attained. The understanding of the teachings allow the mind to be free from "craving" worldly things and to love all things and people equally, since they are understood to be manifestations of the "Creator", the Absolute reality, one's very self: Pure Consciousness.

THE TEACHINGS are the writings of Masters who were able to control their minds and bodies in such a way as to ascend to great psychological and psychic heights. They attained communion with Cosmic Intelligence, the Creator and Sustainer of all things.

Upon doing so, they realized the nature of their own existence and the fact that they, along with the rest of humanity, are one with that ultimate reality. The Sages realized that even though there are many names and forms in creation, all that can be seen is not only a part of GOD, the all encompassing being, but in effect are GOD.

They came back from the lofty heights to assist others in attaining the beatific visions and the ever present peace... *Hetep.* Hetep is the ULTIMATE peace that cannot be disturbed by worldly occurrences.

They said that the heights they attained were attainable by all humans with the desire, will and fearlessness to accept the truth. This truth is not in books, but in the innermost heart.

The teachings are not for everyone, however, since not all humans are spiritually and psychologically ready to control their lower nature (body and ego-mind). Many prefer to believe what they are told at face value and wallow in the ups and downs of their mortal existence, thinking: *"this is all there is to life and when I die, that will be that."*

Those who abide by that form of ignorance will reap the fruits of what they have sown, because existence is essentially a mental process. They who can control the mind will have a greater opportunity to attain immortality, not of the body, but of the true essence, the ultimate reality which is GOD: Pure Consciousness.

Ancient Egyptian teachings:

"I am the Mind - the Eternal Teacher. I am the begetter of the Word - the Redeemer of all humankind - and in the nature of the wise, the Word takes flesh. By means of the Word, the world is saved. I, Thought - the begetter of the Word, the Mind - come only unto they that are holy, good, pure and merciful, and that live piously and religiously, and my presence is an inspiration and a help to them, for when I come, they

immediately know all things and adore the Universal Spirit. Before such wise and philosophic ones die, they learn to renounce their senses, knowing that these are the enemies of their immortal Souls."

"A SAGE is someone who loves impersonally, someone who realizes in their deepest heart that there is no reality outside of the supreme nameless GOD."

Egyptian Proverbs

A SAGE KNOWS all the time that he or she is a part of GOD as are the trees, birds, insects, rocks, air and stars. The SAGE lives within the idea, *"My spirit is using this body and all things are part of me and I of them; I am not in the universe; it is the universe that is within me."* Therefore, the SAGE does not die when the body dies.

"Under and in back of the Universe of Time and Space and Change, is ever to be found The Substantial Reality: the Fundamental Truth."

Egyptian Proverb

Religion is

The term religion comes from the Latin word roots *"RE"* which means *"BACK"* and *"LIGON"* which means *"to hold, to link, to bind."* Therefore, the essence of true religion is that of linking back, specifically, linking its followers back to their original source: GOD. Human beings, their spirits having come from the Universal, all pervading consciousness, GOD, have forgotten their origin and therefore wander the earth without knowledge of their true divine nature. Religion is supposed to be a process of assisting men and women to reconnect with the Creator, GOD. The human entity (soul) has been deluded into believing that it is composed of a mind and body that exists once, and that will die one day. Actually, it is not really a process of re-connection so much as remembering one's true identity. It's as if we have contracted amnesia. This is the true meaning of the Biblical statements:

"Is it not written in your law that ye are Gods?"

Jesus

"The kingdom of the Father (GOD) is spread upon the earth and men do not see it!"

Jesus

Although religion in its purest form is a Yoga system, the original intent and meaning of the scriptures are often misunderstood, if not distorted. If religions were devoid of corruption and properly understood and practiced, most would provide a suitable system to *"Yoga"* their followers.

It is a well known fact to religious scholars that the original scriptures of the western Bible included teachings which closely follow the Egyptian Mysteries-Yoga system, and the Indian Philosophical Yoga Vedanta system. At the Nicean council of Bishops in 325 A.C.E., the doctrine of self-salvation was distorted to the degree that the masses of people were convinced that they needed a savior as a "go between" to reach GOD. As their minds were thus conditioned, they forgot that they, the individuals, were as we are today, responsible for our own fate. A new religion, Christianity, was thus created by the Nicean council under the direction of the Roman Empire and the emperor decreed the destruction of all other philosophies, religions, and doctrines. It was at this time that references to reincarnation and the ability of each individual to become a Christ were either deleted or misrepresented.

Many writings which were called "Gnostic" or "Knowing" gospels were "deleted" from the standard text by Roman Emperor Constantine. In the *Essene Gospel of Peace,* translated by Edmund Bordeau Shakely in the early twentieth century from a copy which was locked away in the Vatican, Jesus states that his teachings are to help guide those seeking to attain his level of consciousness, that is, Cosmic Consciousness, to become as he was: Christ. The same teaching is found in the *Gospel of Thomas,* one of several early Gnostic Christian texts which were found in Egypt. It was one of the texts that were edited by the Nicean Council and the Roman emperor Constantine. Thus, the phrase *"being saved through Jesus"* means that an individual may effect his or her own salvation by studying and following the teachings of Jesus and not that we need Jesus to act as mediator between ourselves and GOD to attain salvation.

"Salvation is accomplished through the efforts of the individual. There is no mediator between man and his/her salvation."

Egyptian Proverb

For 300 to 600 years after the Nicean council, the Roman emperors, and later on, the Christian leaders, set about to destroy any vestige of religious doctrines that did not comply with the doctrines of their new religion. The crusades, inquisitions and excommunications were later attempts to promote ignorance among the masses of people. Other documents and relics lie in the well guarded basement of the Vatican to this day.

The ancient Egyptian Cult of *Auset* (ASET) was so strong that it was the last to be overcome. Its teachings were assimilated into Christianity as the "Virgin Mother Mary and Child". This Madonna and child represent the African Goddess ASET (*Auset*) and her child Heru (*Heru*) who was born of an immaculate conception. ASET suckling Heru is a common symbol in art and mythology throughout Africa and East Asia. It represents the importance of the mother, nurturing principle in the making of a human being, as well as the nurturing that must take place in order for one to give birth to one's spirit, our immaculate conception, out of one's animal (lower self) existence.

Yoga in India - Early Indian Philosophy

The earliest known civilization of India, the Indus Valley culture or Dravidians, developed the first advanced philosophical system in India. As in Egypt, Dravidian philosophy and mythology centered around the male and female fertility and sexuality, the root of yoga systems, which relate to the sublimation of sexual energy, Kundalini. This is evidenced by the Dravidian stales of "vegetation" Gods in ithyphallic (erect penis) poses (one called: *"The Black One"*) and those of female Goddesses with plants growing out of their wombs. Its precepts developed into the Tantra Yoga, Jain, Hindu, Buddhist and Vedanta philosophical systems and are similar in most respects to the Egyptian mythology of *"Asar, The Lord of the Perfect Black"*, an ithyphallic vegetation God, and the sacred cow goddess Hetheru-Aset, the Goddess of fertility and sexuality.

Jain Philosophy (c. 1,200 B.C.E)

1- The Qualities of Matter- The universe is a living organism, imperishable in its true essence.

2- Mask of Personality- The personality of a human being is only a mask covering the true being which lies within the person. The Latin word "Persona" denotes a mask which is worn by our soul. This mask must be separated from our true self. "Per" means "through" and "sona" means "sound." Thus, "person" literally means "through sound", referring to the sound (vibrations) of the "voice" of GOD.

3- Cosmic Man- The materialized spirit is the first man; the spirit is eternal. The universe is spirit within and without and therefore, has no beginning and will have no end.

4- Doctrine of Bondage- The spirit in humans is held by Karma, the law of
Causation: you reap what you sow; what you do comes back to you. Every cause has its effect; every effect has its cause. Everything happens according to the law. Chance is a name for the law not recognized.

5- Doctrine of Release- Attainment of purity, self detachment from the body and the world (psychological, don't depend on the senses, body, or emotions for existence) leading to enlightenment.

Vedanta Yoga, and Samkhya Philosophy (c. +1,000 B.C.E.- Present)

Vedanta philosophy originated from the ancient spiritual scriptures of India called the *Vedas*. More specifically, Vedanta refers to the end of the Vedas or the scriptures commonly referred to as *The Upanishads* which constitute a summary or distillation of the highest philosophy of the Vedas. Vedanta philosophy, as it exists in the present, is a combination of Buddhist psychology, Hindu mythology and ancient mystical philosophy.

Having its original roots in the philosophy of the oneness of GOD who manifests in a myriad of ways, Vedanta achieves a balanced blend of all the philosophies and has been adapted by the present day Sages to teach to modern day society. Vedanta, which includes the 16 Yogas (8 major, 8 minor) adapted from the Buddhist Wheel of Life, developed as an alternative to the patriarchal and racist Brahmanic system. Major Tenets:

Vedanta Philosophy is summed up in four *Mahavakyas* or *Great Utterances* to be found in the Upanishads:

1- *Brahman, the Absolute is Consciousness beyond all mental concepts.*
2- *Thou Art That* (Referring to the fact that everyone is essentially this consciousness).
3- *I Am Brahman, the Absolute* (To be spoken by people referring to their own essential nature).
4- *The Self is Brahman* (The Self is the essence of all things).

Compare to the Bible

On the essence of GOD: *"GOD is everywhere and in all things."**

On the name of GOD: *"I Am That I Am."**

Jesus speaks of his own origin and identity: *"I and the Father (GOD) are ONE."**

*From The Bible (c. 1- C.E.)

Compare the preceding statements in the Indian Upanishads and the Christian Bible to the following Ancient Egyptian scriptures (*Metu Neter,* Sacred Speech) taken from the *Egyptian Book of Coming Forth By Day* (c. 10,000-5,000 B.C.E.) and other hieroglyphic texts:

Nuk Pu Nuk. (*"I Am That I Am."*)

In reference to the relationship between GOD and Mankind:

Ntef änuk änuk Ntef. (*"He is I and I am He."*)

The following statements from the Egyptian *"Book of Coming Forth By Day"* illustrate the attributes of GOD (NETER) and the concepts of Monotheism and Absolute existence.

1- *"I was One, I became three"*
2- *"Atum-Ra-Ptah,* **(are)** *three in ONE."*
3- *"God is one and alone, none other exists with Him; God is One, the One who has made all things."*
4- *"GOD is a Spirit, a hidden Spirit, the Spirit of Spirits...The Divine Spirit."*
5- *"GOD is from the beginning and He has been from the beginning; GOD existed from old and was, before anything else had being. GOD existed when nothing else existed, and what now exists, GOD created... Before creation, not was created the earth, not were created men, not were created the Gods, not was created DEATH."*
6- *"GOD is truth, and GOD has established the earth thereupon."*
7- *"GOD is life and through Him only Humankind lives. GOD gives life to men and women, breathing the breath of life into their nostrils."*
8- *"GOD is both Father and Mother, the Father of fathers and the Mother of mothers. He begets but was never begotten, produces but was never produced; He begat Himself and produced himself."*
9- *"GOD creates but was never created; He is the maker of his own form, and the fashioner of His own body."*
10- *"GOD endures without increase or diminution. GOD multiplies himself millions of times, and He is manifold in forms and members."*
11- *"GOD made the universe and all that is within. GOD is the Creator of what is in this world and what was, what is and what will be."*
12- *"GOD is the Father of Gods; GOD fashioned men and formed the Gods."*
13- *"GOD is merciful unto those who reverence Him, and He heareth they that call upon Him."*
14- *"GOD KNOWETH they who acknowledge Him; GOD rewardeth them who serve Him and protects them who follow Him; they who SET Him in their HEART."*

15- *"GOD's RAYS are the guides of millions of men and women."*
16- *"GOD gives the whole earth unto those who love Him. Gods and Goddesses bow down in adoration before GOD's soul."*
17- *"GOD is more hidden than all the Gods."*
18- *"No man or God can know GOD."*

19- *"The (Sun) Disk is his (GOD's) symbol ."*

20- *"GOD is not Mind, but Cause that the Mind is; GOD is not Spirit, but Cause that Spirit is; GOD is not Light; but Cause that Light is."*

The Sundisk of Ra representing the primordial point in the center and creation in the outer circle.

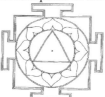

Shakta Yantra of India showing the Egyptian Sundisk and pyramid in the center.

* The Rig Veda is a compilation of religious doctrines which are known to have partially originated with the invaders (Aryans) who came into India around the years 2,000 B.C.E. to 1,500 B.C.E. and attempted to impose themselves on the Dravidian civilization which was well established in India by the year 2,500 B.C.E. As has been noted earlier, Egyptian influence and civilization had spread throughout the region from which the Aryans originated. Thus, the religious and philosophical teachings brought into India by the Aryans are found to be similar to the original Egyptian and Indian philosophies. The main differences would seem to lie in the writings of the Rig Veda which pertain to social custom which have been characterized by many modern scholars of the Rig Veda as *"racist"* and *"sexist"* in character due to their development of a *caste system* in which those who were *"dark skinned"* and women in general were classified as *"beings of lower status"*. It will be noted that like the Ethiopians and early Egyptians, the Dravidians were black skinned curly haired people. This situation was similar to that which had occurred in Egypt with the invasion and influx of Asiatic and Indo-European invaders.

Compare the 20 Egyptian statements above to the following passage from the Indian Rig Veda*:

"He is the all-pervading Being manifesting himself in all things. He has innumerable heads, eyes and feet. It is He that has encompassed the whole universe, and it is He who transcends it... That Being is the whole cosmos, all that was and all that will be. He manifests Himself in the form of the universe. He is also the lord and giver of immortality... So vast is His glory but He, the universal Being, is greater than all that. The manifested world forms but a small portion of His Being, in main He is unmanifest and Immortal."

Author's note:

One will note that the attributes of GOD in the previous Egyptian statements correspond to those of the Hindu, (Samkhya and Vedanta), Buddhist and Taoist philosophical systems of the Far East denoting the idea of an <u>*"Absolute"*</u> GOD force or energy encompassing all existence. The description given for "GOD" also refers to the mental state which GOD represents. Thus, the true essence of our soul is described by the sages as a guide for understanding what the goal of spirituality is.

Vedanta philosophy continued:

<u>Major Tenets of Vedanta</u>

1- Absolute Reality is that which is unchanging.

2- The Absolute Reality is named *Brahman.* The manifesting universe is an appearance only, an illusory modification of Brahman. Therefore, it never had a beginning and will never have an end because it is only an appearance.

3- Brahman or the Ultimate reality, GOD, Supreme Being, is ALL that exists. All the objects of the world and universe even though appearing to be different are really one entity. All physical reality is an illusory manifestation of Brahman which Brahman sustains but yet is detached from at all times just as the sun sustains life on earth and yet is detached from it.

4- Brahman is Pure consciousness. All that exists is essentially Brahman: *"Sat-Chit-Ananda"* - Existence - Knowledge - Bliss. GOD gives things existence; God is conscious of those things (therefore they exist) and GOD gives "bliss" to the experience of living.

5- The mind, body and senses of human beings are illusions. The essence of everything in the universe, including the human soul, is pure consciousness. Even though objects appear real, tangible and permanent, it is in reality transient and illusory.

6- Brahman is the world and also assumes the role of millions of individual life forms (people, animals, insects, etc.). The Individual Soul is termed Atman.

7- Atman and Brahman are one and the same. Therefore, everyone's soul is part of the universal essence, Brahman.

8- Through a veil of mental ignorance, the individual soul (Atman) believes it is an individual entity (Jiva), separate from everything else when it is indeed part of everything. The mental veil of ignorance comes from erroneous subconscious impressions which cause the person to believe they are a body instead of a spirit and therefore, they search for happiness and fulfillment in the illusory pleasures of the world. This leads one from one unfulfilled desire to another.

9- Vedanta seeks to transform the subconscious of the individual through gradually increasing philosophical and practical discipline. Its goal is to remove the veil of ignorance by asserting that the only reality is Brahman. When this reality is "consciously realized" by intuition (through meditative experience), the veil of ignorance is lifted. Once the veil of ignorance is removed, the initiate subsists in a transformed psychological and spiritual state where they abide in the real universal, omnipresent, expansive state of consciousness termed: *"Jivan Mukta"* which means: one who is liberated while still alive. *Jivan Mukta* is an individual who has sublimated their ego-sense in favor of becoming one with the Absolute reality. No longer knowing themselves as an individual, they are one with GOD: *Brahman.* This is the state termed as *Moksha* or *Kaivalia* (liberation).

The term *"Illusory Modification"* can be better understood from a simile given by Vedanta philosophy. A person enters a dark room and steps on something which appears to feel like a snake. The person is very scared because he believes the information from his senses. The person turns the light on and finds that there is only a rope. It was due to ignorance (the darkness) that the rope was perceived to be a snake. In the same way, it is our ignorance about our true nature which allows us to perceive the multiplicity of the world as a "reality." The *"objects of the world"* are perceived as separate entities instead of what they truly are: *Brahman.* This ignorance is based on the information our brains gather from the senses rather than from that gathered through the higher intuitional capacities. The light represents intuitional wisdom of the truth whereby the questions (based on our incorrect and ignorant assumptions and ideas): Where did the snake come from?, What kind of snake is this? Who does the snake belong to?, Is the snake poisonous?, become irrelevant. In the same way questions about the origin of the world, humanity, etc., become irrelevant since time, space and physical reality are illusions, only Brahman exists. One sees oneself as Brahman therefore, one sees only oneself in existence. Relatives, people, the sun, planets are all oneself. Illusory modification made it seem like there was a multiplicity of different objects in existence.

Vedanta Philosophy holds that there are four planes of existence and that the human being is really a composite of three bodies and five sheaths or layers. In this manner, the divine self (Brahman) expresses itself in the form of nature and living beings.

The Planes:

      1- <u>Gross Plane:</u>   **Consisting of the gross elements and the senses.**

      2- <u>Subtle Plane:</u>   **Consisting of subtle elements that may be perceived through extra-sensory perception.**

      3- <u>Subtler Plane:</u>   **The intellect; here the ego is transcended and one experiences higher forms of being.**

      4- <u>Subtlest Plane:</u>   **This is the level of the causal body.**

The Bodies:

      1- Physical Body.
      2- Astral Body.
      3- Causal Body.

The Five Sheaths (coverings):

      1- <u>**Food Sheath**</u> (*Anandamaya Kosha*)**.**
      2- <u>**Pranic Sheath**</u> **- Vital energy** (*Pranamaya Kosha*)**.**
      3- <u>**Mind Sheath**</u> (*Manomaya Kosha*)**.**
      4- <u>**Intellect Sheath**</u> (*Vijnamaya Kosha*)**.**
      5- <u>**Bliss Sheath**</u> **(one transcends the ego and body and experiences the spirit).**

The three bodies and the five sheaths may be compared to the Egyptian belief of the nine parts of the spirit including the BA or Supreme Soul. When it is considered that the Vedantic system of India proposes eight parts plus the Supreme Self or Atman - Brahman, the similarity appears almost exact in theme and number.

The practice of Yoga, as it developed in India (+1,000 B.C.E.-100 B.C.E.), is classified as a science with eight steps; their correspondence to the Egyptian system will become evident:

1- <u>Self control (yama):</u> Non- violence, truthfulness, chastity, avoidance of greed.

2- <u>Practice of virtues (niyama):</u> Actions to avoid in order to maintain yama.

3- <u>Postures (asana):</u> To condition the body and prepare the mind and body for meditation.

4- <u>Breath control (pranayama):</u> Controlling the breath is controlling the Life Force; controlling the Life Force is controlling the mind.

5- <u>Restraint (pratyahara):</u> Disciplining the sense organs to avoid overindulgence and physical temptation of the body: food, sex, drugs, etc.

6- <u>Steadying the mind (dharana):</u> Practice focusing the mind. Concentrating the mental rays on one subject over a short period of time.

7- <u>Meditation (dhyana):</u> When the object of concentration engulfs the entire mind and concentration continues spontaneously.

8- <u>Deep meditation (samadhi):</u> Personality dissolves temporarily into the object of meditation, experience of super-consciousness.

In the Yoga Sutras of Sage Patanjali (c. 200 B.C.E.), the following instruction is given for the practitioner of yoga:

योगश्चित्तवृत्तिनिरोधः

YOGASH CHITTA VRITTI NIRODHAH.

Sutra 2: Yoga is the intentional stopping of the mind-stuff (thought waves).

This is desirable because:

वृत्तिसारूप्यमितरत्र

VRITTI SARUPYAM ITARATRA.

Sutra 4: "At times when the mind stuff flows indiscriminately, "the seer" becomes "identified" with the thought-waves."

Patanjali goes on to say that due to the identification of the seer (our true self) with the thoughts, we believe ourselves to be mortal and limited instead of immortal and immutable. He further says that there is no need to worry because through the steady practice of yoga (dispassion, devotion, mind control exercises of meditation), even the most unruly mind can be controlled. Thus, the individual will discover their true self when the *"Chitta"* (thought waves) are controlled. It is as if one looks at oneself through colored sunglasses and believes oneself to be that color. In the same way, Yoga is the process of uncovering the eyes from the illusion of the mind's thought waves.

Chronology of Egyptian Philosophy

*The Sky GOD- Realm of Light-Day - NETER
Androgynous - All-encompassing -Absolute, Nameless Being, later identified with Ra-Heru (Sphinx)
Yoga of Spirituality (Ra-Buto) 10,000+ B.C.E. to 600 A.C.E.

*Pyramid Texts - Egyptian Book of Coming Forth By Day - 42 Precepts of MAAT
Asar-Heru. God is the soul of all men and women. 10,000 B.C.E.-5,500 B.C.E.

*Amun -Ra - Ptah (Heru) - Amenit - Rai - Sekmet
(male and female Trinity-Complementary Opposites)
5,500+ B.C.E. to 600 A.C.E.

*The Gods of Heliopolis
Shu - Tefnut
Geb - Nut
Asar - Aset
Set - Nebethet
Heru - Hetheru
5,500+ B.C.E. to 600 A.C.E.

*The Gods of Memphis
Ptah (Atum-Heru)- Sekhmet
Nun (primeval waters) -Nunet (heaven).
Huh (boundlessness) and Huhet (bound)
Kuk (darkness) and Kuket (light).
Amon (hidden) and Amonet (manifest).
5,500+ B.C.E. to 600 A.C.E.

*The Gods of Hermopolis
Male and female principals in creation:
Existence - Non existence
Endlessness - End
Inertness - Movement
Darkness - Light

Chronology of Indian Philosophy

Pre - Aryan
Yoga of Spirituality (Kundalini)
Dravidian-Indus Valley Culture
+2500 B.C.E - 1,500 B.C.E

Aryan Influence
Vedas - Atman - Brahman- Maya
Path of Ritualism and social castes.
1,500 B.C.E.-1,000 B.C.E.

Jainism
1,200 B.C.E.

Upanishads
Non-dualism, non-ritualistic philosophy of renunciation of a world of illusion and pain.
800 B.C.E.

Vasudeva - Krishna Cult
Devotion to Deity
800 B.C.E.-500 B.C.E.

Samkhya Philosophy
Complementary Dualism Philosophy
700 B.C.E.

Greek and Mongol Influence
1200 B.C.E.-700 B.C.E.

Buddha
Non-ritualistic, non-dualist, non-deistic philosophy. 500 B.C.E.-600 B.C.E.

Mahabharta-Bhagavad Gita
Yoga Sutras of Patanjali
Uniting the principals of previous philosophies as way to Moksha: Karma yoga, Bhakti yoga and Jnana Yoga forming the basis for a synthesis: Hinduism. 500 B.C.E.-200 B.C.E.

Laws of Manu
200 B.C.E.

Tehuti (Thoth-Heru) 5,500+ B.C.E. to 600 A.C.E. ***The Osirian Resurrection** Yoga mixed with religion 4,500+ B.C.E. to 600 A.C.E. ***The Goddess Principle** Aset-Hetheru-Neith-Mut-Sekhmet-Buto 5,500+ B.C.E to 600 A.C.E.. **Four main principles of the Egyptian concept of GOD, Human Beings and Creation: 1- The androgynous nature containing male and female. 2- Heru-Neter is the universal spirit that manifests in every period of Egyptian religion and represents the ultimate reality behind all manifestations of creation which are simply an interplay between complementary opposite principals often described and named as male and female deities. The same "Great Goddess" principal is represented in different forms or aspects. 3- Men and women are personifications of GOD: spirit and matter (Sphinx), the two principals which together make up all things.* *4-GOD and Creation are ONE. Thus From earliest times 10,000 B.C.E. to the downfall of Egypt 600 A.C.E., the same theme is found throughout Egyptian Philosophy. All of the major cosmogonies and Deities come from the same origin set down in the pyramid texts.*	**Hinduism** 100 B.C.E. **Vedanta Philosophy** 200 A.C.E. **Shaivism and Vaishnavism** **Puranas-Agamas** Hindi Scriptures. 200 A.C.E.- 500 A.C.E. **Tantras** Non-sectarian spiritual scriptures. 500 A.C.E.-600 A.C.E. **Yoga Vasistha** Union of Vedanta (Non-dualism) philosophy and Samkhya 750 A.C.E. **Shankara - founder of Advaita Vedanta (radical Non-dualism)** 800 A.C.E. **Moslem Influence** Kabir (poet-saint) - Integration of Hinduism with Moslem teachings. 1,450 A.C.E. **Sikhism** 1,500 A.C.E. **Sri Aurobindo** Founder of Integral Yoga. 1,900 A.C.E. **Modern Vedanta** Attempts to integrate dual and non dual philosophy, Buddhist psychology and yoga. 1,800 A.C.E. - Present

Below: a summary of the Yoga system of Patanjali and the Philosophy of Buddha. Each represents the many paths to union with the divine which may be used integrally according to the psychological makeup (character) of the individual. All tenets within these philosophical systems are present within the Egyptian philosophy of MAAT 5,000 B.C.E.

Wheel of Yogas of Patanjali. **(250 B.C.E.)**	**The Buddhist Wheel of Life** **(600 B.C.E)**
Eight Inner Yogas 1- <u>Chakra Yoga</u> - Union through attunement of the energy body energy centers. 2- <u>Jnana Yoga</u> - Union through wisdom. 3- <u>Bhakti Yoga</u>- Union through divine love. 4- <u>Prakriti Yoga</u>- Union through power (Life Force). 5- <u>Samadhi Yoga</u>- Union through meditation (communion) with the divine. 6- <u>Karma Yoga</u>- Union through working for GOD as selfless service to humanity.	**The Noble Eightfold Inner Path to** **Nirvana** 1- Noble Path of Creation. 2- Noble Path of Preservation. 3- Noble Path of Wisdom. 4- Noble Path of Love. 5- Noble Path of Power. 6- Noble Path of Peace. 7- Noble Path of Work.

7- <u>Satya Yoga</u>- Union through eternal life. 8- <u>Raja Yoga</u>- Union through mental control - meditation on the divine.	8- Noble Path of Eternal Life.
Eight Outer Yogas	
1- <u>Laya Yoga</u> -Union through development of oneself. 2- <u>Sattwic Yoga</u>- Union through food. 3- <u>Pranayama Yoga</u>- Union through breath control. 4- <u>Shat Yoga</u>- Union through water. 5- <u>Ha Yoga</u>- Union through the Sun. 6- <u>Mantra Yoga</u>- Joy- Union through repetition of sacred words. 7- <u>Hatha Yoga</u>- Union through health. 8- <u>Laya-Kriya Yoga</u>- Union through the earth (earth energy, sexual energy - kundalini).	**<u>The Noble Eightfold Outer Path to Nirvana</u>** 1- Noble Path of Food. 2- Noble Path of Air. 3- Noble Path of Water. 4- Noble Path of the Sun. 5- Noble Path of Joy. 6- Noble Path of Health. 7- Noble Path of Earth. 8- Noble Path of Man.

Due to the extremely close social and ethnic connection between north east Afrika and India, Egyptian and Indian philosophies (Jain, Vedanta-Upanishads, Samkhya) show a large number of Mythological, Linguistic, Phonetic and Social correspondences, many of which will be discussed at length throughout this volume and in future volumes. The following page contains a partial listing of some of the most important correspondences which are of equal symbolic, mythological and philosophical value.

Comparison of Kemetic (Egyptian-Ethiopian) Philosophy and Indian (Hindu-Buddhist) Philosophy showing symbolic, linguistic, mythological and philosophical correspondences.

<u>Kemetic Philosophy (from EGYPT)</u>	**<u>Jain, Vedanta-Upanishads, Samkhya, Buddhist Philosophies (from INDIA)</u>**
* Nefer, Sema, Ankh, Hetep *	** YOGA **
1- NETER	*1-Brahman, Darmakaya*
2- Maat-cosmic order.	*2- Mahat- cosmic mind*
3- Lotus (1000)	*3- Lotus (1000)*
4- Heru	*4- Krishna, Buddha*
5- Asar and Aset	*5- Shiva and Parvati*
6- The Sacred Cow	*6- The Sacred Cow*
7- Tat (Tehuti)	*7- Tat*
8- The Eyes of Heru	*8- The Eyes of Krishna, The Eyes of Buddha.*
9- Ankh	*9- Aum, Ardanari (Iswara)*
10- Black Dot	*10- Bindu*
11- Sahu	*11- Sadhu*
12- Buto-Cobra Goddess.	*12- Bhujanga (cobra), Bhuta (to be, become).*
13- Annu	*13- Anu*
14- Ra (fire), (sun symbol of God)	*14- Ra (fire), (Surya - sun God)*
15- Ra - Rai	*15- Prana - Rai*
16- Ra (sun).	*16- Ravi (sun).*
17- Virgin Birth of Heru.	*17- Virgin Birth of Krishna and Buddha.*
18- The castration of Asar.	*18- The castration of Shiva.*
19- In the form of Asar, Heru is "The Lord of the Perfect Black".	*19- Krishna is "The Black One".*
20- Hetheru- Destructive aspect of Aset.	*20- Kali (Durga)- Destructive aspect of Parvati (Shakti).*
21- The Nine Parts of the Spirit.	*21- The Three Bodies, The Five Sheaths and The Supreme Self.*
22- The Primeval Waters (Chaos)- Nun	*22- The Primeval Waters (Chaos)- Nara*
23- The Journey of Ra.	*23- The Cosmic Dance of Shiva.*
24- Cosmic Egg.	*24- Cosmic Egg.*
25- God abides in the body of all things.	*25- God abides in the body of all things.*
26- The Beautiful West.	*26- The Buddha of the west.*
27- Male (Geb, Asar)- passive principal and Female (Nut, Aset)- active principal.	*27- Male (Purusha)- passive principal and Female (Prakriti)- active principal.*
28- Slime.	*28- Maya.*

29- The Aset Pose.	29- The Kali Pose.
30- Castration of Asar.	30- Castration of Shiva.
31- Above as Below.	31- Above as Below.
32- Mount Meru- Dwelling place of GOD.	32- Mount Meru- Dwelling place of GOD.
33- Seven energy centers in the body.	33- Seven energy centers in the body.
34- The Bull of Asar and Min.	34- The Bull of Shiva.
35- Stilling the heart- Meditation from the Book of Coming Forth by Day.	35- Cessation of mind stuff- Meditation from the Yoga Sutras of Patanjali.
36- Swastika- GOD encompassing all four quarters of creation.	36- Swastika- GOD encompassing all four quarters of creation.
37- Trilinga of Asar.	37- Trilinga of Shiva.
38- Memphite Theology and Creation Story.	38- The Creation Story from the Indian Laws of Manu.
39- Amun, Amen, Ama- Egyptian Creator God, and the Dogon Creator GOD, Amma.	39- Ammaiappan (Dravidian name of GOD).
40- "The Lord of the Perfect Black" Ithiphallic Egyptian vegetation God (Asar).	40- "The Black One" Ithiphallic Dravidian vegetation God.
41- Manu.	41- Manu.
42- Mystical Nile River.	42- Mystical Ganges River.
43- Sun: GOD, Supreme Being - Moon: mind, intellect, wisdom.	43- Sun: GOD, Supreme Being - Moon: mind, intellect, wisdom.
44- Ba- soul (originates from the Universal Ba-Neter Neteru, Atum).	44- Atman- soul (originates from Universal Spirit.- Brahman).
45- Metu Neter- Sacred Speech (all Egyptian hieroglyphics are called Metu Neter).	45- Upanishads, Mahavakyas or Great Utterances.
46- Story of Heru and Set.	46- Story of The Uncle Who Tried to Kill The Newborn.
47- Hekau (words of power).	47- Mantras (words of power).
48- Egyptian Magic.	48- Indian Siddha and Tibetan Buddhist philosophies.
49- Hoeing of the Earth.	49- The Teaching of the Field and Its Knower.
50- Hetep.	50- Om Tat Sat.
51- Ka.	51- Ka.
52- The Veil of Aset.	52- The Veil of Maya.
53- Hetep Slab.	53- Lingam-Yoni.
54- Shu - God of Air, Supporter of Heaven.	54- Varuna - God of Wind, Supporter of Heaven.
55- The World (Cosmic) Lotus rising out of Asar.	55- The Cosmic Lotus rising out of Vishnu.
56– Om	56– Om
57– Haari Om	57– Hari Om

The Philosophy of Buddha (c. 600 B.C.E.)

The Buddha or *"The Enlightened One"** developed a philosophy based on ideas which existed previously in Jain philosophy and the Upanishads. Buddha recognized that many people took the teachings to extreme. Teachings such as that of non-violence which stressed not harming any creatures were understood by some as not moving so as not to step on insects or not breathing in without covering the mouth so as not to kill insects or microorganisms. Prior to Buddha, other teachings such as those of the "Brahmins" and "Sanyasa" (renunciation), where one was supposed to renounce the apparent reality as an illusion, were taken to extremes wherein some followers would starve themselves to the point of death in order to achieve spiritual experience. Others became deeply involved with the intellectual aspects of philosophy, endlessly questioning, "Where did I come from?, Who put me here?, How long will I need to do spiritual practice?, Where did Brahman (GOD) come from?", etc. Buddha saw the error of the way in which the teaching was understood and set out to reform religion.

Buddha emphasized attaining salvation rather than asking so many questions. He likened people who asked too many intellectual questions to a person whose house (lifetime) is burning down while they ask "How did the fire get started?" instead of first worrying about getting out. Further, Buddha saw that renouncing attachment to worldly objects was not necessarily a physical discipline but more importantly, it was a psychological one and therefore, he created a philosophical discipline which explained the psychology behind human suffering and how to end that suffering, a philosophy emphasizing "BALANCE" rather than extremes. He recognized that extremes cause mental upset-ness because *"One extreme leads to another"*. Therefore, mental balance was the way to achieve mental peace. This psychological discipline became the Noble Eight-fold Path which was later adapted by the Indian Sage Patanjali and developed into the eight major Yoga disciplines of Indian Yoga.

The Buddhist Wheel

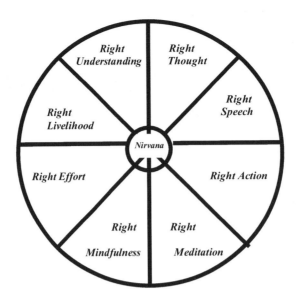

*In much the same way as the term Christ refers to anyone who has attained "Christhood", the term Buddha refers to any one who has attained the state of enlightenment. In this context there have been many male and female Christs and Buddhas throughout history.

The Setting in Motion of the Wheel of the Law:

The Noble Truth of Suffering is:

The reason for all suffering is participation in the world process:

One is unhappy because one invariably expect to find happiness in worldly things.

The Noble Truth of the Cause of Suffering:

The cause of suffering is <u>Ignorance</u> (Avidya).
You have a fundamental misconception about reality.
I see no other single hindrance such as this hindrance of IGNORANCE, obstructed by which mankind for a long, long time runs on, round and round in circles (Ittivutaka).

The Noble Truth of the End of Suffering:

The End of Suffering is ENLIGHTENMENT (NIRVANA).
The way to Nirvana is the basis of Buddha's teaching.

The Noble Eight-fold Path:

The Noble Eight-fold Path is the practical means to disentangle the knot of ignorance and illusion.

<u>1- Right Understanding</u> is learning how to see the world as it truly is.
<u>2- Right Thought</u> is understanding that thought has great power on oneself and others and that whatever one focuses on gains more life; one becomes it.
<u>3- Right Speech</u> is knowing what to say, how to say it, when to say it, and when to remain silent.
<u>4- Right Action:</u>   Guidelines for controlling one's behavior and allowing calmness of mind to pursue Enlightenment:

1. Not intentionally taking the life of any creature.
2. Not taking anything which is not freely given.

3. Not indulging in irresponsible sexual behavior.
4. Not speaking falsely, abusively or maliciously.
5. Not consuming alcohol or drugs.

5- Right Livelihood is making a living in such a way as to benefit oneself and all other beings.
6- Right Effort is determination and perseverance in one's spiritual discipline to transcend one's lower nature.
7- Right Mindfulness is learning how to be aware of everything that one does at all times, not acting automatically, reacting to events as an animal.

8- Right Meditation is a way to transcend into higher forms of consciousness including:

> *"The four stages with form" and*
> *"The four stages without form."*

These comprise successive levels of introvertedness:

> *Joy, Equanimity, and Mindfulness.*

The Kabbalah (c. 100 B.C.E -1000 A.C.E)

The Kabbalah is an ancient sacred science of the study of Creation and man as developed by Jewish initiates. In the Bible, it is stated that Moses, who wrote the laws and guidelines for Jewish society, was knowledgeable in all of the wisdom and magic of Egypt; he was an Egyptian priest. The similarity between the 10 Commandments and the 42 Laws of Maat and the similarities with other scriptures will be noted upon simple comparison. The Tree of Life represents the ten aspects of Creation which in turn represent the ten aspects of GOD and the essence of the human soul. Figure A comes from a stale in the Egyptian Temple of Kom Ombo. Below is the traditional diagram of the Kabalistic Tree of Life. As in the Egyptian mystical system, the Kabbalah states that the tree of life is within the human being.

The tree corresponds to increasing levels of evolving consciousness and the Chakras or psychic energy centers. As in the Egyptian system of philosophy, if the various levels are explored and mastered, the human will know the true name and number of all that exists and have command of all the inner human forces (love, hate, greed, passion, etc.) and will know the names of spirits (Gods) and the seven forces (or powers). This is equal to the Egyptian teaching of achieving control over the Neters inside one's self and the doctrine of Hekau or words of power. Further, upon reaching the highest level, KETHER, which is equivalent to the Egyptian NETER, the human will attain cosmic consciousness and immortality. In the Kabalistic system, as well as the Egyptian, the same symbol for the Sun and Solar Life Force power is used: a dot surrounded by a circle.

Egyptian: Ra; Kabalistic: Tipheret ⊙

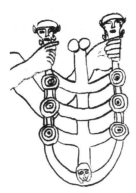

A- Kabbalistic style relief from the temple of Kom Ombo in Egypt.

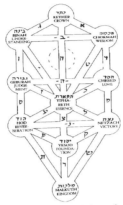

Kabbalistic Tree of Life

Chinese Philosophy: The Tao. (c. 600 B.C.E)

The Egyptian word for Eternal Spirit is *"SHEN"*. In the Chinese Mystical Philosophy, SHEN means Eternal Spirit. Historical evidence shows that the early Chinese dynasties (Shang Dynasty c.1,523 B.C.E.- c.1,927 B.C.E. and Chou Dynasty c.770 B.C.E.-c.221 B.C.E.) were linked to north-east Africa and the area now referred to as the Middle East. As the Middle Eastern inscription read, Asar, at the time he ruled Egypt, extended the Egyptian culture to the farthest reaches of Asia.

The *"Tao Te Ching"* (c. 600 B.C.E.) was the first written record outside of Egypt which discussed the use of breathing exercises just before the written appearance of the Yoga Sutras of Patanjali (c.350 B.C.E.) and the teachings of Buddha (c.B.C.E.550). TAO philosophy was also the first known teaching outside of Egypt which held as the main idea that all creation is composed of two opposite but complementary forces which were called *"Heru and Set"* in Egypt and *"Ying and Yang"* in China. The TAO or *"The Way"*, is a philosophical exposition of Chinese mystical philosophy. It stresses the understanding of the interplay between the two major forces that comprise the universe (male and female), the way to be in harmony with them (virtue), and the experience that lies beyond the "pairs of opposites": unity with all that exists.

Chi is the Chinese name for the single Life Force which exists all throughout the universe. The first writings in reference to Chi begins with Huang Di in c.2690 B.C.E.-2,590 B.C.E. Knowledge about the human energy centers (Kundalini Chakras) outside of Egypt comes from China in the form of snakes which are coiled three and one half times. This is the well known symbol which gained popularity through the Indian Kundalini Yoga System.

EGYPTIAN YOGA VOLUME 1

Like Indian Hatha Yoga, Chi Kung is a system of meditation and physical exercises for the development, sublimation and channeling of the Life Force energy, CHI (Sekhem, Prana, Kundalini), in order to promote spiritual transformation.

According to the Shaolin Temple system where Chi Kung and Kung Fu were first developed, there must first be "internal purification" before there can be Chi Kung or Kung Fu training; that is, before the exercises can be performed effectively, the initiate or aspirant must follow a rigorous system of virtue and self control almost identical to the Egyptian system:

*Student must prepare himself for five restrictions:

> *1. He must not be Frivolous.*
> *2. He must not be Conceited.*
> *3. He must not be Impatient.*
> *4. He must not be Negligent.*
> *5 He must not be Lascivious.*

and seven detriments:

> *1. Fornication depletes the energy.*
> *2. Anger harms the breathing* **(CHI, Life Force Energy flow).**
> *3. Worry numbs the mind.*
> *4. Over-trustfulness hurts the heart.*
> *5. Overdrinking* **(alcoholic beverages)** *dilutes the blood.*
> *6. Laziness softens the muscles.*
> *7. Tenseness weakens the bones.*

*From *Kung Fu History and Philosophy* **by David Chow.**

According to Robert Smith's *Secrets of Shaolin Temple Boxing,* some of the Temple rules were as follows:

1. A student must practice without interruption.
2. Boxing must be used for legitimate self defense.
3. Courtesy and prudence must be shown to all teachers and elders.
4. A student must be forever kind and honest, and friendly to all his colleagues.
5. In traveling, a boxer should refrain from showing his art to the common people even to the extent of refusing challenges.
6. A boxer must never be bellicose.
7. Wine and meat should never be tasted.
8. Sexual desire cannot be permitted.
9. Boxing should not be taught rashly to non-Buddhists lest it produce harm. It can only be transmitted to one who is gentle and merciful.
10. A boxer must never be aggressive, greedy or boastful.

The three Ancient Egyptian symbols shown (A, B, C), represent the following: Fig A., representing the Egyptian "Division of the Heavens", shows the concept of two complementary forces that exist in the universe and are observed everywhere. Thus, it represents the duality of creation wherein GOD, the universal consciousness, has created the appearance of two dynamic principles. These principals at work in the universe (male-female, Yang-Ying, up-down, life-death, etc.) are two divisions of the one reality. Each therefore, is an inseparable part of the other and only appears separate to those who are spiritually immature. Fig B is the Egyptian symbol showing the two opposite forces, Heru (good) and Set (evil), with identical eyes and space. It gives the idea that good and evil are balanced and complementary, adding up to a whole (reality). Fig. B is virtually identical to the Chinese symbol of the Tao or *"The Way of Nature"* (*Ying and Ya*ng), shown in Fig D. The Chinese philosophical system called the Tao is equivalent to the Kemetic (Egyptian) philosophical system of MAAT.

The ancient Ethiopian-Egyptian symbol (Fig C) represents the eternal Trinity principal. GOD is the sustaining factor enabling the other two to exist but most importantly, GOD is all three. This is the meaning of the statement which is found in the "Egyptian Book of Coming Forth By Day" in which GOD states: *"I was one and then I became three."* (Father-Son-Holy Ghost, Ra-Asar-Heru, Father-Mother-Child, the seer - that which is seen - sight itself). Furthermore, Fig C represents the Trinity within humans wherein there is a Heru and Set aspect of consciousness which may be harmonized and brought into balance by the third aspect, represented by the God of Air (breath), SHU.

Above: Egyptian symbol for Shen. Below: another Egyptian symbol for Shen.

Shen is a rope or snake shaped into the form of a circle or loop tied by a knot.

The coiled serpent, the Indian symbol of Kundalini energy.

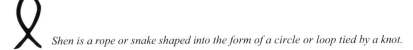

Chinese symbol for Shen

Fig. A   Fig. B   Fig. C   Fig. D

*The Ka'bah monument is a shrine which holds a meteorite. It is venerated by the Muslims. The meteorite is fitted to the monument, a square stone structure, by means of a metal band in the shape of a female genital. This black stone is regarded as the *"hand"* of Allah. The Islamic mythology of the *"hand"* follows the Egyptian creation story in which Atom creates by means of uniting with his own female part, his hand.

The Origins of Islam (c. 600 A.C.E.)

The word "*Islam*" means to surrender. In its religious application, Islam refers to "surrendering to the will or the law of God." Islam is seen by theological scholars to be a reformation of the older Arab religions, which themselves were influenced by Egyptian philosophy during the time of Egyptian the conquest of the Middle East.

Mohammed, the founder of Islam, was opposed by other Arab leaders in the earlier stages of the development of his "new" religion and was forced to flee into Egypt and Ethiopia where he and his followers further developed Islamic philosophy. While living there, Mohammed married an Ethiopian woman. Orthodox Islam departed from the concept of the feminine, Goddess principle so evident in Egyptian philosophy, to a patriarchal religion, much like orthodox Christianity. However, their recognition of the importance of the female principal is evidenced in the *Ka'bah* monument, the most sacred Islamic monument, located in the city of Mecca. The Ka'bah has a female vulva carved on one side*.

Mohammed said he had been given the word of GOD by the Angel Gabriel in a revelation. These teachings are presented in *"The Koran"*, the Holy Book of Islam. The major tenets of Orthodox Islam are:

1- There is only one GOD, unitary and omnipresent. GOD is separate from creation and manages it from afar.
2- The plurality of Gods or the extension of GOD's divinity to any person is strongly rejected.
3- GOD created nature through a primordial act of mercy, lest there would be only nothingness.
4- God governs creation. All areas of creation were given laws to follow. The following of these laws creates perfect harmony. The breaking of them creates disharmony. Since there are laws, there is no need for miracles. *The Koran* is the highest miracle which no man will match.
5- The ultimate purpose of humanity is to serve God in order to reform the earth.
6- God has four functions:

> **Creation,**
> **Sustenance,**
> **Guidance,**
> **Judgment.**

7- After death, those who lived by the laws will go to the Garden (Heaven); those who did not will go to Hell.

The Origins of Esoteric (mystical) Islam: SUFISM (c. 700 A.C.E)

Sufism emerged in the Middle East shortly after Islam became established as a dominant religion in that area. The name "*Sufi*" comes from "Suf" which means "wool." The name Sufi was adopted since the acetic followers of this doctrine wore coarse woolen garments (sufu).

To the followers of Orthodox Islam, Sufism has almost always been regarded as heresy since its main goal is to lead the Sufi follower to have *"Mystic Knowledge of GOD."* Sufism is based upon the fundamental Islamic tenets of living in harmony with others but beyond these ideas, the Sufis hold that:

A- GOD, as creator of the universe, transcends it.
B- GOD cannot be expressed in words.
C- The inner light (one's own soul-spirit) is a sufficient source of religious guidance.
D- The Universe and GOD are actually one.
E- Since humans are part of creation, a human being can, through mystical discipline, become one with GOD.
F-The Sufi mystic is described as a pilgrim on a journey following a path of seven stages:
> **1- Repentance**
> **2- Abstinence**
> **3- Renunciation**
> **4- Poverty**
> **5- Patience**
> **6- Trust in God**
> **7-Acquiescence to the will of God**

G- As in Christian Mysticism and the Bhakti Yoga of India, some Sufis practice devotion by employing the energies of love and directing them solely toward the divine (union with GOD). Through rituals such as reading, listening to poetry and other works of literature, and devotional dancing (The Whirling Dervishes), an ecstatic mental-emotional feeling develops which can be used to sublimate and direct psychic (spiritual) energy to becoming attuned to and attaining union with the divine forces.

H- Sufism incorporates teachings in reference to the subtle spiritual body which may be compared to the Egyptian teachings of the "Pillar of Asar" and the seven powers (energy centers in the body), and the Chakras of Indian Yoga. These are:

Energy Centers

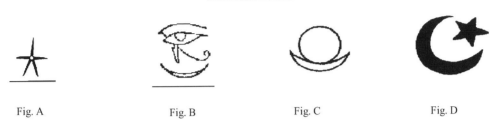

| Fig. A | Fig. B | Fig. C | Fig. D |

From top to bottom: The Egyptian symbol of A. The star, always five pointed, B. The eye of Thoth (Tehuti) and Heru representing a star and the moon (united opposites, completeness, Supreme Being), C. Sun and Moon (same as previous). D. Symbol of Islam.

The main doctrine of Islam and Sufism is encompassed by the word *"Islam": Submission To GOD*. This same doctrine exists in the pyramid texts of Egypt 10,000 B.C.E. - 5,000 B.C.E in the following teaching:

"Give thyself to GOD, keep thou thyself daily for God, and let tomorrow be as today."

Sufi	Egyptian	Indian
The Teacher	*Ikh*	*Sahasrara*
The Mysterious center	*Sekhem*	*Visuddha*
The Secret Center	*Kheper*	*Anahata*
Center of the Self	*Ob*	*Manipura*

Historical evidence and Sufi Mystic literature clearly show that Sufi followers had relationships (cultural, ethnic and social ties) with Egypt, the Essenes (Jewish tribe of Jesus) and the Hindus and Buddhists of the Far East. Thus, it is not surprising that the energy center system of Sufism is closely related to the Tantric systems of Egypt and India. The original Tantric traditions of Egypt and India concentrated on four energy centers instead of seven.

Druidism and The Environment of Religious Development in Africa and Eurasia. (c. 1,500 B.C.E - 700 A.C.E.)

It is evident that the period designated by "Egyptologists" as "Dynastic" represents only the last portion (5,500 years) of Egyptian history and shows an overall decline in every level of society. It must be noted that the period between the years 1,500 B.C.E and 700 A.C.E were marked by a steep decline of the Egyptian society which had existed for thousands of years before, and the rise and fall of the Aryan, Greek, Roman and Persian (Asiatic - European and Arab) empires. The Egyptian Sages realized the growing threat coming from the Asiatic invasions along with the declining moral structure of society due to the unceasing military and social struggles against Asiatics invaders. It was during this time that the Sages and other members of Egyptian society began to leave Egypt in large numbers. Coincidentally, this period saw the greatest growth in intellectual expositions of ancient mystical philosophy outside of Egypt (Ex. Buddhism, Hinduism, Taoism). One of the many exoduses was that of the Druids. The Druids were Egyptian followers of the Egyptian teachings who migrated to Gaul (northern

Europe) and the British Isles. They instructed the Gauls and the Celts (warlike tribes of northeastern Europe) in the following philosophy:

      1- The soul is immortal.
      2- At death, the soul passes into the body of a newborn child.
      3- We are all descendent from the Supreme Being.

In the year 1,030 B.C.E., a Celtic King by the name of Canute issued an edict against the Druids and their cult. As with other cults such as that of Socrates of Greece and Jesus of the Essenes who had learned the ancient mystical wisdom from Egypt, they were feared by Roman imperial as well as local political and military leaders who sought to control the masses by keeping them in a state of perpetual ignorance about their true nature and the power which lies within all humans to attain ultimate freedom.

Egyptian symbols also used by the Druids

Pyramid enclosing the swastika, an ancient Egyptian symbol for Heru as the God of the four quarters (Creation).

Upside down pyramid known in Egypt as the triangle of Heru and in India as the Yoni Yantra which represents the pubic area of the female (womb of GOD) from where all things come: creation, female principal, etc.

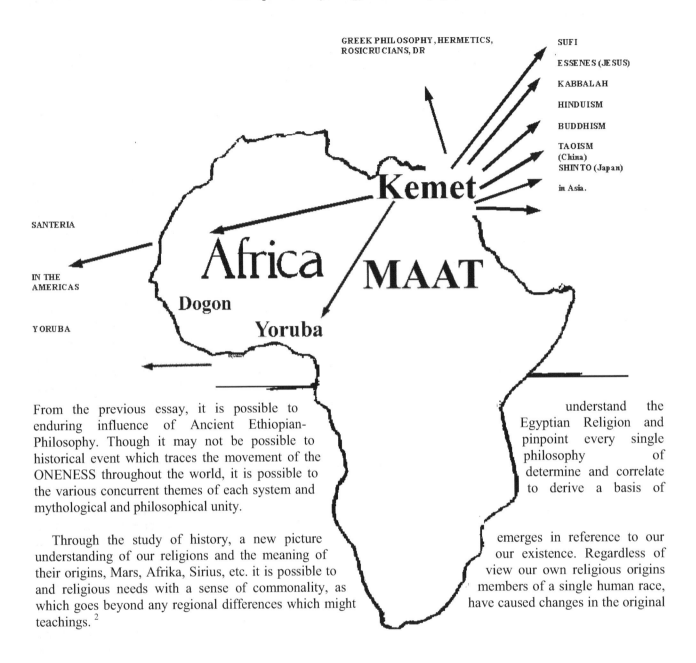

GREEK PHILOSOPHY, HERMETICS, ROSICRUCIANS, DR

SUFI

ESSENES (JESUS)

KABBALAH

HINDUISM

BUDDHISM

TAOISM (China)
SHINTO (Japan)

in Asia.

Kemet

Africa

MAAT

SANTERIA

IN THE AMERICAS

YORUBA

Dogon

Yoruba

From the previous essay, it is possible to enduring influence of Ancient Ethiopian-Philosophy. Though it may not be possible to historical event which traces the movement of the ONENESS throughout the world, it is possible to the various concurrent themes of each system and mythological and philosophical unity.

Through the study of history, a new picture understanding of our religions and the meaning of their origins, Mars, Afrika, Sirius, etc. it is possible to and religious needs with a sense of commonality, as which goes beyond any regional differences which might teachings. [2]

understand the Egyptian Religion and pinpoint every single philosophy of determine and correlate to derive a basis of

emerges in reference to our our existence. Regardless of view our own religious origins members of a single human race, have caused changes in the original

Zulu, Dogon, Yoruba, and Fon Mythology and Philosophy.

At about the time when the Sphinx was constructed (50,000 B.C.E.- 10,000 B.C.E.), North-East Africa (Ethiopia-Egypt) was an abundant, lush rain forest in which many groups lived. The Sahara desert was only in its beginning stages of formation. As time passed, climactic changes became more pronounced leading to the formation and expansion of the Sahara desert. As the annual rainfall became reduced with each passing

---

[2] NOTE: For more on the relationship of Ancient Egyptian with other religions in Asia and Africa see the book
THE AFRICAN ORIGINS OF CIVILIZATION, RELIGION, MYSTICISM AND YOGA PHILOSOPHY by Dr. Muata Ashby.

millennium, many civilized groups and tribes found it necessary to leave the North-Central African area (Sahara) in order to survive. Two of these groups were the ZULU and the DOGON.

The ZULU culture currently live in the southern part of the continent now referred to as "Africa", but stories of their origins have survived in their mythology. One ZULU tradition claims that they originated in the stars and arrived on earth after living on the planet Mars. The move to the earth was needed because there was a war on Mars which left the planet uninhabitable. Recent evidence has been found by the American Viking Space Program that corroborates this claim and the evidence indicates possible kinship ties between the ZULU and the Ethiopian-Egyptians. In the late 1970's, the Viking spacecrafts which were sent to photograph Mars revealed a complex of pyramids and a giant "Sphinx Face" which stares out into space.

The Dogon culture, who now reside in western Africa, adhere to a cosmogony and mythology which closely follows the Egyptian systems. As with the Ancient Egyptians, the Dogons revere the star Sirius as the origin of humanity and the role of Heru, the savior, is given to the God named Nommo. A detailed description of the cosmogony and mythology will be found in the book *"The Pale Fox"* by Marcel Griaule and Germaine Dieterlen who studied with the Dogon Masters for over 15 years. Like the Zulu, the Dogon also acknowledge their ancient origins from North-Eastern Africa.

The Yoruba people also reside in Western Africa. The Yoruba religion has many similarities with the cosmogony, Gods and divination systems of Egypt. For example, one Yoruba creation story is almost identical to the Egyptian one which is described in the Shabaka Stone (see page 47), later referred to as Memphite Theology. It describes the beginning as being a "watery and marshy place". The "Supreme Being" created the "Great God" whom he directed to create the world. As in the Judgment of the Egyptian Book of Coming Forth By Day, the idea of a "Judgment after death" is also held by the Yorubas. It is believed that after death the spirit of the person goes in front of GOD in order to give account of her or his life on earth. As in Egypt, the Yorubas believe that some will go to live with relatives in a good place, while others will end up in a bad place. Thus it is said:

> *All of the things we do when on earth,*
> *We will give account for in heaven.....*
> *We will state our case at the feet of GOD.*

The Fon Nation of West Africa views the snake as the creator and sustainer of creation. Through its 3,500 "coils" above the earth, and 3,500 "coils" below the earth, the snake represents energy in perpetual motion, energy without which creation would immediately disintegrate. This description recalls the Primeval Serpent of Ancient Egyptian mythology and the Kundalini of India, with her "coiled up" cosmic energy which sustains all life. Another Fon story tells that a serpent carried GOD everywhere in its mouth in the making of creation. This is reminiscent of the Egyptian story of *"The Serpent in the Sky"* (see page 66). Also, the main character in Fon mythology, *Legba,* seeks to reconcile the rift between heaven and earth which occurred in primeval times. These stories resemble those of Heru who travels the land teaching and enlightening the people.

Throughout Africa, the snake with two heads in the form of a circle or a serpent in the form of a circle swallowing its own tail represent eternity, life, continuity, constant rejuvenation, etc. It should be noted that one of the goals of Kundalini Yoga is to develop the Life Force energy of the serpent and to tie up that serpent (energy) into a circuit wherein energy does not escape, thereby accumulating it, resulting in the rejuvenation of the body and raised consciousness.

CONCLUSION

When comparing ancient mythologies and philosophies, it is necessary to approach them all with an open mind and the idea that no matter how discordant or flamboyant they may appear to be, there is a basis of truth which underlies them all. In the study of religions and philosophies, it may be necessary to discount local variations of mythological stories in order to view the commonality of their themes. Likewise, when analyzing writings by those who claim to have had mystical experiences, it is necessary to discount the inconsistent aberrations which may be due to their particular mental state (being unenlightened) at the time. Once local and regional variations in mythological stories and hallucinatory or delusory descriptions of mystical experiences are stripped away from the religious and philosophical traditions, it is possible to gain insight into the underlying unity of religious thought wherein the major themes have survived to the present day. These include:

1- The human being is more than what meets the eye. Beyond the body, there is an eternal soul which aspires to achieve greater heights than what ordinary life suggests.

2- That Soul is immortal.

3- There is one Divinity (GOD) which expresses in many ways; the soul seeks closeness with that divinity (mystical experience).

4- Mystical experience requires the seeker to cultivate a state of mind (consciousness) that leads to the awareness of that which lies beyond the realm of ordinary senses.
5- Mystical experience requires the seeker to develop a lifestyle based on virtue, and both mental and physical health.

6- Mystical experience leads to an expanded state of consciousness and awareness of reality.

7- Mystical experience is a necessary part of the existence and evolution of the soul.

8- When the soul is deprived of mystical aspiration through its own ignorance, mental activity which is the primary method of expression of the soul may become unstable. Mental illness and other mental aberrations may result in depression, wars, crime, etc.

The Sages realized that the coming world age necessitated the dissemination of ancient mystical wisdom in a form which the masses of people could more easily have access to and understand. Thus, hieroglyphic writing and oral tradition (teachings kept in the memory of the Sage and initiates) gave way to written versions of the same teachings. These written versions constituted intellectual expositions of mystical wisdom which already existed in both oral history as carried on by the Egyptian Sages and also in Egyptian hieroglyphic form.

The development of Hieratic writing in Egypt, Cuneiform in the Middle East and Sanskrit in India were among the first in a series of new writing systems which espoused the same philosophy that had existed in Egypt for many thousands of years. Schools of mystical philosophy grew up around such names as Socrates, Pythagoras and Plato in Europe, Zoroaster in Persia, Moses and Jesus in the Middle East, Buddha and Patanjali in India and Lao Tzu in China. The writings of the Greeks acknowledge the fact that they studied mystical philosophy in Egypt. From the current analysis, Kemetic (Egyptian) philosophy appears to form the basis of Christianity, Hinduism, Vedanta, Sufism, Buddhism, Taoism, Druidism, and the Kabbalah. The similarity of the tenets of the other systems suggests a common origin. They are but aspects of the same philosophy of

ONENESS.

•

"The Primordial Point, The Origin of Creation"

Common Features of Mystical Experience: The Goal of Mystical Philosophy

Common features which seem to characterize the mystical experience have been noted in the philosophical and religious scriptures of many countries. The following realizations may come in a single experience or may occur several times either spontaneously or while engaged in formal Yoga and meditation practice. They may occur spontaneously, once in a lifetime, or several times and may remain as a permanent feature of one's consciousness. They often come in the form of something that suddenly "dawns" on one. The enlightenment experience may occur in an "instant" and in the following moment the "thinking" mind reactivates and makes sense of the experience. Some common realizations are listed below.

1- All of a sudden one knows that there is only one consciousness that exists and that it is one's own.

2- One discovers that all that exists depends on one's consciousness. One knows that creation (the world) "depends" on one's consciousness. The world is seen as a projection which one has created.

3- One knows that one's consciousness (soul) is the same one which underlies and supports all other human beings. All souls are one.

4- One knows that this consciousness is distinct from the ego-personality of others, that it is their true inner self, their soul, of which even they are unaware; one's soul is one with every other soul.

5- Immortality; one knows at once that one is immortal, infinite, boundless.

6- One may experience lasting effects from the mystical experience which may fade in time. For example, one may experience a sensation of being one with other people.

All mystical experience is said to proceed from the action of the primal Life Force (Egyptian-Ra-Buto, Indian-Kundalini) which causes evolutionary changes in the physical and subtle nervous systems and mental understanding. If not prepared, the onset of mystical experience may cause emotional imbalance, disease or insanity. For this reason, training in spiritual and occult teaching and the adjustment of one's life in order to integrate the expansion of consciousness is desirable.

From the description above, it is evident that the mystical experience of "oneness" with the absolute goes beyond the concepts of the mind and lies beyond any form of physical experience even in the most subtle forms where psychic powers such as telepathy, out of body experiences and communion with divine personalities occur. The individual ego-personality is for that time "dissolved" into "Absolute being". Upon returning to the "normal" or mundane state of everyday consciousness, the personality of the spiritual aspirant is little by little changed, molded into a higher form of consciousness. In the mystical state, consciousness goes beyond previous concepts of its previously perceived notions of reality including its ideas about "GOD". This occurs because in order for consciousness to perceive time, space and physical reality, it must be conditioned to perceive something called time, space and physical reality. During the mystical experience, it becomes absolutely clear through one's own "intuitional realization" that physical reality is only a reflection of the true reality. One has now proven to him or her self the validity of the teachings.

Conditioning occurs when the unconditioned consciousness enters the body and interacts with the world through the perception instruments of the senses and forgets its unconditioned state. In the process of conditioning, the consciousness (soul) not only believes that it perceives matter, but also believes it itself is something physical. This is the state of duality in which the soul, through its identification with the mind and body, becomes bound to the rules of physical reality which apply to the mind and body. In the unconditioned state reached through mystical experience, *Hetep* ⬓, the previous notions of duality wherein one experiences opposites (male and female: life, ☥ *Ankh*), dissolves into the ocean of existence, *NETER* ⌐ (Being).

During the mystical state, the mind is temporarily disengaged from (conditioned) consciousness. Consciousness has returned to its original state of being (unconditioned): free from identification (conditioning) with time, space, body, mind and ego. The initial onset of a mystical experience sometimes causes extreme awe and fear. With time, the experiencer will become comfortable with the experience and may begin to desire to remain in that state. The mystical state is characterized by an initial feeling of rapture in which there is a "pleasurable" feeling of release from the bonds of the body, followed by a blissful feeling (continuation of the experience). Meditation may be used as a deliberate way to seek a mystical experience and to train the mind in order to reproduce it at will, eventually possessing a form of "double consciousness" wherein the Absolute and relative realities are equally perceived. When the ego-consciousness is fully established in its innate mystical "being-ness" apart from its physical manifestation as a person, then it is said to be free, liberated, saved; complementary opposites (Ankh) fuse into "Being" (NETER-oneness), and then go even beyond any concepts of duality. Absolute "being" therefore, lies beyond rapture and bliss and beyond all thought categories.

CHAPTER 3: Modern Physics and Ancient Egyptian Physics

"The Ancient Egyptian God Ptah"

"The noblest employment of the mind is the study of its Creator."

Ancient Egyptian Mystical Wisdom

Modern Physics

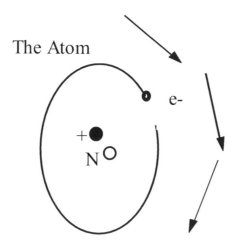

The Atom

Modern Physics appears to be "proving" Ancient Mystical Philosophy. In the past 20 years, studies that have tried to find the smallest particle or to explore the outer limits of space have come up with answers which support the ancient mystical philosophical view of the cosmos and the constitution of the human being.

Science is discovering that the Universe is infinite in all directions, both at the atomic (micro) level and at the planetary (macro) level. It is also finding that what we call "matter", is not what it appears to be. In fact, studies suggest that matter is 99.9% empty space surrounded by an idea (information, thought), consciousness. Contrary to popular belief, quantum physicists have found that they cannot explain what matter is nor what holds it together. The remaining 1% of matter which appears to be visible is also theorized by quantum physics (modern physics) to be an optical illusion. The "Atom" is said to be composed of a positively (+) charged "Particle" called a "Proton" and a particle with no charge (N), called a "Neutron", in the center. These two particles are said to be surrounded by an electron which carry a negative (-) charge and revolves around the nucleus. See Fig. 1. All matter is found to be composed of the same Protons, Neutrons and Electrons. The difference in appearance comes from the different numbers of "particles" in each "ATOM" and also from the combination of different atoms with varied combinations of the three particles. Further, it is known that electrons have no weight and that there is a vast "empty space" between the protons and the electrons that circulate around them; also that there is "empty space" inside of the protons, neutrons and electrons. Therefore, what we are seeing and touching by use of our senses is not at all what it appears to be.

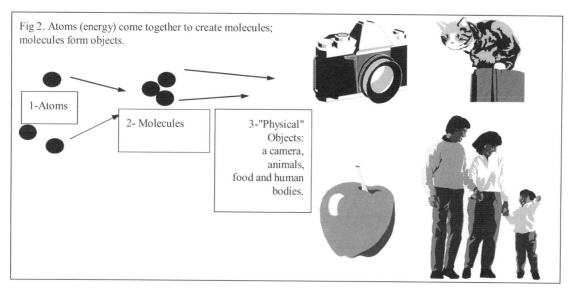

Fig 2. Atoms (energy) come together to create molecules; molecules form objects.

1- Atoms

2- Molecules

3- "Physical" Objects: a camera, animals, food and human bodies.

If matter is in reality energy, then what holds it together and causes it to appear as the varied "physical"objects of the universe? Matter/Energy is held together by consciousness. Consciousness is the underlying support of all things in the universe. Matter cannot exist without consciousness to give it form and to be the perceiver of its existence, because matter is only an illusion projected by the conscious perceiver who uses sensory organs to perceive with and a mind to interpret that which is perceived.

What we seem to perceive with our senses is in reality, only different aspects of the same substance. That is, when energy "vibrates" at a high speed (frequency), it appears as a light (less dense, less weight) material such as gas or electricity. When it "vibrates" at a lower speed, it appears as a solid (dense material) object such as rocks or metal. The higher the vibrations are, the more subtle the "material" will appear to be. The slower the vibrations are, the more solid, rigid and static it will appear to be. When matter vibrates at very high rates, it goes beyond the gaseous state; then matter appears as rays such as sun - rays or X-rays. At higher rates of vibration, it would be so subtle that it could fit in between the "empty spaces" in the slower vibrating matter. It could pass through it or "reside" in it. This is the subtle realm of the "spirit" body which "inhabits" the "physical" body. The object of all spiritual movements is to "identify" one's consciousness, one's concept of who one is, with the "subtlest reality" rather than with the gross physical reality because the physical one is perishable and transient, whereas the subtlest one is transcendental and immortal. In fact, it is the "subtle" spirit from which "gross" matter is created. For this reason, keeping a "light" lifestyle which promotes higher mental vibrations, a "light" diet and "light" thoughts are important as will be seen in further chapters.

The new generation of physicists beginning with Albert Einstein has developed a "new physics." They now believe that matter, that is, everything which can be perceived with our senses, including our bodies, is an "ILLUSION." If we were to look at matter the way it truly is, we would see structures that appear as small planets and moons circling them at lightning speeds. Even the most solid looking structures are really moving; everything is in perpetual motion. Further, we would see that matter seems to come out of nowhere and then goes back into "nowhere-ness." As all "matter" is composed of the same "stuff," the different objects we see in the world are merely different combinations of the same material substance common to all things; this is what is meant by an illusion or appearance of multiplicity and variety. The "new physics" says that matter is nothing more than energy.

Above: *Waves of energy are particles and particles are also waves. Both are energy in different form.*

Particle accelerator experiments attempted to break down atoms into smaller units by colliding them at great speeds. Scientists found that when a positively charged proton (matter) and a negatively charged proton (anti-matter) are crashed together, particles turned into energy (wave patterns) and then back to matter again. Energy and matter are therefore, interchangeable. This interchangeability of matter and energy is represented in the famous formula $E=mc^2$ by Einstein who initially developed this theory mentally (without experimentation). Therefore, even the most solid looking objects are in reality ENERGY in motion at different vibratory rates.

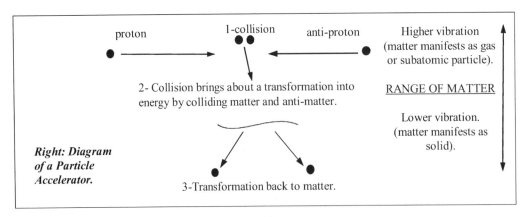

Further, modern science has discovered that even objects of the world which appear to be separate, such as human beings, are in reality "exchanging pieces of each other" on a continuous basis. That is to say, every time we breathe out we are expelling atoms and molecules from our internal organs. Therefore, every time we breathe, we are sharing pieces of our bodies with other people and with the environment. For example, air that is breathed by someone in India may be breathed by someone in the United States two days later and vise versa. Thus, the physical world which appears to have defined boundaries is only an illusion. In reality, the world is one interrelated mass of atoms and energy which is being "caused" to move and interact by some "unknown" force.

> *SPACE:* Once considered as a void in which "nothing" exists, space is now known to be composed of extremely subtle matter. Modern physics has proven that space "bends" when close to an object with high gravitation such as a dense star. Therefore, the modern understanding of space, that is, the space between two people as well as the space between stars must be understood in a new way. Like ordinary "physical" matter, space itself must now be considered a "substance" which unites and binds the cosmos. Therefore, there are no "voids", "cavities" or "empty spaces" in the universe. All is ONE. Indian philosophy uses the term *"ether"* to describe this space.

The Ancient Mystical Philosophy of an all encompassing "force" that binds the universe together was espoused thousands of years ago in the Egyptian philosophy of SEKHEM, the Indian idea of PRANA, the Chinese idea of CHI and in the philosophies of other cultures. Philosophy further states that this "FORCE" can be controlled through mental discipline. Modern science has now, based on scientific evidence, postulated the existence of a substance called *"DARK MATTER"* which is described as an "unseen, unfelt substance that makes up to 99% of the Universe." This means that not only is the world one interrelated mass, but that it is a part of the greater mass called the "Universe".

This theory supports the ancient philosophical idea that the "Created" Universe really does not exist except as perceived through the mind of the individual. It is a manifestation of the Supreme Being that ebbs and flows in a time frame that encompasses an untold number (perhaps billions) of years. It is "created" and "destroyed" periodically. This supports the theory of a *"BIG BANG"* and the *"Expanding-Contracting Model of the Universe."* The last "Creation" is thought by scientists to have occurred several billions of years ago. In the future, they theorize that the universe will close in on itself (contract), and all the planets, stars, etc. will return one point, as represented by the point in the symbol of Ra. Then, a new "creation" or big bang will occur again.

This is the same information stated in age old philosophical scriptures dating from the beginning of "historical" times.

Those who are alive now, will not witness that "dissolution" since it is theorized that it will not occur for millions of years in the future, however, the implications of what it means are crucial to the understanding of the nature of reality (the cosmos) with which humans are intimately related. In fact, Ancient Mystical Philosophy states that the "Created" universe is only an appearance for the generation of a stage upon which the human experience may occur. In addition, this "illusion" that has been created by our conditioned minds, is a "reality" only to the extent that we "believe" in it.

Thus, reality appears to be a relative idea. Ancient Mystical Philosophy states that the true essence of things can be seen by the liberated mind which sees what lies beyond the information given by the senses and that those whose minds are not liberated will experience the "physical" world as if it really "exists." For example: there is no blue sky. It only appears to be blue because of the limited human sense of vision.

Modern science has now accepted that so called "physical reality" cannot exist outside of the person conducting the experiments. An older theory held that the person conducting the experiment could be considered separate and apart from the phenomena being observed. Modern science now holds that nature and all phenomena occur because of an experimenters ability to conceptualize the phenomena and to interpret it. Therefore, the observer is part of the phenomena being observed. Consequently, modern science now uses a new term for the experimenter. The new term is <u>Participant.</u> Thus, the experimenter is really a participant in the experiment because his or her consciousness conceives, determines, perceives, interprets and understands it. No experiment or observed phenomena in nature can occur without someone to conceive that something is happening, determine that something is happening, perceive that something is happening (through instruments or the senses), and finally to interpret what has happened and to understand that interpretation. Therefore, the most recent theory in modern physics is that matter, that is to say creation, is composed of not only energy in varying degrees of density (vibration), but that it is "intelligent", or it might be better understood by saying that matter and energy are manifestations of Cosmic Intelligence (consciousness).

Egyptian Physics

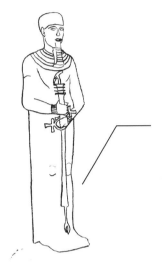

Ptah-Horus with the Was-Djed staff holding an Ankh in each hand. Ptah symbolizes all Life, Stability and Strength.

The Illusion of Time According to The Teaching of Mer-Ka-Re

Einstein's theory of relativity showed that time is not a constant, fixed, and tangible factor we are so accustomed to. In fact, the concept of time depends on the perception of the individual who is experiencing the passage of time. The very fact that time does not have a fixed point of reference is acknowledge by physicists to be a factor of its illusoriness. The concept of time developed out of a need to explain the way in which events seem to occur in a sequential manner, but modern physics has proven this idea to be an illusion of the human mind. In fact what we seem to experience is not the passage of time, but the motion of the Neters (opposite but complementary forces) as they (we) interact with each other. The Neters (cosmic energies and elements) are ever engaged in perpetual change which the human mind confuses as the passage of time. Einstein was not the first to state a theory of relativity. The theory of time relativity was stated in ancient Egyptian spiritual texts and later in Indian spiritual texts thousands of years before Einstein. In the following text, *"Instruction to Mer-ka-Ré"*, a pharaoh teaches his son about the importance of performing righteous actions in this lifetime because he will be judged by the assessors of Maat who exist in a different time reference than the one which is known of by ordinary humans:

"You know that they are not merciful the day when they judge the miserable one..... Do not count on the passage of the years; they consider a lifetime as but an hour. After death man remains in existence and his acts accumulate beside him. Life in the other world is eternal, but he who arrives without sin before the Judge of the Dead, he will be there as a Neter and he will walk freely as do the masters of eternity"

Creation, Matter and Physical Reality According to the *Shabaka Stone* Inscription.

The nature and composition of *"matter"* or what is termed *"physical reality"* and the concept of *"consciousness"* were understood and clearly set down in the hieroglyphic texts which date back to 5,500 B.C.E in the theological system of Memphis, Egypt as follows:

In the beginning only NETER (GOD of Gods) existed and nothing else. Then Neter became three, Amon - Ra - Ptah.

The *"Shabaka Stone"* states:

"Ptah conceived in his heart (reasoning consciousness) all that would exist and at his utterance (the word - will, power to make manifest), created Nun, the primeval waters (unformed matter-energy).

Then, not having a place to sit Ptah causes Nun to emerge from the primeval waters as the Primeval Hill so that he may have a place to sit. Atom then emerges and sits upon Ptah. Then came out of the waters four pairs of Gods, the Ogdoad (eight Gods):

Nun (primeval waters) and Nunet (heaven).
Huh (boundlessness) and Huhet (that which has boundaries).
Kuk (darkness) and Kuket (light).
Amon (the hidden) and Amonet (that which is manifest).

The Neters (Nun, Nunet, Huh, Huhet, Kuk, Kuket, Amon, Amonet) are the lips and teeth of (GOD'S) mouth which speaks the names of all things which come into existence . . .

. . . The Heart and tongue have power over all the limbs. GOD is found as the heart within all bodies, and in the mouth of each Neter and all humans as the tongue (will), of all things that live. . . It is GOD who thinks (as the Heart) and who commands (as the tongue). . .

. . . That which the nose breathes, the eyes see, the ears hear; all of these (senses) are communicated to the heart. It is the heart (mind) which makes all knowledge and awareness manifest, and then the tongue is what repeats what the heart has thought. . .

. . . All divine utterances manifested themselves through the thoughts of the heart and the commandments of the tongue. . .

. . . Justice is done to they who do what is loved, punishment to they who do what is hated. Life is given to they who are peaceful, death is given to the criminal. . .

. . . In truth GOD caused the Neters to be born, the creation of the cities, establishment of the nomes, the establishment of the Neters in their places of adoration. . . GOD made their likenesses according to their desire. Thereby, the Neters entered into their bodies*, the variety of wood, all types of mineral, clay, and all things that grow from these and in which they have taken place, foods, provisions, and all good things... He (Ptah) is Heru."

Thus, through the Shabaka Inscription, we are instructed in the following wisdom:

1- Creation came into being through the mind (thought) of Ptah (the GOD of Gods) and his utterance (power).

2- GOD created "Energy - Matter" (Nun), and then formed the principals by which they would be governed (four pairs of opposites).

Below: The Egyptian

"Four Qualities and the Four Elements".

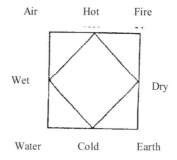

3- Atom (Sun and Fire God) performs the work of creation by sitting on Ptah, taking the creative thought, and then acting on the command of GOD. Therefore, "ATOMS" are the creative thought from GOD which "obey" GOD'S will, ie. *EXISTENCE.* GOD gives existence; human consciousness allows perception of and gives meaning to that existence.

4- GOD is conscious of creation, therefore, creation exists.

5- Consciousness, the "HEART", (what modern physics would call "intelligence"), is the underlying reality behind all existence and all human experience. The senses receive the information from the environment and thereby, register knowledge and existence. In fact, the world (creation) exists because consciousness (soul-intelligence) projects its existence through thought power. There can be no existence without consciousness to perceive it. GOD IS the Neters and the Neters are creation.

6- Heru and Ptah are one in the same.

Below: Atom, "The Great He-She", the Androgynous Egyptian God who created that which Ptah command by mating with himself. Atom creates by uniting with his female half, symbolized by his hand. Thus, as in the Indian mythology surrounding *Ardhanari-Purusha*, creation arises from GOD's "masturbation". Creation "emanates" from GOD's very essence. Creation is GOD.

*The understanding that GOD is located within the "bodies of all things" is also found in the ancient Yoga text *"Yoga Vasistha"* (first recorded in c. 750 A.C.E.):

"Just as there is butter in every kind of milk, similarly the Supreme abides in the bodies of all things."

Thus, the universe is mental as is stated by the God Djehuti-Hermes:

"The Universe is Mental, they who grasp the mental nature of the universe are far along the path of self mastery."

Creation itself is **THOUGHT** and it is sustained by **THOUGHT** power. Another name for the God Djehuti-Hermes (God of writing, wisdom and scribe of the Gods) is Thoth. The similarity of the word "Thoth" to the word "thought" is striking since Thoth (thought) is the determiner of fate in the karmic scales of MAAT. Thoth represents the mind. Mental advancement (raising consciousness, understanding) is the key to understanding creation.

6- GOD is the underlying reality (consciousness) behind all events of the world . GOD is that which is perceived and also the perceiver. Therefore, only GOD exists. Nature does not exist as a separate entity from GOD. The soul of all things is GOD (NETER).

7- GOD is the underlying reality (consciousness) behind all objects that exist (wood, minerals, foods, provisions, and all things that come from these).

8- The doctrine of life (mental peace) and death (criminal behavior - mental unrest).

The Mind of GOD Conceives Creation as a Dream Within a Dream

From the Ancient Egyptian Scriptures...

"In the form of Khepra, Ra (NETER) declares that before him, nothing existed; Time, Space, the realm of matter, Nun, the primeval waters (unformed mater) did not exist. His power was not exhausted by that single creative act, he continued to create millions and millions of new forms out of that which he had already created.

Khepra

Just as a dream can be experienced within another dream, GOD creates new forms of existence (world systems, universes, life forms, etc.), as successive mental thoughts within thoughts. Modern physics would see this concept as a multi-dimensional movement of energy. Energy is neither used nor wasted, only reformulated into ever changing, infinity. In one of the most important, but not well known ancient Indian Vedantic texts called *"Yoga Vasistha",* also known as *"Maha Ramayana"*, there is a story illustrating the same idea of creation as expressed by GOD in the form of Khepra. A seeker of enlightenment meditates on his own existence and finds that he is meditating upon someone who is having a dream. The dream subject being meditated on discovers he is a dream of someone else and so on until the root personality or subject is reached. That root personality is GOD. In the same way we exist through many incarnations creating the projection of a body and a surrounding world but in reality each of us is GOD having innumerable dreams. In the Yoga Vasistha as well as the creation of Khepera, creation occurs due to the power of the mind to think and believe in what is thought. Since the universe proceeds from the mind of GOD, through a dream process as it were, it follows that all things, our mental ideas as well as what is called physical reality are in reality emanations from the cosmic mind of GOD. Therefore, it follows that attunement of the individual human mind with that cosmic mind will bring forth union with the cosmos (Maat). Thus, by getting back to the source of the original thoughts of the mind, it is possible to find enlightenment. This task may be accomplished by simple but intense reflection on the nature of reality. As we are innately divine Neters (Gods), we too can create with our mind, not only ideas but new physical realities as well, through the practice and exercise of our heart (mind) and tongue (will). It is only because we have been convinced by the world that we are puny animals in need of salvation and assistance from outside of our-selves that we exist in a degraded, depressed state. Therefore, from an even higher perspective, it must be understood that our concepts of GOD, the cosmic mind that creates and causes existence to appear to exist, is only a projection of GOD.

Thus the mind of NETER, GOD, is the source of all creations, and everything that springs forth from them. This is the mystery of mysteries that must be known, not only "intellectually", but intuitionally. All philosophical, religious and scientific ideas originate from this one source. All other mysteries or ideas are only lower mysteries which proceed from within this simple truth. The pursuit of intricate religious, philosophical or mystical systems is thus likened to a dream within a dream, the pursuit of an illusion if they do not lead to this simple truth. As Creation is vast and capable of providing the mind with endless subjects and intricacies, it is easy to get caught in "illusions." Therefore, the most important ability to develop is *"the ability to distinguish the real from the unreal."* It is important therefore, to understand that spiritual freedom cannot be attained from reading the material in this or any other book. The information is needed but the goal goes beyond thoughts, so if a person thinks "I read the wisdom book so now I am enlightened," then that person is probably not truly enlightened. Enlightenment is not something one can "read" or "think"; it's something one KNOWS. When spiritual transformation occurs, there will be no question about what it is or how it feels. It has nothing to do with egoistic feelings of superiority over others due to one's "high wisdom" or other delusions of self importance. It is however more like waking up in the morning and realizing one had a vivid dream which seemed "so real" but upon waking up (enlightenment), the dream of life disappears and there is a new reality, a wonderful reality beyond any past imaginings, a reality which transcends any notions of one's individual self.

Ancient philosophy tells us that the creation story is re-played every moment of every day. Every time our heart beats, a new moment of life is created. Everyday the sun rises, another day is created. Modern science agrees with this assessment. In less than one year, 98% of all the atoms in the human body are replaced with completely new ones. In less than a year and a half we have a completely new body. Therefore, the body and brain do not meet the criteria of reality as that which is unchanging. They are ever changing and illusory. They, along with the mind, are changeable with time. Therefore, the only reality is that which sustains them, that which keeps them working and allows them to have the illusion that they really exist. The only unchanging reality is the spirit.

The meaning of the word "PHYSICS" is "the study of the composition of Nature". The word "Nature" comes from the Ancient Latin word *"NATURA"*. The word *"Natura"* originates in the Egyptian words *"NETER"* (GOD) and *"NETERU"* (GOD'S manifestations). The early Greek students of physics, such as Thales and Democritus, learned the science of the study of GOD from the Egyptian masters who instructed them to *"Know Thyself"*. Since each human being is a Neter, a manifestation of GOD the most direct way to know GOD (NETER) is to study GOD'S manifestation, NETERU - ONESELF, because NETERU cannot exist without being sustained at every moment by NETER. Therefore, NETER can be found in NETERU. It is only due to the rampant, untrained thought processes that control the direction of the mind, that GOD (NETER) is not perceived by us (Neteru). Therefore, the study of NETER through NETER'S manifestations in NETERU requires the mastery of our thought faculty, Djehuti, and the understanding of laws by which nature exists (MAAT).

From Memphite theology (5,000 B.C.E.) we learned that the Neters are in reality the myriad of forms which Ptah (GOD) assumes. Therefore, the idea of explaining the physical world was set forth in terms of principles (Neters), represented by objects, personalities or animals, which exhibit and exemplify certain characteristics and tendencies that are found in nature as well as in human beings. This differs from the traditional western view of explaining the physical (material) world in terms of it being a concrete, absolute reality composed of "elements" because, according to the ancient scriptures, there is only one element that exists: GOD. Through philosophical examination and modern scientific experimentation, that idea of the world being an absolute reality is found to be illusory. Thus, the laws of existence by which the "physical" universe manifests and works is understood as interactions of opposite but complementary principles (Heru and Set).

The Egyptian conception of the dynamic principles in nature is contained in the *"Diagram of Opposites"* (5,000 B.C.E.). It contains the principles of Creation, Air-Fire-Earth-Water, and the basic mechanism by which they interact, Hot-Dry-Wet-Cold. The qualities are further elaborated in the cosmogonies as outlined on page 24 (see inset) of this text where creation is seen as an elaborate interaction of complementary opposites. Similar ideas are found in Indian Ayurvedic medicine (1,000 B.C.E.) with the five elements or principles in nature (Earth-Water-Fire-Air-Ether) and in the Chinese idea of the two forces (Ying-Yang) which arose from the Ultimate One (Tao) and the five elements (Wood-Metal-Fire-Earth-Air) in 1,050 A.C.E.

NOTE: For more on the mystical teachings of Ancient Egyptian Physics and the mysteries of matter see the book *THE HIDDEN PROPERTIES OF MATTER: Egyptian Physics and Yoga Metaphysics* by Dr. Muata Ashby.

✓ *The creation myth from the Shabaka Stone which constitutes the main tenets of Memphite Theology are similar in many respects to the creation story from the Indian mythology associated with The Laws of Manu. Manu is a Sage-Creator God of Indian Hindu-Vedic tradition who recounts the process of Creation.*

✓ *The Self Existent Spirit (GOD) felt desire (Kama). Thus from a state of rest, the creative force, God Kama, is created. Wishing to create all things from his own body, GOD created the primeval waters (Nara) and threw a seed in. From the seed came the golden cosmic egg. The Self Existent Spirit developed in the egg into Brahma (Purusha) and after a year of meditation, divided into two parts (Male and Female).*

✓ *In Egyptian mythology, the word Manu signifies "The land of the setting Sun" and "The Beautiful West". The west is the abode of GOD and the resting place of all souls.*

EGYPTIAN YOGA VOLUME 1

BASIC EGYPTIAN PHYSICS:

5
NETERS

NETERS = Creation of elements (air, fire, water, earth), different objects with name and form arise because of the interaction of different elements which are themselves composed of the same thing-consciousness). Creation of the qualities of matter - hot, dry, wet, cold, etc., the physical and astral universe which is composed of matter in various degrees of vibrational existence from gross (solid-lower frequency) to subtle (waves-higher frequence).

4
ATOM

Under the direction of Ptah, Atom creates all things. Neters, qualities of matter.
Atom (the will-power to create) who is both male and female, does the will of Ptah (mind).

3
NUN

Formed matter devoid of will to become anything in particular.

2
PTAH (HERU)

Mind-Consciousness, creates all (100%) matter through thought - first condensed matter (Nun- unformed matter-energy).

1
NETER

(Nameless One, Hidden One, Formless One, Self-existent Being, intangible, beyond time and space, pure consciousness, intelligence underlying and supporting all matter).

CHAPTER 4: Who is GOD?

NETER NETERU
GOD AND CREATION

(NTR)

"GOD is the father of beings.
GOD is the eternal One... and infinite and endures forever.
GOD is hidden and no man knows GOD's form.
No man has been able to seek out GOD's likeness.
GOD is hidden to Gods and men... GOD's name remains hidden... It is a mystery to his children, men, women and Gods. GOD's names are innumerable, manifold and no one knows their number... though GOD can be seen in form and observation of GOD can be made at GOD's appearance, GOD cannot be understood... GOD cannot be seen with mortal eyes... GOD is invisible and inscrutable to Gods as well as men."

***Portions from the Egyptian Book of Coming forth by** Day and*
the papyrus of Nesi-Khensu

Creation

•

The CREATOR is seen as a dot, with all the potential to do and be anything, the origin of all things seen and unseen; the origin of countless Bas (individual souls), pure potentiality, non-dual, there are no pairs of opposites (male-female) in existence yet.

From the center outward, the CREATOR, *AMEN*[3], "PROJECTS" itself onto itself. AT THE TIME OF CREATION, THE OUTER CIRCLE, THE COSMOS, IS CREATED.

TIME AND SPACE COME INTO BEING, LITERALLY, "*HAPPENING*" NOW HAPPENS. THIS IS THE AURA OF GOD, NOW THE RECEIVING FEMALE PART. THE DOT MAY NOW BE REFERRED TO AS THE LORD, FATHER, MALE, GOD ETC., AND CREATION MAY NOW BE CALLED GODDESS, MOTHER, FEMALE.

WHEN CREATION IS CREATED FROM THE ONE, AN APPARENT DIVISION OCCURS, NOW THERE EXISTS TWO PRINCIPLES; THESE ENCOMPASS THE NOTION OF DUALITY: MALE AND FEMALE, MOVER AND MOVED, VIVIFIER AND VIVIFIED, POSITIVE AND NEGATIVE, GIVER AND RECEIVER, ALL TOGETHER IN ONE BODY CALLED "*THE ALL* ".

ONE PART "GIVES" THE LIFE FORCE AND THE OTHER RECEIVES THE LIFE FORCE AND THEN RETURNS IT BACK TO THE SOURCE IN A PERPETUAL CYCLE. NOTHING IS GAINED OR LOST.

THE COSMOS AND EVERYTHING IN IT INCLUDING ALL LIVING BEINGS ON ALL PLANETS AND PLANES OF EXISTENCE ARE REALLY ONE SUPREME BEING VIEWED AS SEPARATE ENTITIES BY OUR CONDITIONED MINDS. THEY ARE STILL ONE WHOLE. THIS SYMBOL IS CALLED *RA:* ☉

The Sundisk symbol is seen in almost every Yantra (symbolic diagram containing mystical knowledge, often used for meditation) of the Indian Hindu and Tantra religious-mythologies; it is known as the Bindu (seed, primordial, origin of all things).

The NETER NETERU is not to be considered a Neter. Models or diagrams are always faulty because of the limited human mind and because we are trying to use words to understand a world which one needs to "BE" in order to "KNOW". *NETER NETERU* is also the UNIVERSAL BA. It is the BA or SOUL from which ALL souls come, including ALL human souls (individual Bas). The *NETER NETERU* not only "created" creation but SUSTAINS it at every moment. The Sun, our hearts, the earth, exist and go on every day because it is sustained by GOD; in the same manner as the sun supports life on earth, GOD supports the sun and the Universe.

The *NETER NETERU* is not located in the realm of time and space as are the other Neters and the three worlds, Earth, Dwat (Intermediate world) and Heaven as they are known in the Kemetic (Egyptian) system or Physical, Astral, and Causal as they are known in the Indian Vedanta System.

The NETER NETERU is what causes TIME, SPACE and the appearance of physical objects to exist.

---

[3] AMEN, (AMUN, AMON) is the name of the primordial GOD of predynastic Egypt signifying *"The Hidden One"*, *"All encompassing One"*, *"Self Created One"*, *"The Nameless One"*, *"The ALL"*, etc.

GOD IS ABSOLUTE REALITY, the *NETER NETERU:* GOD IS the Universe, its cause and what lies beyond as well. The Absolute *NETER NETERU* is truly beyond the description of words or models. In order to truly understand and "know" the Absolute, one must be "ONE" with the Absolute. One must be pure of heart. One must transform one's ego-personality into a Godlike one in order to "KNOW" GOD, which is the same as knowing one's true nature:

"Men are mortal Gods, Gods are immortal men." (Egyptian proverb)

"Know ye not that ye are Gods." (Jesus).

All creation and the ABSOLUTE realm is one. Through the "Veil of ASET", it APPEARS as though Creation is DUAL, consisting of heaven and earth, good and evil, negative and positive, male and female, Ying and Yang, Creator and Created and so on. This appearance however, is an illusion created by the ignorance of our conditioned mental process which identifies with our limited individual self (Ba), instead of with the source:

The NETER NETERU.

Accomplishing this shift in identification of "who one thinks one really is", is in effect the process of removing the veil of ignorance. It is the process of becoming what one already is: Heru, Christ, Buddha, a Saint, a Sage etc.

This accomplishment represents the ultimate blissful existence of life (*htp* - supreme peace and satisfaction) and is to be pursued while one is still in the physical body. This is the ultimate sublimation: Hetep *(htp),*

 ,

of the physical nature into the divine nature within all humans. *Htp* is also the name of *PTAH (Pth)* if written backwards. Ptah is an aspect of GOD, the Supreme Being, who represents the creative force that brings creation

into being. ━━┷━━

The symbol of Hetep (above) represents an offering mat with a loaf of bread (divine food) in the center, symbolizing that the Gods are satisfied and at rest, at peace. This is not the peace of solitude or of silence but a peace borne of desire-lessness which one feels when one has all one's needs fulfilled. This state of being does not arise through worldly pursuits, but through the intuitional realization of one's own true identity. Then, there will be no mental agitation due to desires or psychological needs which most people mistakenly try to fulfil through interaction with the world. In the state of Hetep, one is fulfilled regardless of one's affairs.

Know that there is one God who manifests in many ways; the Neters (cosmic forces) are within us and in all that is seen and unseen; as the children of God we have their powers; know that the same power in the cosmos is also in MAN; therefore, as we learn about the cosmos, we learn about ourselves. The more we learn about others the more we learn about ourselves.

"Make your self the object of intense study and you will discover God."

<u>*Egyptian Proverb*</u>

A coveted experience at the end of physical life on earth is the complete rejoining with the Absolute, Universal *BA* (GOD, *NETER NETERU,* Supreme Being) to continue our journey through eternity.

In chapter 17 of the *"Book of Coming Forth By Day"* (+5,500 B.C.E.), it is explained that all the Gods (Neters including Asar and Heru) and *"The Great GOD inside the common folk"* are really one GOD (RA). Further, it states that they are benefited who do achieve communion with Asar (the Great GOD inside) while on Earth.

Ra and Ra Harakty (Ra-Heru) are the name that was given to the *"Nameless One", GOD,* in later Egyptian times (Dynastic period). Its association with the sundisk gave a concrete, visual image for the purpose of public worship. In the hieroglyph to the left, Ra-Harakty (Ra-Heru) is shown holding the Ankh (symbol of life).

❘ "NETER"; ❘❘❘ "Neters", "Gods"; ☉ "Ra"; ♀ "Ankh."

The Primal Androgyny

"Souls, Heru, son, are of the self-same nature, since they came from the same place where the Creator modeled them; nor male nor female are they. Sex is a thing of bodies not of Souls."

Above: The Egyptian creator GOD Amun (also spelled Amen or Ammon), depicted in the form of a ram-headed human. Amun was represented first without form as the "Hidden Force" creating and supporting all things, then as a Ram headed human as above and finally, in a fully anthropomorphic form. In all forms Amun wears the characteristic headpiece: the Sundisk (Ra) and tall plumes (Heru-Ptah). Thus, Amun also encompasses the qualities of Ra, Heru and Ptah, hence the title "Amun-Ra-Ptah, Three in one". The Ram is also a symbol of the human soul (Ba), therefore, the true identity of every human soul is not the individual ego-personality but Amun or the Universal Ba.

Heru was considered to be a symbol of the androgynous soul, as were Asar and Ra-Atum. In the Shabaka inscription, Ra-Atum represents the Egyptian version of the Primal Androgyny. The Androgyny is one who has achieved balance and harmony in themselves, becoming at peace with one's own complementary opposite forces, one's "male" and "female" halves. Atum is depicted as looking at "him / her" self. Atum created by "mating with him/herself", thereby expressing the idea that GOD was one and from that original oneness came the "many forms." In this way spirit creates male and female although spirit itself is neither and both at the same time. Thus, the indwelling spirit of all living and non-living things is androgynous.

Above: The God-Goddess Ardanari-Iswara from India, the Androgynous spirit within every human being.

The Hindu God / Goddess *Ardhanari*, the Universal spirit, is the soul of all humans and of all creation. Ardhanari also represents the primal Androgyny, the right side being male and the left being female. Notice the Ankh at the level of the sexual genitalia. The Ankh, from the remotest times of Egyptian philosophy, represented the union of the male and female principles which bestow life. Thus, the same symbol that was used in Egypt (+10,000 B.C.E.) was later used in India (+1,000 B.C.E.) in Hindu mythology, again showing correspondence between the Egyptian and the Indian philosophies.

Who Are The Gods? The Neters Of Creation.

The Neters, (Gods) are cosmic forces throughout and in which the universe operates. They are to be thought of as expressions of the divine will of the GOD of Gods, the Supreme Being, *NETER NETERU* (Neter of Neters). The Neters keep the divine order in the universe and operate the great plan of nature: to promote the development and evolution of all creatures in the universe.

The Neters follow the dictate of GOD. They act in a set way as prescribed by the *NETER NETERU*. They cannot act independently of the order set by GOD. They are expressions of that order.

ⵏⵏⵏ, The Gods.

The Neters (Gods) represent aspects of GOD who operate in the universe and in us. Present inside everyone, they must be realized and developed by us for the journey on the Spiritual Path.

In Indian Hindu Mythology as in Kemetic (Egyptian) Mythology, there are ultimately millions of Gods. From an Absolute perspective, the number may be unknown because all objects in creation are given existence by NETER, therefore, all objects (including people) are Neters.

Actions pleasing to the Neters are those which are in harmony with the Universe. Those actions which are displeasing are the ones which go against the natural laws of the universe. Unpleasant consequences are derived from actions against cosmic order. The goal of life is to consciously come into harmony with the cosmic order by regaining one's true identity. The Neters may be categorized into three groups:

   The *Metaphysical Neters* represent the principles of the Universe. They are Ra, Amun and Ptah, the "Trinity", also known as *"Nebertcher"*: *"Everything is Amun-Ra-Ptah, three in one."* These are a direct creation from the Neter of Neters: *NETER NETERU.* They are responsible for the direction (management) of creation at every moment (previously discussed in the chapter on Egyptian Physics, Chap. 3).

   The *Cosmic Neters* are seasonal. They are variable in relation to the requirements of the Metaphysical Neters, obeying the laws of life in general. Examples of Cosmic Neters are: Shu, Geb, Nut, Asar, Set, Aset and Nebethet.

   The *Natural Neters* are represented in the functioning of natural objects such as the God Hapi for the Nile and the God Apet for gestation.

NETER NETERU, Supreme Being, through Amun-Ra-Ptah, first created Shu, the air, and Tefnut, the principle of humidity. Next, Shu and Tefnut united to beget Geb (earth) and Nut (sky). Nut arched her back over Geb and they begat Asar, Aset, Set and Nebethet (see diagram on page 57). The other God principles are produced thereafter from this group. All male Gods are aspects or particular manifestations of the Supreme Being in the male perspective. All female Goddesses are manifestations of the Supreme Being in the female aspect. Male cannot exist without female and vice versa. This female / male complementary principle which underlies creation is the basis of all Yoga.

Most important to the process of Yoga are the God principles *Saa* and *Hu.* These are the God principles within us that control the sense and intuitive understanding faculties. Saa: Divine intelligence. Hu: Divine food upon which Gods live (virtue, truth, justice, order, peace).

The Realm of Light

In pre-dynastic times (before 5,500 B.C.E.), Egyptian doctrine held that there is a realm of light (beyond our physical universe) where food, clothing and our bodies are of light, and further, that we will exist for all eternity as beings of light along with other beings of light. This realm of light may be likened to the modern esoteric notion of an "Astral Plane" or the even subtler "Causal Plane" of existence. The physical realm (earth) is a reflection or shadow of this astral reality.

In dynastic times, the doctrine of the realm of light and of a single GOD of whom creation is composed survived in the earliest religious texts. In chapter 64 of the *Egyptian Book of Coming Forth By Day,* GOD is referred to as *"The One Who Sees by His Own Light"* and *"Atum in the western horizon and Heru in the east". H*ence, the *"Lord of Two Faces",* who is in reality only ONE, is very much similar to the TAO, the singularity which is composed of two opposite but complementary forces. The main observable difference between the pre-dynastic and post-dynastic philosophy of Egypt is that there were fewer deities in the predynastic time. Like other religious philosophies that developed later, this period did not include a complex system of Gods, cosmogony or rituals. In this respect, Egypt's predynastic philosophy is most similar to the simpler forms of Buddhism and Taoism which do not incorporate the idea of "deities". The individual who purifies him / herself through the teaching is considered to be the only deity.

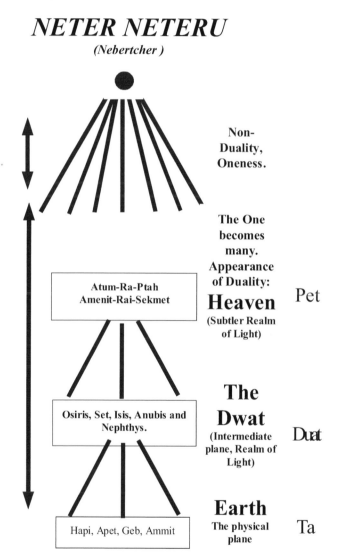

NETER NETERU
(Nebertcher)

Non-Duality, Oneness.

The One becomes many. Appearance of Duality:

Atum-Ra-Ptah
Amenit-Rai-Sekmet

Heaven   Pet
(Subtler Realm of Light)

Osiris, Set, Isis, Anubis and Nephthys.

The Dwat   Duat
(Intermediate plane, Realm of Light)

Hapi, Apet, Geb, Ammit

Earth   Ta
The physical plane

Just before the beginning of the first dynasty (c5,000 B.C.E.) the followers of Egyptian philosophy began to represent the divine forces of GOD which operate through nature in zoomorphic forms. At the beginning of the first dynasty and afterwards until the end of Egyptian civilization (c. 600 A.C.E.), the followers of Egyptian religion, which had used Gods from the pre-dynastic times represented as animals, developed and incorporated new myths using anthropomorphic in forms.

One of the most popular doctrines was that of Asar, Aset and Heru. These Gods were mentioned in pre-dynastic times, however, the additional myths which were added to them (such as the Osirian Resurrection) resulted in increased popularity and gave the local priests the opportunity to add to the teachings handed down previously and to cope with the new political and social changes throughout Egypt.

In some respects, however, the changes represented a downfall from the original teaching. For example: the "realm of light" mentioned above came to be known by some as the "Land of Asar" (The West) where after death, souls would go to work in the fields for Asar for all eternity. This "distasteful" prospect caused some to fashion dolls (Ushabti) whose spirits would do the work for them. Some of these new doctrines and erroneous practices no doubt created new opportunities for unscrupulous priests and others with some degree of spiritual knowledge.

In fact, written evidence shows that over the last 5,000 years of Egyptian history, the amount of spiritual leaders (priests and priestesses) who governed the country was reduced as military and political leaders assumed command. It must be understood that in the earlier times, Egypt was managed by the spiritual leaders who were instructed in the temples (universities) thus attaining a balance of spiritual, intellectual and physical maturity. The political and military leaders lacked such balance. This, coupled with the changing character and composition of Egyptian society which occurred as a result of intermingling with other societies and the Asian invasions, created a situation of gradual decline in the mental and spiritual health of the masses and lay government officials.

However, the mystical implications of the principals of the Osirian Resurrection and the mythology surrounding the various Gods of the Egyptian pantheon are still in accord with the pre-dynastic teachings.

Left: "Shiva Nataraja, Lord of Dance." The Indian God Shiva is seen here dancing the cosmic dance which sustains creation. In his hair are a new moon and a skull, signifying life and death occurring at the same moment, always becoming (creation is a continuous process-not something that was done long ago). In one hand he holds a drum. This drum of time beats on and its sound keeps out the knowledge of eternity (human ignorance about cosmic reality). In another hand he holds a flame. This flame burns away the veil of time and space and brings back the knowledge of eternity. Shiva dances on the body of a dwarf demon. This signifies his constant victory over the dwarf demon (evil) which allows the establishment of cosmic order over chaos. The halo surrounding him is a symbol of creation, destruction and rebirth.

Below: "The God Ra on His Barque." Creation is sustained by the journey of Ra in his Mandjet (barque). Ra possesses two barques: "The Barque of Morning and The Barque of Evening." Ra is seen often travelling with the other major deities in his barque (Thoth, Hetheru, Maat, etc.). In order to sustain creation, Ra journeys across heaven (cosmos) but must continually defeat the serpent Apophis (evil) in order to do so. Apophis attempts to destroy Ra (creation) each day. Therefore, the battle against evil (chaos) is a continuous one since it cannot be destroyed. Chaos and order are integral components of creation. Creation cannot exist without the two. They are complementary opposites; the dissolution of either would mean the dissolution of creation. This signifies the ongoing battle within every human being. The challenge is to maintain a dynamic balance between good and evil.

NOTE: For more on the Ancient Egyptian mystical teachings of the nature of Divinity see the books *MYSTERIES OF ASET* and **EGYPTIAN YOGA Volume II: The Supreme Wisdom of Enlightenment** by Dr. Muata Ashby.

The Mind, Truth and Reality

"That which is the Fundamental Truth, the Substantial Reality, is beyond true naming, but the Wise men call it the All."

<u>*Egyptian Mystical Wisdom*</u>

Introduction to Maat.

Pert em Hru

The philosophy of Maat: **ꜣ** (symbolized by the feather) is contained in the most ancient writings of Egypt, even those preceding the dynastic or Pharaonic period (4,500 B.C.E.-600 A.C.E). The most extensive expositions of the philosophy may be found in the writings which have in modern times been referred to as "The Egyptian Book of the Dead." It was originally known as "Rw Prt M Hrw" or "Ru Pert em Heru." This is translated as: "The Utterances for Going Forth into the Light." In Egyptian mythology, Heru (Heru) not only means "Light" but also "Day". In fact, Day and Light are two of the most important attributes of the GOD Heru who is understood as the highest potential of every human being. Therefore, the title may also read "The Guide for Becoming Heru." The writings were named "The Egyptian Book of the Dead" by modern egyptologists who obtained them from the modern day dwellers of the area (north-east African Arabs) who said they were found buried with the ancient Egyptian dead. In the interest of simplicity and consistency, the name "Egyptian Book of Coming Forth by Day" will be used throughout this text.

The philosophical definition of MAAT is:

"That which is unchanging; it was the same in the beginning of time,
it is the same now and will be the same forever."

The philosophy of Maat has been described as: Truth, Justice, Righteousness, Order. Based on the above definition of Maat, it is very easy to see that there is little "truth" in the physical world and upon further examination, a more profound idea emerges: Nothing in the world is static, not our bodies, buildings, not the land, not youth, not planets, NOTHING; the only constant thing is CHANGE. Change is the only reality. Many people realize this superficially but for most, it has not been consciously accepted as a "rule" of this reality. Nature has instituted change to direct us to the changeless, to cause us to seek out our imperishable reality. But this Absolute reality is not to be found anywhere in this world. We must know this because without this knowledge, we will continue to pour our hearts (and Life Force) into trying to make situations that last forever, only to become frustrated and heartbroken when they end, usually in a manner other than we had hoped for.

TRUTH IS UNIVERSAL. Let not the use of the symbols and hieroglyphs herein contained confuse you. Look past them and past all languages to find the truth. The TRUTH is universal; yet it can only be determined by you the individual, because the ultimate truth can only be understood through experience, not discussion. Any symbol or language used to describe or discuss the truth is incidental to the truth. There is only one truth and many roads lead to it. A true seeker will find the truth through any road he or she chooses, as long as the person seeking it (truth) truly wants to find it, and to apply it in his or her life. Those who choose to remain ignorant in the face of the truth will remain slaves to the narrow ideas of their own mind, the uncontrolled wants of their own body, that of their friends, country, and unjust economic systems, or corrupt religious organizations.

"The closer you get to the truth the simpler it is."
"Truth is not simple except to those who know everything."
"The wise person who acts with MAAT is free of falsehood and disorder."
"The law is cold, truth is cold."
"ASET is blindfolded because justice is unprejudiced!"
"Truth has the force of emotion BEHIND it."
"Truth and knowledge produce courage."
"The laws of God are the first thing the seeker will find on the way to the truth."

What is Reality?

"Let not be shut in my Soul, let not be fettered my Shadow, let be opened the way for my Soul and for my shadow, may it see the great God. May I look upon my Soul and my SHADOW."

Egyptian Proverbs

The *Khaibit* (shadow) is the reflection of GOD; it is a projection of that which is real, of that which is the truth. GOD created and continues to create out of GOD's own self, GOD's own shadow. GOD, being both male and female thinks of him /herself as a being who is looking at its own shadow (the universe). Here in creation, the infinite planets and galaxies are but a mental creation of GOD, GOD's Shadow. As the human soul is essentially a piece of GOD as it were, it also has a shadow. GOD manifests (is reflected) in each individual. However, this reflection becomes refracted proportional to the degree of mental conditioning that one has. Just as a ray of light which passes through a glass prism becomes refracted and produces many rays, so too GOD'S expression in an individual is refracted by the ignorance of the mind producing many "different" situations and objects. To the extent that the soul is a prisoner of the physical desires and mental ignorance which do not allow it to be in tune with the mind of GOD, it (human mind) is fettered to a mortal, physical body, and thus is unable to see its soul.

GOD is the only reality that exists, the ABSOLUTE REALITY, but it appears to the ignorant (conditioned) mind that the world, our bodies, and the universe exist outside of GOD. We believe ourselves to be separate objects and entities. This is relative reality. In reality, <u>EVERYTHING</u> is <u>ONE.</u> Relative reality is the state most people are caught up in. Relative reality is an illusion. It exists only in our minds. GOD not only created the world but GOD IS the world. Everything we perceive with our senses IS GOD. We must transcend relative reality to "Live" within "Absolute Reality." To not only understand this greatest teaching, but to "KNOW" it means complete bliss and happiness. Yoga is a scientific process to accomplish the goal of transcendence: liberation, salvation, self-realization.

Relative reality is what is referred to in Hinduism and Buddhism as "MAYA."

THE POINT MUST BE WELL UNDER-STOOD THAT: THE MEANING BEHIND THE WISDOM OF CALLING THE PHYSICAL WORLD AN ILLUSION DOES NOT MEAN THAT IT DOES NOT EXIST (ONE ONLY HAS TO TRY WALKING THROUGH A WALL TO REALIZE THE ERROR IN THIS FORM OF THINKING), BUT RATHER THAT IT EXISTS IN A FORM OTHER THAN THAT WHICH WE BELIEVE IT TO BE. WHAT WE BELIEVE TO BE PHYSICAL OBJECTS ARE REALLY EXPRESSIONS OF GOD. OUR SOUL, THROUGH THE PROCESS OF MESKHENET (KARMA), DRAWS TO US THOSE OBJECTS (PERSONS, THINGS OR SITUATIONS) THAT WE (OUR SOULS) NEED TO FURTHER OUR SPIRITUAL EVOLUTION OUTWARD.

The preoccupation with matters such as race relations, wars, crime, social status, physical appearance, and all other intricacies of human interaction are, as we will see, manifestations of a limited (ignorant) intellect which has not been able to transcend the pettiness of the apparent world condition in order to see the larger reality, the Absolute reality that lies beyond the apparent differences that seem to exist in the world. Yes there are practical realities in the world to be dealt with in one's physical existence, but these are not to be accepted as Absolute realities, for acceptance of these as Absolute realities leads to bondage to them. Rather, an attitude of detachment, dispassion and study should be developed so as to not be affected by either situations of adversity or prosperity, since after all, these two seemingly opposite concepts are really two aspects of the same reality. One's mind is equally agitated in a state of joy as in pain. Both situations take the focus of the mind away from GOD (supreme peace) toward transient realities. For example, someone who has just won the lottery can have a mind that is as agitated as someone who has just lost all their possessions. In the former case, the person worries about protecting the money from theft, what to say to family members who want to "borrow" some to tide them over, what to buy and what investments to make to ensure that it lasts a lifetime. In the latter case, this person has the opposite worries of how to borrow or steal some money. Neither of these two persons experience mental peace because true mental peace does not depend on external situations; it is an internal affair.

When the mind is turbulent with worldly concerns, it is like the turbulent water in a lake caused by gusty winds; it cannot reflect the sky accurately. However, the calm mind becomes like a calm lake, able to reflect the sky (true reality). This can only be accomplished through the process of conscious transcendence, achieved through sustained practice of the disciplines of Yoga. Through the process of transcendence, new positive subconscious impressions of the Absolute reality will be created in the mind which will lead us to different perceptions of physical reality.

"Those who live today will die tomorrow, those who die tomorrow will be born again; those who live MAAT will not die."

"The reality of a thing is its relation to the Creator, not that which we see; it was created by the word of the Creator, this word is its true name; to know a thing's true name is to know its true power, to pronounce it exactly is to release its energy."

"Truth is but one; thy doubts are of thine own raising. It that made virtues what they are, planted also in thee a knowledge of their pre-eminence. Act as Soul dictates to thee, and the end shall be always right."

<u>Egyptian Proverbs</u>

Body Consciousness

Most people in the world believe themselves to be a physical body and mind but upon deeper examination, one finds that this notion does not hold up to the definition of reality given by MAAT. Therefore, it is only an illusion.

If we are the body, then which part are we---the hands, kidneys, feet, eyes or the skin? Are we the spinal cord or are we the sexual organs? Upon reflection, it becomes obvious that if we were to lose any of these, we would still continue "living." Even if part of the brain were damaged or lost, life could continue. Documented experiments with animals have shown that a head can be severed from the body and later replaced. We are not the senses because we are still there when we lose sight or hearing, etc. Our senses contribute to our ignorant concept of reality by supplying the mind with limited (erroneous) information as to the nature of reality. Therefore, neither the body parts nor the senses constitute the essence of what we call consciousness. We are not the mind, otherwise it would be impossible for us to talk about *"training ourselves"* to be this or that, or to change into this or that way of thinking. We are not the vitality of the body because "we" are still there when the body feels weak as well as when it feels strong.

The body, senses, mind and vitality (Life Force, Sekhem, Prana) should be seen as extensions of our individual consciousness (mind-ego). They are tools, instruments of our own creation for the purpose of achieving entry and interaction with the "physical reality." The body is to the spirit what a car or an ox is to the body, a valuable tool. We definitely should take care of the car or ox to the extent that they are useful to do work and serve our body, but we should not identify ourselves with them saying: "That is me, I am the car, I am the ox." In the same manner, it is ridiculous for us to identify with our physical body, senses and ego, thinking or saying they are us when our true nature is the universal spirit.

What is the Mind?

 The mind is the cause of bondage and release. The mind is that which judges the various experiences

we face at every moment. In a world created out of a combination of dense and subtle energy and various states of consciousness, it is necessary to have an instrument that will discern and discriminate between good and evil, hot and cold, here and there, etc., in order to carry on the affairs of life. This process of discrimination is what causes the appearance of distinct and different objects and situations. Therefore, the process of discrimination is a dualizing process where out of the one reality, energy, there seems to be "many realities." From this standpoint of apparent duality, the idea arises that we are separate "thinking" individuals and we are also separate from the universe. In this state of ignorance, we interact with the world in an action-reaction mentality, following our lower nature (anger, greed, hate, etc.), instead of incorporating our higher nature (feeling of oneness) which, when balanced with the lower, will lead one to experience universal love, sharing and peace.

The experience of oneness is likened to the experience of peace because there are no desires to create unrest in trying to act on them or not trying to act on them. Therefore, the experience of oneness is considered to be the state in which all apparent realities cease to exist. This is the original state. The experience of "duality" or discrimination is the state in which opposites exist and therefore, the struggle between those opposites exists as well.

The waves of the mind, resembling the body of a serpent, are like a roller coaster ride for the soul. A mind free of these waves has achieved supreme peace and understands the unity of all creation. In another sense the coils of the serpent of the primeval waters represents the cosmic mind and its thoughts which stir up the ocean from its calm and thereby creates waves of different shapes and sizes (the names and forms of Creation.

The hieroglyphic symbol of the serpent characterizes the idea of duality. The serpent, although it appears as one unit, that is to say, it has no arms or legs, has a double tongue and a double penis. Thus, the mind, as symbolized by the serpent, has two aspects: a discriminative (dualistic) quality as symbolized by the serpent Apopis, and a synthetic (unifying) quality called the *"Serpent in the sky"*. The *Serpent in the sky*, representing the higher mind-intellect, is the centipede of Heru, the God of light and protector of Asar (Ra). In the Ancient Egyptian texts, APOPHIS *or APOPIS or APEP* is the enemy of Ra, the sun. Ra represents light, warmth, Life Force, truth, spirit, etc. APOPIS and its fiendish friends represent darkness, physical and moral evil, etc. It is important to understand that APOPIS is a "constant" enemy of Ra, who fights him everyday, trying to stop him from shining. The implication is that those who wish to be like Ra (those on the spiritual path) must, like Ra, be prepared to fight Apopis at every moment. Thus, there must be continued self effort and one must develop endurance if one is to achieve success as Apopis a persistent adversary. Apopis represents the "lower self", the mind and body which indulges in emotionality, greed, deceit, sense pleasures etc. Apopis also represents adversity in life as well. Consequently, those situations or people who were seen as "evil" (contrary to Maat) are called children of APOPIS as in the following text:

> *"...children of the serpent Apopis, the impious who haunt the wilderness and the dessert..."*

Apopis is defeated by they who are armed with the burning and destroying heat of the sun (fire, light), that is, they who possess MAAT (truth and righteousness) and Djehuti (light, insight, wisdom). As the burning body is consumed by the flames of the fire, so too will the illusion of duality be consumed by the light (fire) of truth (oneness). Just as the dream world loses its reality upon one's waking up, so too the illusion of Apopis (duality) dissolves when the forces of light are shed upon it.

The Serpent Power

Spiritual movement is the development of the higher mind in order that it may carry one's consciousness to the discovery of truth rather than illusion. Thus, as we change the patterns of conditioned thoughts, we break away from our circular cyclical pattern of existence and enter into a spiral pattern of growth and transformation, as represented by the awakening of the coiled serpent, Kundalini.

This is BUTO, the cobra Goddess, better known as the Uraeus of Ra. Buto is winged. She is the ruler of eternity as she holds the symbol of the shen at the far right. Thus the mind (serpent) is transformed

from an instrument which is mortal and powerless to a state of freedom (wings), all power (sundisk), and eternity (shen).

Below: The coils of Goddess Kundalini.

Kundalini as the symbol of Cosmic Energy. 18th century, India. The Indian Goddess of female energy (Kundalini) rises from the lotus (India 18 Cent.). As with Goddess BUTO of Egypt, Goddess Kundalini of India is also represented by the serpent. The power of Kundalini resides at the base of the spine, awaiting conscious awakening.

Above: The hieroglyph of the "Vertebrae".

Below: From the *"Egyptian Book of Coming Forth By Day,"* This episode is known as "The Slaughter." The soul of Ankhwahibre does battle with Apopis who is sitting atop the vertebrae (Back - Djed Pillar of Asar) implying that Apopis seeks control of the spiritual energy present in the spiritual subtle channels of the back.

The initiate does battle by invoking the fire of wisdom and therefore asserts the absolute reality he has discovered in himself: *"I am Ra, continually praised...I am he in whom is the sacred eye.."* (See eye of Ra). The "Back" is where unbounded spiritual energy (Buto-Uraeus) resides. The initiate is admonished to "develop the fire of the back."

"The Serpent In The Sky." A human figure sits atop a Uraeus with the hieroglyph symbol of Hetep (Ptah-Heru, supreme peace) above the head. The controlled and transformed mind (conscience) sees unity and divinity in all things and identifies with the spirit instead of the mortal body. They who possess the serpent in the sky fly on its back, beyond the limitations of physical reality.

Above: From the tomb of Pharaoh Tutankhamon, a visual exposition of the idea expressed by the God Tehuti-Hermes: "As above, so below", as two serpents enclose the cosmic form of man (the universe). That which is above (spirit) is eternal, that which is below (matter) is also eternal. The serpent of the earth and the serpent of the sky encircle the lower as well as the higher self. The lower self and the higher self are complementary halves of the whole if brought into harmony.

The center area at the base of the spine is highlighted with a line and by the ram-headed hawk positioned with arms raised (in adoration "Ka") toward the sacral region of the spine - the root energy center (chakra).

In India, the revered ancient Sage Shankaracarya in the book "Vivekacudamani" stated:

"The Self is within, and the self is without, the Self is before and the Self is behind, the Self is in the south, and the Self is in the north, the Self likewise is Above and Below... The embodied consciousness is none other than the Universal Consciousness."

The Ego Is

Our EGO is our identification with our body. As soon as we are born, we are told and begin to believe that our arms, legs, skin, thoughts, ideas, etc. are what constitute the totality of our existence. In addition, through the process of reincarnation, we have had this false identity hammered into our heads as it were. Hypnotized by our surroundings and convinced by those around us, we believe we are mortal flesh and blood and nothing more.

The ego says things like: *"I feel sorry, I feel hungry, I am happy, I want this, I want that, My body is good looking, I want to get a lot of money for myself because then I can buy many things and then I will be happy, My name is so and so, I come from my parents and from nowhere else, My country is such and such, I am separate from other people, I am separate from the earth and the universe, and my thoughts are my own creation, nothing inspires them except my own mind, There is no such thing as a spirit, Life is flesh and blood and nothing else so while I'm here I will live it up till the day I die, for you only live once. I... I...I...My...My...My."*

The ego or personality is the source of human pleasure and pain in the world experience. All pleasurable or painful perceptions are a production of the EGO aspect of the mind and an untrained (conditioned) mind is often lost in the maze of world experiences.

The re-trained (unconditioned) mind is the source of release or freedom from the fetters that hold the spirit chained to the events of the world, and our perceptions of them.

To become ONE with GOD, we must discard our ego sense. We must discard the notion that we are individuals living in the universe and that we are separate from everything else. We must understand that we are not the body, not the mind, not our senses, not anything we can feel or touch.

The process of cleansing the Ego-Personality and attaining a purified heart, is the process of YOGA---to leave behind the ego and to develop the higher self. The ego is a tool as are our bodies and it is to be used by us to assist in our survival and evolution. This occurs by training the ego to serve one's best interests instead of allowing it to run our lives; it must be our servant, not the master.

Through denial (sublimation) of the ego, it is possible to partake in the cosmic true self. One may:

"Become a transmitter like Ptah and do the work of they who reside in their caves."

Egyptian Proverb

One may become a conduit of the divine power of GOD and do the work of the Neters by becoming in harmony with them.

"Become the KA of Heru and the Neters."

One may become merged with the spirit of Nature (GOD), thereby living on in immortality when the physical body dies.

The Pyramid and Coffin Texts further admonish us to:

> *"awaken the Neter quality* (**Godhood**) *in man... to free him... save him from the Osirian Path* (**passion and reincarnation**)*...*

> *...conquer the enemy* (**ego-personality**) *because by doing so, the ONE* (**GOD**) *may shine forth through the purified Ba* (**soul**) *in splendor."*

The Philosophy of Sleep and The Four States of Consciousness

There are three distinct states of consciousness which everyone is familiar with: waking, dream and deep sleep. We go through each of these three states everyday, changing our perception of reality with each different state. This waking state of consciousness we are so used to with the image, concept and name for ourselves is not as solid and real as we think it is. When we fall asleep, the waking consciousness is left behind and we take on a new "identity." In the dream state, the new identity thinks that everything that is happening in the dream is "REAL", but upon waking up one realizes that "nothing" really happened. In the deep sleep state where there are no dreams, we are absorbed in the transcendental state which is beyond time and space. Upon waking from the deep sleep state of consciousness, we do not remember anything but we experience a feeling of deep rest and re-creation of our emotional and psychological selves.

In all of the three regular states of consciousness just described, there is one constant factor, a constantly changing state of mental awareness. Change therefore, implies that these three states do not qualify for the definition of Absolute reality (MAAT) as previously discussed. Whatever it is that we call "us", our "essence", that which makes us "unique", that which "thinks" thoughts and has desires, that which we call a "soul," the innermost "I," is really the unchanging witness of all the three states. Through "ignorance" of its true nature however, the soul "identifies" with the three different states of mental consciousness. Thus, it becomes is bound to the reality with which it is currently involved; thus it is always being caught in one of these states of consciousness at any given point in time.

The waking, dream and deep sleep states of consciousness are only illusory mental states. No one can maintain a perpetual mental state of wakefulness, dream or deep sleep. All of these states are therefore illusions, transient projections of reality which we must transcend, as the search for our true self is really a search for the thing about us which is constant, these three states are only a reflection of the truth. However, they offer a clue to the truth, the one constant, our innermost self which is the spectator in all modes of consciousness (waking, dream and sleeping states). There must be a fourth state then, of Absolute truth, beyond these three familiar states.

Just as it is possible to wake up in the morning from the dream state into the everyday state of waking consciousness, it is possible to wake up from the "normal day to day consciousness" into a higher state of consciousness (enlightenment). Thus, what we currently perceive to be our day to day consciousness becomes another form of the dream state of consciousness.

The problem occurs when we forget that we are really "dreaming" and get caught up in the events of the dream, believing that what is happening is "real"; we lack the higher state of consciousness. This situation can be equated to watching a movie. If we remember throughout the movie that we are just onlookers, we remain detached from the experiences of pain or pleasure being portrayed by the actors. Our emotions remain intact as long as we remember that we are only watching a movie and that no one is really getting hurt or really happy. However, the moment we forget to keep that mental distance we become caught up in the movie. When we *"IDENTIFY"* with the actors, we suffer or experience joy along with the characters being portrayed; thus, we cry or laugh with them. In reality however, the actors who are portraying the characters did not experience true suffering or joy. It was our identification with the illusion created by the movie that caused us to suffer or experience pleasure, when in fact, nothing really happened.

Similarly, in our practical life, as we identify our souls-consciousness (the actor) with our ego-mind and body (the character) we find ourselves on a roller coaster ride of emotions, alternating between extreme pleasure and extreme pain.

We need not have studied high philosophy to have already figured out that nothing lasts forever and that what goes up will eventually come down and vice versa. This wave like form of existence is also represented by the serpent Apophis. Therefore, as with the roller coaster ride at an amusement park, the only way to fully enjoy the ride (life) is to think of it as a temporary occurrence, knowing that at the end of its ups and downs, one will be unharmed. One must know that the soul is unaffected and unchanged by the ups and downs which are experienced by the ego-personality.

In order to maximize one's sleep experience and gradually introduce conscious awareness during the dream state, one should spend a few minutes affirming one's intention to remain conscious during the dream experience and to remember the dreams. Fall asleep on the right side, with one's right hand between the pillow and the face. The left hand should be placed on the left thigh. Even though it is likely that the body will move out of this position during the night, one should still attempt to fall asleep in this position. This position will allow the left nostril to be open, thereby allowing "moon" breath, which is most beneficial during this time for spiritual and physical health. As soon as one wakes up, one should bring one's consciousness to the present moment and then recall the dream events and write them down. The symbolism and events may carry important intuitional messages which may be readily apparent individually or over a period of time when seen as a group of dreams.

In ancient times, dreams were seen as communications between one's waking self and one's astral (dream-intermediate) self. As such, under the proper guidance and understanding, one could expect to receive insight into one's life problems and assistance in determining one's direction in life, the assistance coming from one's higher self or from benevolent Neters. It is important not to overindulge in dream deciphering since the dreams state is after all, only another variant state of consciousness (relative reality), and not the Absolute state. It must be realized that until one is fully enlightened, dreams are colored by one's mental illusions and therefore must be viewed with a dispassionate and detached eye.

From an initiatic point of view, the waking state of consciousness is the most important because it is only when we are awake that we can make a conscious effort to learn spiritual teachings and it is in the waking state that we can most easily control our thoughts and actions in an effort to achieve self-discovery (enlightenment).

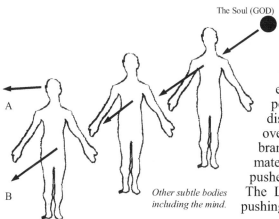

Circuit   Power Station

The Soul (GOD)

A

B

Other subtle bodies including the mind.

Physical Body

Mental Energy

Mental energy is supported by the eternal Life Force which pervades all things. It is the same energy that makes the grass grow, the sun shine and manifests in people as the desire to survive, live on and to seek happiness. A seed of a plant may fall in any given plot of land. So too the individual soul may incarnate in any given body. In order to grow well and reach its full potential, the proper nutrients such as minerals in the soil and enough sunlight must be available. If they are not, there is a possibility that the plant may become stunted or susceptible to disease. If the plant's internal life force is strong enough, it may overcome the added obstacles to its growth by extending its branches and or roots to a better location in order to acquire the materials it needs to succeed. Like plant life, the human mind is pushed to be born, to grow, to survive and to reach its full potential. The Life Force energy (Ra, spirit) is ever-present and relentlessly pushing the mind and body to grow (evolve) whether the mind is willing or able to deal with the changes in life or not. The spirit wants to reach its full potential (Heruhood), but in becoming identified with the ego, it seeks fulfillment in illusory endeavors, mental concepts and earthly relationships. These lead to anger, passion, greed, selfishness, etc. which in turn produce more situations of illusion, disappointment, pain and suffering, all of which lead to the dissipation of mental energy which weakens the will and intuitive as well as intellectual faculties. The weakened mind becomes blocked with mental complexes which cause irregular (disharmonious) vibrations, leading to boredom, despair and depression which in turn affect physical health. Therefore, it is of paramount importance to create the proper conditions and engage in practices that will promote the expansion of consciousness rather than its contraction.

Left: the diagram of a household light bulb. It works by creating a "resistance" to the flow of electricity which is generated by the power station. The power station sends energy in a circuit. One line is positively charged and the other is negatively charged. This flow of electricity in the lines is called the current. If the light bulb (appliance) was not there or if the lines were to cross and touch each other without passing through the appliance, there would be no resistance to the flow, thereby causing a "short circuit" in which the current would travel so fast that it would burn up the lines. If the resistance is too high (blown bulb), the flow would be restricted and the appliance would not function. Therefore, a particular balance of resistance must be maintained in order to effect the proper functioning of the appliance.

The human body is much like an appliance in that it receives spiritual energy from the soul through the mind and transforms it into physical energy to perform physical work. Feelings of peace, contentment, harmony, equanimity, dispassion and understanding allow the proper flow of spiritual energy.
Feelings of anger, hate, fear and passionate desire cause blockages in the flow of spiritual energy through the parts of the spirit, mind and body thereby causing illness. Also, depletion of energy occurs when the energy dissipates or flows out (open circuit) of the body due to mental attention on worldly objects (attachment), desire, worry, passion, sexual ejaculation. These activities hasten the death of the individual because the energy is "used up" sooner. Therefore, one aim of concentration and meditation is to prevent the foolish loss of energy (closed circuit).

Reincarnation occurs when the soul decides to "switch off" it's identification with a particular bulb (death), and then to send its light (Life Force) power to another bulb (body).

Far left: Ordinary flow of energy through the body is outward through the mental attention on the senses and mental desires (A) and sexual ejaculation (B). This mode of energy flow serves the purposes of gratification of the senses and procreation of the species.

Mental Health

Since the spirit is our true essence, our condition of existence with a physical form may be seen as an aberration from the original essence. The original essence is a state of infinite expansion in consciousness, immortality, indestructibility, etc. From this perspective it is easy to understand that the mind may develop mental complexes (blocks) when confronted with a limited human experience. Therefore, our coming to earth in itself is understood by Sages to be the source of the primary and fundamental state of illness: dis-ease. Mental complexes are as varied as the numbers of individuals, however, all of these originate in the attachment of the soul to the physical illusion of reality culminating with the ultimate mental complex: the identification with the physical form or body. The spirit forgets it is spirit and begins to believe it is a physical, mortal body. In finding out that as a human personality it cannot have "its" way, or in falling prey to the idea that someone is "hurting it" and may even "kill it", the mental complexes intensify. Due to its misunderstanding of what it perceives (pain, bondage, death) and what it intrinsically knows deep down (freedom, completeness, immortality), dis-ease (conflict) arises. The conflict is exacerbated because of our inability to accept life as it is unfolding. Due to our ignorance about our true essence, we do not understand that all situations we encounter during our life time are products of our own desire, produced by us in order to provide us with some specific experience so that we can evolve. Therefore, we end up "fighting against" life and developing feelings of regret instead of understanding that we came here of our free will and "created" the situation in which we find ourselves. Thus, instead of employing our energy to the task of improving our mental power by sublimating our egoistic desires, we dissipate it and waste it in useless endeavors which cannot provide fulfillment. The stronger the attachment to the ego, the larger the conflict will be and consequently, the larger the disappointment will be and the more profound and more severe the illness. The cure for this condition is the development of wisdom which inevitably leads to detachment from that which is "unreal" (physical existence) and attachment to that which is "real".

In order to sustain this illusion (physical existence) and all of the mental and physical activity related to it, the spirit "sends" energy to the physical form in order to sustain it. Energy comes in various forms: mental, subtle, physical. The proper flow of energy promotes good health and the improper flow of energy leads to illness. Therefore, the mental and physical health of the individual is required for the proper processing (flow) of energy in the mind.

Disease is therefore an imbalance in the flow of energies of the body which are controlled by the mind and which emanate from the soul. Healing is accomplished by re-balancing the energies and vibrations of the mind and body, thereby fulfilling the needs of the soul (spirit). This may be accomplished through changes in one's lifestyle and mental attitude. Specifically, administering herbs whose ingredients have balancing qualities with respect to the particular ailment, effecting harmonious vibrations to cause a harmonious effect in the energies of the body(s), psychotherapy (wisdom Yoga), spiritual counseling to promote understanding of reality as it truly is to reduce the conflict in the mind and meditation (quieting the mind) to allow the direct flow of energy from the soul. Due to the misunderstanding of reality, we believe we are ego personalities instead of spiritual beings having a physical, human experience. The identification with the ego causes us to live in fear (mental block) of the future. Spiritual counseling should attempt to help the individual to reconcile his or her perception of Absolute reality and relative reality, thereby removing mental blockages which had accumulated due to misunderstanding reality as it truly is. Healing techniques should be used in an integrated and balanced fashion, depending on the needs of the individual.

In much the same way as an ordinary household appliance transforms energy into useful functions, the body acts as a transducer of cosmic energy (sexual energy). The soul acts to coalesce a conglomerate of elements into the form of a physical body. In doing so, the infinite cosmic energy (Ra) is transformed through the resistance of the coalesced matter (body). As in household electrical appliances (which also work through the principle of resistance), if there was no resistance, energy would flow freely with too much current and burn out the system (household appliance or human body). Therefore, the mind and body must be gradually trained and made accustomed to greater and greater levels of energy by increasing the level of consciousness and reducing the level of resistance in a balanced fashion. This may be accomplished through repeated exercises in the control of the sexual energy, increasing purity of mind through the practice of virtue and purification of the body through a pure, nutritional diet and exercise.

The Project of Spiritual Unfoldment

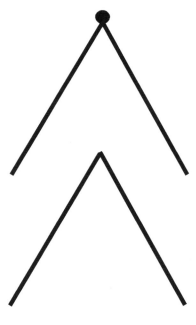
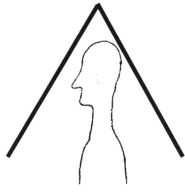

The project of spiritual achievement is to transcend the three regular states of consciousness and to become established in the source of all consciousness which is the spirit. The key to ending ignorance is to acquire wisdom. Through the development of a meditative mind (conscious of all actions and thoughts) which is based on the understanding of reality as it truly is, it is possible to transcend the common states of consciousness and to discover what lies beyond.

Transcendental Self consciousness, containing ALL (enlightenment). The Transcendent Self encompasses all other mental states.

Expanded level of Intellectual and Psychic consciousness, where higher forms of meditation such as Samadhi, Kia, Satori and psychic phenomena (magic).

Level of ego-personality and body consciousness. One believes oneself to be an individual, unconnected to anything else; unaware of any other realms or levels of his/her own consciousness. Thus, the individual is only aware of his/her limited surroundings.

NOTE: For more on the mystical teachings of Ancient Egyptian MAAT Philosophy of see the books *Healing the Criminal Heart and The Wisdom of Maati* by Dr. Muata Ashby. For more on the mystical teachings of Ancient Egyptian Psychology see the books *EGYPTIAN YOGA VOLUME II: The Supreme Wisdom of Enlightenment* **and** *Meditation: The Ancient Egyptian Path to Enlightenment* by Dr. Muata Ashby.

CHAPTER 6: DJEHUTI: Gnosis or Thought?

"To the Supreme Divinity (GOD), Gnosis is no beginning; rather Gnosis doth afford to us the first beginning of Its (GOD) being known."

<u>*Egyptian Mystical Wisdom*</u>

EGYPTIAN YOGA VOLUME 1

GNOSIS MEANS KNOWING SOMETHING INTUITIVELY WITHOUT HAVING TO THINK ABOUT IT.

Egyptian God of Wisdom Djehuti His animal symbols are the IBIS bird and the Baboon.

Having information and having knowledge are not necessarily the same thing. There are two forms of knowledge: direct and indirect. Indirect knowledge is something you learn and are convinced of intellectually. Direct knowledge on the other hand, is something you experience. It is something which requires no thinking to be understood. . . it is <u>"being"</u> (knowing) knowledge as opposed to learning or "thinking" knowledge. One may learn about a flower by reading but one does not become the flower. To know something intuitionally is in effect, to become it within one's consciousness. In order for Gnosis to occur, it is necessary to become "identified" with the object of study. One may accomplish this through concentrated thought and meditation, however, there are millions of individual objects in the universe. To become one with each of them would take at the very least, millions of life times. The simpler way is to achieve supreme wisdom (Djehuti) by identifying (becoming one in consciousness) with NETER, GOD, who is the source of all objects in existence. Becoming one with or merging with NETER is therefore, the same as becoming one with all existence, having all knowledge, all power --- omnipresent, omniscient, omnipotent.

Much in the "WORLD" is information we have been told; much is information gathered by our senses which are specially made to gather information from the physical realm, to the extent that they can. This forms the basis of what we believe to be "real" and "true." This process constitutes our "psychological conditioning" into certain modes of behavior and certain beliefs. This is the formation of a limited intellect. However, if our senses were designed differently, for example, if we had the eyes of an owl, the canine sense of smell, the hearing of a bat, our perceptions of the "WORLD" would be quite different. Our perceptions would lead to different beliefs about what the "WORLD" is and therefore, our experiences would be quite different. Similarly, if we could see things (matter) the way a particle accelerator or an electron microscope sees it, we would live in a world of pure energy held together by that which is unseen: consciousness.

Due to their limitations, the human senses miss a whole other reality which lies beyond ordinary sense perception. The "Absolute Truth" (GOD) which underlies all things in the "physical" realm cannot be sensed with the ordinary senses, designed only for the world of duality.

Therefore, in order to KNOW, that is, to have GNOSIS or experiential knowledge of the transcendent and divine essence of anything, we must be able to connect with its divine essence to perceive "*its connection with its creator.*" Any other essence that may be compiled by the use of senses or other information gathering devices will only be an illusion. In order to perceive Absolute, non-changing Truth, we must become one with that Absolute Truth. This is the essence of our journey home. The Absolute experience of our divine nature will provide us a state of supreme peace *(Hetep)*. We will have completed a circuit (come full circle) from Amen which is the "hidden" reality from where all human souls come to Geb, the "manifest" physical reality and then back to Amen.

To do this is to become Godlike, even while still alive. The true way to know GOD is by looking within and not out, because our deepest self is GOD, regardless of sex, race, creed, or religion. Therefore, in order to "know"

GOD, it is necessary to "BE" GOD. In the Egyptian *"Story of Sinuhe",* the King (who is a symbol of a perfected human being, a Heru), is said to have:

" flown to heaven and united with the Sundisk, the divine body (of the King) *merging with its maker."*

In the Egyptian system, the faculty of wisdom is symbolized by the Ibis bird. The faculty of truth is symbolized by the feather (Maat) of the Ibis.

In the Indian philosophical system, the Goddess of wisdom, Saraswati, is often shown seated on a white swan.

The Ibis of Egypt and the Swan of India are both white in plumage, signifying the purity of conscious thought permeated with wisdom, truth and righteousness.

For the sake of clarity, from here on the Supreme Being will be referred to as "GOD" with all capitals and all the other aspects, divine principles or projections of the Supreme Being will be referred to as "Gods."

Above: Egyptian Goddess of Wisdom, Aset (Aset). Her symbol is the feather of the hawk.
Above right: Hindu Goddess of wisdom, truth and learning, Saraswati. Her image is shown on a white swan indicating purity of consciousness.

Ancient Egyptian Teachings about the nature of "knowledge."

A Devotee of ASET is:

"One who ponders over sacred matters and seeks therein for hidden truth."

"While ALL is in THE ALL, it is also true that THE ALL is in ALL. To him who truly understands this truth hath come great knowledge."

"Salvation is the freeing of the soul from its bodily fetters; becoming a God through knowledge and wisdom; controlling the forces of the cosmos instead of being a slave to them; subduing the lower nature and through awakening the higher self, ending the cycle of rebirth and dwelling with the Neters who direct and control the Great Plan."

"Men and women are to become God-like through a life of virtue and the cultivation of the spirit through scientific knowledge, practice and bodily discipline."

EGYPTIAN YOGA VOLUME 1

"Make your life the subject of intense inquiry, in this way you will discover its goal, direction, and destiny."

"To Know God, strive to grow in stature beyond all measure; conceive that there is nothing beyond thy capability. Know thyself deathless and able to know all things, all arts, sciences, the way of every life. Become higher than the highest height and lower than the lowest depth. Amass in thyself all senses of animals, fire, water, dryness and moistness. Think of thyself in all places at the same time, earth, sea, sky, not yet born, in the womb, young, old, dead, and in the after death state."

"The Mind being builder doth use the fire as tool for the construction of all things, but that of man only for things on earth. Stripped of its fire the mind on earth cannot make things divine, for it is human in it's dispensation. And such a Soul, when from the body freed, if it have fought the fight of piety-to Know God and to do wrong to no one-such Soul becomes entirely mind. Whereas the impious Soul remains in it's own essence, chastised by its own self."

"Those who hath learned to know themselves, hath reached that Good which doth transcend abundance; but they who through a love that leads astray, expend their love upon their body; they stay in Darkness wandering, and suffering through their senses things of Death."

"Indeed they who are yonder (those who live righteously will join GOD after death), will be living Gods, punishing anyone who commits a sin. Indeed they who are yonder will stand in the boat (barke of RA) causing the choicest offerings in it to be given to the temples. Indeed he who is yonder will become a sage who will not be hindered from appealing to GOD whenever they speak."

"Whoever has eaten the knowledge of every God, their existence is for all eternity and everlasting in their spirit body; what they willeth they doeth."

NOTE: For more on the mystical teachings of wisdom and the process of spiritual inquiry into the question "Who am I" see the book *THE MYSTERIES OF ASET: God in the universe god in the heart* by Dr. Muata Ashby.

CHAPTER 7: SYMBOLS

"If anyone suggests that it is disgraceful to fashion base images of the Divine and most Holy orders, it is sufficient to answer that the most holy Mysteries are set forth in two modes: one by means of similar and sacred representations akin to their nature, and the other to unlike forms designed with every possible discordance ... Discordant symbols are more appropriate representations of the Divine because the human mind tends to cling to the physical form of representation believing for example that the Divine are "golden beings or shining men flashing like lightning". But lest this error befall us, the wisdom of the venerable sages leads us through disharmonious dissimilitudes, not allowing our irrational nature to become attached to those unseemly images ... Divine things may not be easily accessible to the unworthy, nor may those who earnestly contemplate the Divine symbols dwell upon the forms themselves as final truth."

Dionysius the Aropagite

In order to understand the hidden meaning of a symbol it is necessary to understand what symbols are and a complete understanding of the principles behind their use. This section will not attempt to give a complete rendering of each Ancient Egyptian symbol since this would require a lifetime of study but it will provide some of the most important Ancient Egyptian symbols and a basic insight into the universal wisdom behind symbols so that a student may begin to decipher their meanings. Due to the nature of the study of symbols this entire volume will introduce various symbols as we progress with our study or Egyptian Yoga.

The previous quotation by Dyonisius provides us with insight on the nature, purpose and dangers of creating images of the divine for the purpose of worshipping.

Making images of GOD and the Gods in human likeness can be either helpful or dangerous for the follower. The mind is a wonderful tool but it easily indulges in emotion and develops attachment to that which it understands and develops fear toward that which it does not.

The danger arises when the mind becomes fixed on "the image" rather than the essence of the symbolic meaning of the Deity to be worshipped. Instead of worshipping those qualities and developing them in one's self, the worshipper might believe that those qualities belong to the statue or painting or are for "some special person who lived long ago." They do not realize that the symbols such as "HERU", "CHRIST", and "BUDDHA" are symbols of the qualities which lie deep within every individual, not somewhere "out there", but "right in here" inside each one of us. So the wise sages chose images that were so far from the norm, that the attachment oriented human mind would not get "hung up" on the "picture" and thereby concentrate on the MEANING. For example: The HAWK is the symbol of Heru, the God of light, vision and speed. When looking at the Hawk, we should be immediately drawn to those qualities (vision, tenacity and speed, freedom, Heru, etc.).

Symbols have great psychological significance because without them there would be no possibility for the mind to exist, function and interact with creation. A deeper examination of symbols reveals that they are more than just representations of images or ideas. The human mind understands things by first making a mental picture of it and then associating that mental concept with other ideas and thoughts. When we think of a chair, a three dimensional mental image appears in the mind as to what a chair looks like. We do not think of the letters that make up the word C-H-A-I-R. Therefore, to most efficiently and quickly convey an idea or thought, symbols are far superior to written forms of communication. After reading this book, the reader will find that having learned about the symbols, just a glance at them will convey the ideas, thoughts and feeling associated with them. When we understand that we are not the body, but spirits, it becomes obvious that all our mental notions are only elaborate symbols. In fact all the objects in creation are really symbols or ideas, not absolute realities. Therefore, symbols are a vital key to understanding the workings of the mind and the nature of existence. In Egyptian mythology and philosophy as well as in other mythological and philosophical systems, it is often necessary to learn about a symbol's meaning(s) by its relation to other symbols. In many cases, symbols from seemingly separate cultures may shed light on the meaning of a particular symbol.

From the most remote times of Egypt, the Symbol of the Hawk was used to represent all-encompassing divinity (GOD, the Supreme Being, creator of all things): omnipotence, omnipresence, omniscience. The Hawk is also the symbol of the human soul. The implication is that the Supreme Being and the Human Soul are identical. Here Heru (the Hawk) is shown holding the Shen, symbol of eternity and the Ankh, the symbol of life.

*The hieroglyph **"Sema" or "Smai"** represented by the union of two lungs and the trachea, symbolizes that the union of the higher and lower self leads to the One.*

*The hieroglyph **"Nefer"**, close in pronunciation to **"Neter"**, expressed by the union of the heart and the trachea symbolizes: that which is the most beautiful thing, the highest good, the greatest achievement.*

*The hieroglyph **"Ankh,"** symbolizes the union of the cross (male) and the circle (female) aspects of oneself, leading to the transformation into an androgynous being. Thus, the two become One.*

*The hieroglyph **"Hetep"**, the supreme peace, the final abode of all who satisfy the desire of their soul: union with itself.*

Christhood and Heruhood

(*The Uraeus* (Halo of Heruhood and Christhood).)   The word "*Christ*" is not a name but a title, like vice-president is a title. "*Christ*" means: "*He or she whose head is Anointed with oil*" or "*The Anointed One*". Heru, Sage, Saint, Buddha, Christ, Krishna, etc. are terms or names to describe the same thing. Heruhood or Christhood refers to certain qualities exhibited by mythological or historical personalities as symbols representing the potential state of enlightenment of every sentient being in the universe.

Christs are those persons who have attained complete purification of their psychological personality. They experience cosmic consciousness, the experience of being one (identifying oneself) with everything. This is a state of supreme bliss that comes from becoming one with one's essential nature: GOD. This is a state which cannot be achieved through the earthly pleasures or relationships. As explained in the Egyptian *"Book of Coming Forth by Day"*, those who live in virtue (*MAAT*) with a pure heart will know all there is to know and be all there is to be; through their Heruhood (attaining the qualities of Heru which are: truth, righteousness and justice, inner vision - The Eye of Heru), they will have defeated the enemies of Asar (greed, ignorance, impiety, egoism) as personified by Set, the evil one.

So, salvation comes from ATTAINING Heruhood, that is, becoming Heru through a life of virtue, wisdom, courage and Self-Knowledge. Those who become **a** Heru, Christ or Buddha have attained the consciousness that survives death and will live on after their death of the body, being free from ignorance which leads to reincarnation.

So there is no *"ONE"* "Christ." Everyone can potentially become a Christ if they follow the path of masters such as Heru, Jesus, Buddha, Lao Tzu, etc. or the path laid out by other modern day masters.

When cosmic consciousness is attained, an anointing occurs with an etheric oil, secreted from the energy centers into the brain and the body's circulatory system including the heart (the mystical seat of the soul). The body and mind are transcended and one experiences a higher level of existence beyond the joys and sorrows of the world. Christhood means to attain the beatific vision of oneself as GOD. One becomes consciously established in the realization that one IS GOD; this is in contrast to the masses of people who are aware only that they are a perishable body of flesh and bones.

Anpu sitting atop the box protecting the parts of the body of Asar.

Anpu, the Jackal:

"He Who traveled between the realms (temporal, subtle, celestial), able to Lead Asar from the Gods Who belong to Earth to Those Who are in Heaven, able to live upon the Horizon, and before Whom even the Gods of the Ennead Tremble."

"Master of the scales."

Anpu led Asar upward from the realm of humans to the realm of the Gods, as he led Aset to Asar' fragmented remains so that she might revive (re-member) him (see Osirian Resurrection).

Anpu (Anpu) is:

"...the dogged intellect that by the watching and waking from sleep, who by Knowing and not Knowing, determines friend from foe."

"Opener of the way."

Anpu represents the intellectual ability within man / woman to recognize the error of passion and the path *"scent of the divine"* towards divinity, from the world of illusion (physical realm) to the world of reality (spiritual self). Anpu is described as being Gold and Black referring to the faculty of discernment which can lead one from below to above (from earth to heaven). Anpu is the son of Asar (Subtle Realm, Netherworld - between heaven and earth) and Nebethet, Goddess of Temporal (physical-material) Realm. He is likened to a dog because the dog has the use of its sight by day and by night. Anpu represents the awakening of wisdom wherein man must, like a loyal dog, allow the entrance of wisdom and love that lead to the GOOD and bark at the evil (ignorance, passion, emotions). According to Memphite theology, Anpu is also an aspect of Heru, representing the spiritual awakening capacity in every human being. Therefore, the power to "open the way" for spiritual evolution is latent inside every human being.

"The KNOWLEDGE of every God is within us."
"The Gods are immortal men, men are mortal Gods."

Ankh and AUM

Above: The ancient Ethiopian-Egyptian symbol: Ankh

Christian Cross Female SHEN Sanskrit: AUM

The Ankh is the symbol of the imperishable vital force of life. Related to the life giving properties of air and water, the Ankh depicts three symbolic principles found in creation: 1. the circle (female member) 2. the cross (male member) and 3. unity (the male member united with that of the female). Life literally occurs as a result of the union of spirit and matter, the circle representing the immortal and eternal part (absolute reality) and the cross representing that which is mortal and transient (illusion-matter). Its similarity to the female symbol alludes to the regenerative, formative properties of the Ankh.

Thus, as with the Ying and Yang symbol of the Chinese Tao philosophy, the Ankh also symbolizes the balance between the two forces of life, positive-negative, light-dark, long-short, female-male, etc. If properly balanced and cultivated, the power of harmony (union of opposites) is formidable. The top of the Ankh, the circle, represents the Shen, the Egyptian symbol of eternity. In Indian - Hindu Mythology, the Ankh is depicted in the pictures of the androgynous God-Goddess ***Ardhanari.*** The left side of Ardhanari is female and the right side is male. In Chinese philosophy, the Shen represents the life force in the cosmos; it is the wisdom-consciousness, the spirit. ***The parts of the Ankh:***

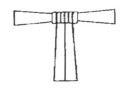

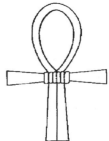

1- Above: The Shen ring: eternity, feminine principal, womb, magnetically charged.

2- Above: The Cross: that which is temporal, time - space principal, phallic principal, electrically charged.

3- Above: The Ankh Knot: That which holds the two principals together, (eternity-temporal, immortal-mortal, spirit-body) creating the human being.

Thus the Ankh refers to life in the form of a human being.

The Ankh is also known as the "key of life." To give an Ankh to someone in thought or deed is to wish that person life and health. A most important feature of the Ankh symbol is that it is composed of two separable parts. That is to say, the loop at the top (female) and the cross at the bottom (male) are only "tied" together as it were. Therefore, it is possible to loosen the bonds (knots) that tie the spirit to the body and thus make it possible for the soul to attain enlightenment. Ankh may be pronounced Aung and used as a Hekau (word of power or Mantra), chanting repeatedly (aloud or mentally) while concentrating on the meaning behind the symbolism. Staring at the symbols either alone or in conjunction with the hekau or simply concentrating on it (alone) mentally will help steady the mind during concentration and meditation.

The Symbol AUM is Sanskrit (from the sacred scriptures of India). It may be pronounced as: OM.

"Om: this eternal word is all, what is, what was, and what shall be."

Indian Scripture

AUM is one of the names of GOD and is said to be the first sound GOD made in the act of Creation: "The Word." It encompasses all possible sounds of creation if pronounced properly.

Above: Post-Dravidian (Aryan period) representation of the ancient Indian Deity, Ardhanari: Pure Consciousness, symbol of the androgynous spirit which is GOD within every human being. Note the Ankh located at the level of the genitals. Ardhanari was also known as Purusha but in later times, the name Purusha became identified with the MALE element of creation only. This was an attempt by the Aryans to integrate the Dravidian philosophy of an androgynous Universal Spirit into the Vedic philosophy which they introduced to India along with the other main male Gods of the Hindu pantheon: Brahma, Vishnu and Shiva. Their female counterparts were relegated to lower status. However, in pre-Aryan times, the Dravidian civilization saw the Universal Spirit as containing both male and female, using the Dravidian name: Ammaiappan. The resemblance of the Dravidian name to the Egyptian Creator GOD, Amun (Amen), and the Dogon Creator GOD, Amma, is evident.

A-U-M-( )

AUM is a 4 syllable word.

A represents the physical reality, the waking state of consciousness where you are aware of the physical body and day to day activities.

U represents the dream state of consciousness where you are conscious of the astral body and the dream state.

M represents the deep sleep state of consciousness where you go beyond the waking and dream states. This is the realm of the causal body. Here one is in contact with the real self, although not at the conscious level.
( ) represents the silence after the 'm' sound is finished. It symbolizes the transcending of the three previous states of consciousness into the realm of experiencing the Absolute Truth of reality which is not possible through the intellectual (thought) process. Our true consciousness, the constant spectator of the previous three states of consciousness may be realized by waking up from these three states through meditation.

Om is a root word for many Hindu and Buddhist mantras. It also may be chanted alone and like all mantras, will work to carry the user into transcendental states of consciousness. It will have the greatest effect if the meaning and the application to the user is well understood.

"Om Tat Sat" (GOD is the only reality).

Bhagavad Gita

"Om is the bow, the soul is the arrow, Brahman (GOD) is the target; let an aspirant discharge the arrow of the soul with an unwavering mind, and be merged in Brahman."

Mundaka Upanishad

OM in India and Ancient Egypt

While *Om* is most commonly known as a *Sanskrit* mantra (word of power from India), it also appears in the ancient Egyptian texts and is closely related to the Kemetic *Amun* in sound and Amen of Christianity. More importantly, it has the same meaning as Amun and is therefore completely compatible with the energy pattern of the entire group. According to the Egyptian Leyden papyrus, the name of the "Hidden God", referring to Amun, may be pronounced as *Om,* or *Am*.

"Om" and "Amun" in Ancient Egypt

Below you will find the ancient glyphs of the ancient Egyptian OM symbol. Note the similarity to the Indian symbol that follows.

 "OM" from the Ancient Egyptian Leyden Papyrus

The ancient African text containing the OM is found in the Leyden Magical Papyrus in which Supreme Being is described as follows:

"Great is thy name, Heir is thy name, Excellent is thy name, Hidden is thy name,. Mighty one of the gods and goddesses is thy name, "He whose name is hidden from all the gods and goddesses is thy name, OM (☦), Mighty Am is thy name; All the gods and goddesses is thy name…"

We know that OM is the name of Amun because of the epithet "Hidden" and OM is the nameless Ancient divinity because of the epithet "name is hidden". OM is also the ancient divinity Neberdjer (All encompassing Divinity) because of the epithet "All the gods and goddesses" so OM is the name given to the most ancient

divinities of Kamit (Egypt) dating to the predynastic era (prior to 5000 BCE). ॐ The Indian Sanskrit

Symbol "Aum" or "Om"

Hekau Or Words Of Power And Prayer

Hekau (mantras) may be safely used by anyone to help steady the mind and to help train it to <u>FOCUS</u> on the wisdom which will lead to mental transformation.

Sounds, words, religious songs or scriptures from any language may be used by understanding the meaning and repeating it for several minutes. It is important to understand that the hekau will be given power by you the user and not the other way around. Therefore, it should have the effect of elevating the mind. The more they are used, the more mental power one will have to put oneself in a calm state and transport oneself to a higher psychological - spiritual plane of consciousness.

It is also important to understand that *EVERY SINGLE TIME* either prayer or hekau is uttered, one is moving closer to one's goal. In fact, every single time one even thinks about GOD, it has the equivalent psychological effect of a visit to church. A deep meditation might be equal to a visit to a temple or religious pilgrimage center.

The following hekau were created by the author; they may be used in Egyptian or English. Hekau may be given out by a spiritual preceptor or you may choose (make) your own. Examples:

Aung sucha Ba Ra.
Life come forth Universal Spirit of Ra Universal GOD.
Nuk apu Ab Maat.
I open my heart to Truth and Righteousness.
Nuk mesu Ra.
I am a child of Ra (Cosmic Consciousness)
Nuk Ba an Khat an Ren.
I am Spirit, not a physical body or a personality.

The following selections come from the *"Book of Coming Forth by Day"*:

Nuk pu NETER
I am the Supreme Divinity.
Ba ar pet sat ar ta.
Soul is of heaven, body belongs to the earth.
Nuk uab-k uab ka-k uab ba-k uab sekhem.
My mind has pure thoughts, so my soul and life forces are pure.
Nuk ast au neheh ertai-nef tetta.
Behold I am the heir of eternity, everlastingness has been given to me.
Sekhem - a em mu ma aua Set.
I have gained power in the water as I conquered Set (greed, lust, ignorance).
Rex - a em Ab - a sekhem - a em hati - a.
I know my heart, I have gained power over my heart.
Un - na uat neb am pet am ta.
The power is within me to open all doors in heaven and earth.
Nuk sah em ba - f.
I am a spirit, with my soul.

These or any other words (religious songs, scriptures) that may occupy the mind so as to quiet the endless stream of thoughts may be used at any time. They may be repeated aloud but are more effective if repeated mentally and silently in concentration as a prelude to meditation.

Prayers may be uttered at any time and should be reflected upon and, like the hekau, should be thoroughly understood before they are used. They are especially effective at the beginning and end of the hekau repetition during meditation, allowing the mind to make a smooth transition between states of relative and absolute reality. In the same way as a practitioner of Indian Vedanta philosophy might greet someone with the mantra *"Om Tat*

Sat", a practitioner of Egyptian philosophy might use *"Hetep"*, as a powerful reminder to oneself of one's true nature and that of he or she who is being addressed.

The Lotus

*Above Left: **Heru sitting atop the lotus and the primeval waters.***
Above right: Krishna* of India on the Lotus*also known as Purusha or Brahma.

In or Kamit (Egypt), the symbol of the lotus encompassed the idea of coming forth into the light. As the Lotus retreats into the waters at dusk and emerges with the light of day, so too, the human spirit blossoms as it emerges from the darkness of ignorance about the nature of its true self into the light of wisdom. The Egyptian number assignment for the lotus is *1,000*. It is notable that in the Indian Kundalini Yoga system, the lotus is the symbol of the seventh energy-consciousness center (Chakra) which is said to have *1,000* petals. The 1,000 petals symbolize the countless number of subtle channels which connect the human being with the universe. The circular shape of the lotus leaves and seed also denotes the ideas of eternity, infinity and immortality, that is our inner Godly nature.

In India, the mystical implications of the Lotus as espoused by Paramahansa Yogananda in "Autobiography of a Yogi" is thus:

"The Lotus flower is an ancient divine symbol of India; its unfolding petals suggest the expansion of the soul; the growth of its beauty from the mud of its
origins holds a benign spiritual promise."

On the previous page, Heru sits atop a Lotus with a flail in one hand, signifying that as the Lotus has risen above the marshy slime to partake in the light and life of the sun, so too they who sit upon the lotus have risen above their lower animal nature and the fetters of time, space and matter. They are beyond change, beyond death, beyond ignorance. They have risen to the level of spiritual supremacy above the slime.

"The God himself, is seated alone, above any such dominion or energy, august and holy, filled abundantly, and remaining in himself without change, as the figure of the one sitting is intended to signify."

Iamblichus (Initiate 100-300 A.D.)

GOD created the universe, time, space and gives himself to them in order that life may exist, not long ago, but at every moment. Creation is a continuous process that goes on at every moment due to the energy provided by GOD. However, GOD is above any creation or energy, sitting atop it, unchanged, ever full, beyond either existence or non-existence; GOD is both and neither at the same time.

Images are tools to help us understand the wonder and majesty that is GOD, but <u>only</u> GOD knows GOD in GOD's true essence. Therefore, in order to see GOD in GOD's essence, we must ascend to our Godly nature of Heru or Aset by developing their qualities within ourselves. In essence, we must consciously become ONE with GOD in order to truly KNOW GOD.

To KNOW GOD, men and women must go beyond thinking into the realm of "intuition" through listening to the teachings, reflecting on them and "making the mind still" (meditation) on those teachings.

The Eye of Ra and The Eye of Heru (Heru)

The Eye of Ra, the URAEUS, represents the Life Force power of the spirit which animates matter. The Uraeus is the right eye of fire and wrath. The right eye is the daughter of Ra, Goddess Hetheru, who commands the destructive power of the Supreme Spirit (GOD). The Eye of the *HIGH GOD* (Ra-Heru) is the Great Goddess of the universe, Hetheru, in her wrathful, terrible aspect. Originally, the eye was sent out on an errand and upon her return, she found that she was replaced by a surrogate. This was the first cause of the wrath of the eye. Since then, the eye can never be permanently or completely appeased. The High GOD (Ra) used the formula to turn the eye into a rearing cobra which he strapped to his forehead to ward off his enemies. This Uraeus head ornament was also used in ancient times to protect the Third Eye region of the head. Located on the forehead between the eyebrows, it is also known as the Third Eye or the Ajna Chakra in the Kundalini yoga system. It can be activated by continued meditation on the area of the forehead. It is a symbol of the Life Force energy, representing not only the visible warmth (fire) of the sun, but also the subtle energy (Life Force) which animates it. It implies that one has mastered (sublimated) the sexual energy, which gives everything life. Developing this energy center allows us to be in contact with the invisible world of the spirit and thus, to see spiritually.

The right eye is the *"burning heat of the Sun."* In Utterance 316 of the Coffin Texts, the eye speaks:

"I am the all-seeing Eye of Heru, whose appearance strikes terror, Lady of Slaughter, Mighty One of Frightfulness."

In other texts the Eye is described further:

"Great will be your power and mighty your majesty over the bodies of your enemies. They will fall howling on their faces, all mankind will cringe beneath you and your might, they will respect you when they see you in that vigorous form..."

The Eye speaks:

... I am-yes-I am a burning flame, but also the boon companion of Ra... I have seized the Gods, there is no opposition to me."

The Left Eye of Heru symbolizes the *"Power of the God of Light."* It implies that one has attained all of the qualities as personified by Heru, that we have vanquished the enemies of Asar (ignorance, egoism, selfishness, disharmony, mental agitation, etc.) from ourselves.

The right Eye of Heru, also known as the Eye of Ra, the Uraeus, represents the Sun (Ra, spiritual energy, Prana, Chi) and the left eye of Heru, the Moon (Aset-nature, mental power, understanding). At once Heru is the synthesis of spirit (Sun) and body (Moon). It is the power to *"see the way"* beyond spirit and matter (absolute reality).

EGYPTIAN YOGA VOLUME 1

The symbol of the two eyes of Heru is most ancient. Having existed in predynastic times (10,000-5,500 B.C.E), it carried over into the philosophy of Hinduism as The Eyes of Krishna, and in Buddhism as The Eyes of Buddha. The eyes imply a form of vision, a state of consciousness beyond ordinary human perception. In the intervening time when Set had stolen Heru' eyes, he took away Heru' vision of unity. Heru therefore saw the world as Set did, through the state of consciousness of a forceful brute, with unbridled emotion, passion and egoism. Heru lost the light (intuitional vision) of the Sun and was dominated by the Moon (earthly passion - vision of Set) which clouded the mind and impeded higher thought and intuition. Therefore, Setian (body consciousness) vision is hostile to Ra (spiritual vision) and must be fought against until it is controlled (sublimated). As stated in the Egyptian Book of coming Forth By Day in Chapter 23, Setian thinking is the greatest force holding the soul in a state of bondage.

At the end of the conflict between Heru and Set, Set (brute force, arrogance, egoism) is sublimated through Djehuti (wisdom). His physical force is directed to the service of Ra as he is given the prestigious position at the head of the Barke of Ra as protector of Ra as he traverses the heavens every day. Each day Ra must do battle with the forces of darkness who would like to stop Ra from shining. These forces are headed by Apopis the serpent. Once Set is controlled through wisdom, he is seen doing battle against Apopis in order to protect the Brake of Ra (see page 58). In this manner, our physical nature, brute animal force, must be placed at the service of the spirit.

The vision of either Sun (spirit) or Moon (matter) alone represents a dangerous imbalance. For spiritual consciousness alone negates physical existence and physical consciousness alone (egoism) negates the spirit. Therefore, a balance must be achieved in order that both spirit and matter may coexist in harmony. This is the vision of Heru, the protective vision (consciousness) which understands that the mystery of the spirit and that of matter are one in the same, that the underlying basis of each one is the same reality. The Eye of Heru therefore, represents the vision of that reality which goes beyond the Sun and the Moon (Spirit and Matter). The Eye of Heru is the protector from all evil. To possess the Eye of Heru, that is, the vision or consciousness of Heru, is to possess all things, to *"SEE"* all things. Fear comes from ignorance and ignorance comes from thinking and believing that the world is composed of separate objects, creatures and human beings and from identifying with the body, believing oneself to be a mortal personality. In seeing (understanding) all things, there is no fear because there is no ignorance. All things are only a manifestation of the "ALL" (one's inner most self) therefore, one cannot hurt oneself. One is really immortal, beyond spirit and matter, therefore, there is no need to fear death. Thus, the Eye of Heru is the greatest protector.

In Vedanta (Samkhya) Indian philosophy, the Moon represents the mind and the Sun represents GOD, the Supreme Being. The Eyes of Krishna are the Sun and Moon. In Kemetic (Egyptian) philosophy, the Moon is a symbol of the God Thoth (Djehuti-Hermes), the God of Wisdom (intellect, higher mind-purified mind). Thus, the implication is that in order to become one with the universe such as Heru or Krishna, the following change in consciousness must occur: The mind (intellect) must merge with the Cosmic Mind (GOD). This change in consciousness may be effected by turning the thoughts of the mind to GOD as opposed to the objects of the world or shifting one's perception of worldly objects and seeing them as expressions of GOD instead of separate, self existing realities. The mind is the Moon. As the Moon is a reflection of the Sun, the mind is a reflection of GOD. Therefore, by changing one's consciousness, one's awareness of reality which has been caught in the extreme of matter, one may move more toward spirituality in order to find the balance between the two and thereby become the master of the two.

When Heru' eye (the moon) was torn out and thrown away by Set, the God Thoth (Djehuti-Hermes) found it and using the formula below, turned it into the Moon. When the parts of the Eye of Heru are added up, gives the answer 63/64 which approximate the whole number 1. One is the number which symbolizes oneness, wholeness, All sight, All knowing, the Supreme Being, The Absolute. As long as the soul is involved in creation (matter), there will remain some small separation between the individual BA and the Universal BA, the ONE. In order to become completely unified, merged into infinity, the individual soul of the enlightened person dissolves into the Universal soul at the time of death, this is complete ONENESS with the divine. The missing part of the Eye of Heru, 1/64, is added by Djehuti through magic. *The Eye of Djehuti.* Thus through the magic of Djehuti (wisdom), the parts (representing our consciousness) may be reconstituted to wholeness. Djehuti is an aspect of Ptah, the Cosmic Mind. In this aspect Djehuti symbolizes the higher consciousness (mind) of those humans who are attuned to the Universal (Cosmic) Mind.

Thus Djehuti speaks:

"I came seeking the Eye of Heru , that I might bring it back and count it. I found it (now it is) complete, counted and sound, so that it can flame up to the sky and blow above and below..."

Therefore, through the Eye (vision, consciousness) of Djehuti (wisdom), the Eye of Heru (inner vision) may be brought back to its original place, that it may attain the heights of heaven and achieve control over the spiritual domain (above) and the realm of matter (below). Djehuti is the God who brings MAAT (truth, righteousness, justice). Thus, through wisdom and righteousness our original condition may be restored. The name for the Eye of Heru may be pronounced as *"Wedjat", "Udjat"* or *"Utchat"* meaning: *"the whole or restored one"* and also *"that which protects."*

In the Pyramid of Unas, the Eye of Djehuti is called *"The Black Eye of Heru."* In the same text is said to Unas:

"Thou hast seized the two Eyes of Heru, the White Eye and the Black Eye and thou hast carried them off and set them in front of thee and they give light to thy face."

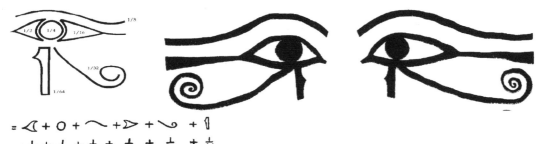

$$= \triangleleft + O + \frown + \rhd + \backsim + \updownarrow$$

$$= \tfrac{1}{2} + \tfrac{1}{4} + \tfrac{1}{8} + \tfrac{1}{16} + \tfrac{1}{32} + \tfrac{1}{64}$$

When the parts of the Eye of Heru (Udjat, left eye) is added up, the result is 63/64 which approximate the whole number 1. As long as the soul is involved in creation (matter), there will remain some small separation between the individual BA and the Universal BA, the ONE.

The Eyes of Krishna

The Eyes of Buddha

The Scroll Is A Symbol Of Hidden Wisdom

From the most ancient times the scroll - a piece of rolled up papyrus or parchment paper containing writings - was considered as the symbol of occult (hidden) wisdom, that is, wisdom or knowledge that is not yet known. In a similar sense it refers to that which is abstract, that which transcends thought.

The Yoga of wisdom is a process of cleansing the mind and intellect (higher mind) from their limited (ignorant - conditioned) vision of the world. To achieve this end, the erroneous subconscious impressions that make us think we are "physical" bodies and not "spirits" must be replaced with correct impressions.

For this reason, <u>Constant</u> affirmation by use of words of power, hekau or mantras, with full understanding should be discussed, reflected upon and meditated upon in order to understand their meaning and to allow that understanding to become part of one's subconscious mind. The Egyptian Book of Coming Forth By Day is a text of wisdom about the true nature of reality and also of "Spells" to assist the initiate in making that reality evident. These spells are in reality Hekau or words of power which the initiate recites in order to assist him or her in changing the consciousness level of the mind. The hekau themselves may have no special power except in their assistance to the mind to change its perception through repetition and in assisting the mind to become still (see Hekau, Meditation). Through these affirmations, the initiate is able to and change the consciousness from body consciousness ("I am a body") to cosmic consciousness ("I am GOD"). This form of affirmatory spiritual discipline is recognized by Indian Gurus as the most intense form of spiritual discipline.

Repetition, either verbally or mentally, of hekau or mantras with full understanding, reflection and meditation will gradually lead to the replacement of old erroneous subconscious and conscious mental concepts. Study of philosophy and keeping company with enlightened personalities are also essential factors during the process of purification.

Unless one is very strong, one is usually influenced by the company one keeps, either in a positive manner or in a negative manner.

"As you believe so shall you become!"

If you IDENTIFY with (believe you are) the Universal BA (Spirit), you will become immortal and eternal; if you identify with your body, emotions, senses and fears, you will remain a mortal personality (Khat) who will not transcend this world at the time of death. You will have to come back again because you are drawn to the physical world to pursue the fulfillment of your desire to be "human.".

The Wings

From the earliest times the symbol of the wings has signified the expansive nature of the soul. One meaning of the word Heru (Heru) is *"That which is up there"* (heaven). Heru as the soul of every human being, is represented as a hawk with a human head. In this way wings are the signature of Heru the hawk, the all encompassing, all pervading being who is the soul of all things and may be found in male and female Neters and humans alike. Thus, we are led to understand that the true nature of every human being is that same Supreme Being (Heru), supremely free, supremely peaceful and immortal, beyond the body, beyond gender, beyond time and space and beyond physical reality, yet including all of these. Another aspect of wings, especially when related to certain deities such as Maat (virtue), is the idea of that state of being which when developed, will allow us to unfurl our own wings and fly as the hawk. People who have achieved altered states of consciousness, spontaneously or through meditation, have reported the ability to "fly" in their minds and spiritual bodies.

The Sacred Cow and The Sacred Bull

From time immemorial, the Sacred Cow has held a prominent place in Egyptian mythology. One of the Egyptian creation stories holds that The Sacred Cow, who was brimming with life, gave birth to creation. Figure A. shows Pharaoh Amenhetep II with the "Power" of the Cow "Behind" him. It should be noted that while the cow is a symbol of the female mother principle, it also incorporates the male principle as symbolized by the sundisk in between the horns. In this aspect, the cow also symbolizes the Goddess Hetheru who is at once the great mother (Aset) as well as the fiery eye of Ra (see "The Eye of Ra", "Min and Hetheru").

In India as with Egypt, the bull symbolizes the erectile-generative power of the male deity. In Egypt, the bull is a symbol of Heru (and all his other forms) and in India, it is a symbol of Shiva.

Figure B. is the God Shiva from India in the androgynous form. It shows the same idea of the human figure (human soul) protected and empowered by the particular deity or God force. In this sculpture entitled *"He is She"* *(Kamakalavilasa)*, female and male are together being supported and empowered by the bovine (cow-bull) creature.

NOTE: For more on the mystical teachings of Ancient Egypt symbolism see the book *RESURRECTING ASAR* by Dr. Muata Ashby.

CHAPTER 8: PARTS OF THE SPIRIT

BA
SAHU
KHAIBIT
KHU
KA
SEKHEM
AB
KHAT
<u>REN</u>

"Oh people of the earth, men and women born and made of the elements, but with the spirit of the Divine within you, rise from your sleep of ignorance! Be sober and thoughtful. Realize that your home is not on the earth but in the Light. Why have you delivered yourselves unto death, having power to partake of immortality? Repent, and change your minds. Depart from the dark light and forsake corruption forever. Prepare to blend your souls with the Eternal Light."

<u>*Egyptian Mystical Wisdom*</u>

The rays of GOD project into "Millions" of humans and objects. In humans, the projection is in 9 main parts. These are the parts of the human spirit:

(1) THE BA:

The Ba is heart-soul which dwells in the KA with the power of metamorphosis. Sometimes described as the "SOUL" and "Higher Self" and it is seen as a spark from the Universal Ba (GOD). The Ba may be dialogued with and can be a spiritual guide to the developing individual. The equivalent of the Hindu "Atman," it is the indestructible, eternal and immortal spark of life. It is not affected by anything that may happen to the senses, body, mind or intellect (higher mind).

Through the mind, the BA (soul-consciousness) "projects" and keeps together an aggregate of physical elements (earth, air, water, fire) into a conglomerate that is called the "physical body." When the soul has no more use for the physical body, it discards it and returns to the Universal Ba if it is enlightened, or it may seek experience in one of the other bodies (spiritual, astral) where it may exist in heaven ("The Realm of Light"). If it is not enlightened, it will tune into another aggregate of elements to make another body (reincarnation).

(2) THE KA:

The abstract personality, ego, spirit-twin subconscious desires, concept of self, ethereal body possessing the power of locomotion and survives the death of the physical body. It is the ethereal double containing the other parts. The concept of the Ka was known in India and the word was also known. The Indian God Brahma had a Ka (soul-twin).

(3) THE KHAT:

The concrete personality, the physical body.

(4) THE AB:

"The conscience (AB) of a man is his own God."

The AB or conscience is the source of Meskhenet (Karma) and the mother of reincarnation. The AB represents the heart. It is the symbol of the mind, the conscience and also the repository of subconscious desires which cause the mind to be in a perpetual state of motion and change (restlessness). As these desires can never be fulfilled by experiences or from objects in the world of time and space, at death, the ignorant soul will harbor unfulfilled desires which will lead to further incarnations in search of this fulfillment. This point is described in Chapter 30, line 3 from the *Egyptian Book of Coming Forth by Day: "My heart, the mother of my coming into being"*. The Ab undergoes examination by Thoth (Djehuti, one's own wisdom faculty) and one's own heart will fashion (mother) one's own fate (come into being) according to one's will, and desires, which are based on one's understanding (wisdom) about one's true self. Thus, the new is fashioned in accordance with what he or she has done during previous lives.

(5) THE KHAIBIT:

The Khaibit or Shadow is associated with the BA from which it receives nourishment. It has the power of locomotion and omnipresence.

(6) THE KHU:

The Khu is the spiritual soul which is immortal; it is associated with the BA and is an Ethereal Being.

(7) THE SAHU:

The "glorious" spiritual body in which the KHU and Ba dwells. When integrated (enlightened), the spiritual and mental attributes of the natural body are united to the new powers of its own nature. The Sahu is the goal of all aspiration. It is the reason for human existence ---to become Godlike while still alive (see GOD and Creation).

(8) THE SEKHEM:

Power, spiritual personification of the vital Life Force in man and woman. Its dwelling place is in the heavens with the KHUS. Sekhem also denotes the potency, erectile power or force used in fashioning one's own glorious new body for resurrection.

(9) THE REN:

The name, essential attribute to the personification of a being. The name is sometimes found encircled by a rope of light called a cartouche which is associated with the Shen, the top part of the Ankh Symbol. The cartouche represents a rope of sunlight or Life Force harnessed into the form of a circle. It is the most impregnable structure to protect one's name against attack. The name of the author is enclosed in a cartouche on the first page of this book.

The Heart (AB)

The heart is:

"An excellent witness." "An ORACLE in everyone."

Egyptian Proverbs

King Thutmose III called the Heart:

" A guide in my affairs...
the Conscience or HEART of a Human is his and her own GOD."

The AB (conscience) is the part of our consciousness which registers our feelings, intent and desires. Since the universe is mental, one's thoughts are of great importance to one's evolution. Thoughts are controlled by one's conscience, one's perception of reality which is dictated by one's level of wisdom, one's knowledge of reality, and by one's subconscious understanding of reality. If one understands oneself to be a mortal individual, one will live in such a manner and will develop mental concepts (conscious and subconscious) which will be reinforced by one's life experiences. One's level of consciousness can be raised by a "conscious" effort to grow in wisdom through the practice of virtue, self discipline (control over the mind) and the study of nature (through science and/or spiritual teachings).

If one reaches the understanding that one is immortal and eternal, one with all other beings, then one will live within that reality. In the judgment of the heart from the *Book of Coming Forth By Day*, it is the heart, one's deepest thoughts and ideas of oneself and reality, which is judged. If one commits crimes knowing they are evil deeds, then one will suffer according to one's own assessment of one's own guilt (heavy heart). On the other hand, if one lived spiritually and virtuously in the knowledge that one is a spirit, acting honestly, trying to do one's best at all times while relinquishing any desire for the fruits (results) of the actions, be they negative or positive outcomes, then one will not "suffer" the consequences of those actions. One should strive to maintain an equally light heart whether a project succeeds or not because one did one's best and that is all that any one could ask, but most importantly, one should strive to maintain such equanimity because ultimately, neither actions nor their fruits (results) can provide true and lasting happiness. They can neither add nor detract from one's essence except in an illusory manner when the mind believes in them. This illusion however, will only lead to mental agitation in the short run and disappointment in the long run. This is the path of ignorance; seeking fulfillment in the world of cause and effect. Thus, one should pursue detachment, then one's conscience will be clear and therefore one's mental involvement in matter (physical body and the world) will not hold one's soul to experience hell (suffering in one's mind by tormenting oneself with one's own fears, unfulfilled desires and remorse which could lead to another incarnation). Other wise, the soul reincarnates in pursuit of the fulfillment of its desires but in the process, suffers the pains and toils of a physical existence. This concept, called *KARMA* in India, was encompassed in the mythology and philosophy of the Egyptian Goddess Meskhenet (5,500 B.C.E.).

The cosmos therefore, provides a mechanism in which one's own conscience dispenses exact justice to itself in accordance with its own actions better than any judicial system on earth. The heart, seen as the seat of the soul, is therefore the most important factor deciding the experiences of the spirit. Only through a purified heart is it possible to ascend to the heights of wisdom and intuitive understanding about the nature of one's own existence.

The living of truth and righteousness, which is MAAT (as symbolized by the feather), should be done while still alive. After death if there are few sins, the HEART will be lighter than MAAT, and the owner is fit for eternal life. However, if the HEART is heavy with sin, anger, fear, ignorance, egoism or if it is too elated or full of desires for worldly pleasures, then it will be heavier than MAAT. It will not be fit for life eternal yet. This HEART did not practice the VIRTUES well enough.

The AB, (conscience), can also be an excellent "GUIDE" or inner "ORACLE" for those who wish to live a life of TRUTH. Those who put aside their pride and egoism can use the higher intelligence within them to find the truth that does not come through thinking. The Ab (higher self, subconscious mind) may be accessed by quieting the thoughts and then asking a question followed by silence once again. The answer will come, seemingly out of nowhere, when the mind is clear.

The mind is not the soul. The mind is limited and subject to ignorance, primarily ignorance about the BA (soul). Those who devote themselves to "the religion of the mind" (those who indulge in sensory pleasures, or those who think themselves to be exalted due to their intellectual prowess, thinking that their mental thoughts and body are all there is to life) will undergo a "death" of the illusory ego at the time when the physical death comes. On the other hand, they who use the mind as a tool and develop the higher, intuitive aspects of it will transcend it (the mind). They will not die. They will have attained immortality.

Developing the power of INTUITION is essential on the spiritual path. This is the only way to become ONE with GOD. INTUITION is PERFECTION while the thinking mind is related to the egotistical vision of one's self as an individual. Individuals are mortals and mortals die; however, INTUITION is the spirit which is eternal and immortal.

The goal is to develop our INTUITIONAL capability and to leave the ego-mind (lower mind) behind. We must train, through wisdom, developing the higher-mind, (intellect) to understand it is a spirit and not a physical body or impure mind.

AB and BA

It is interesting to note that AB spelled backwards is BA. These two words, however, are more integrally related than just in their spellings. Our ignorance causes us to be fearful to the point that we perform negative "deeds" which we later regret after listening to our conscience. In order for us to connect with the BA (our

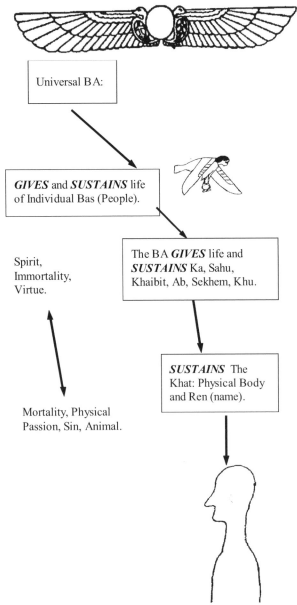

Universal BA:

GIVES and **SUSTAINS** life of Individual Bas (People).

Spirit, Immortality, Virtue.

The BA **GIVES** life and **SUSTAINS** Ka, Sahu, Khaibit, Ab, Sekhem, Khu.

Mortality, Physical Passion, Sin, Animal.

SUSTAINS The Khat: Physical Body and Ren (name).

real self), we must purify the AB. We must strive to grow in peace and purity of heart by listening to the inner voice of the soul.

"Strive to see with the inner eye, the heart. It sees the reality not subject to emotional or personal error; it sees the essence. Intuition then is the most important quality to develop."
                                                                    Egyptian Proverb

It is interesting to note that recent documented experiments at top medical research institutes and hospitals in the United States show that the major cause of heart attacks in modern society is not related to dietary problems, but to *HEARTACHE.* This heartache is caused by feelings of emptiness inside, a lack of meaning in one's life due to a lack of purpose, job dissatisfaction, a feeling of unhappiness and a feeling of mistrust of others. These are all ego based ailments that are caused by living in a manner that is against one's "grain." One is unable to perceive the universality of all people and believes that one is separate from everything and everyone. One becomes caught up in the idea "it's me against the world." This comes from our identification of our self with the ego-mind-personality and the body which are mortal and subject to error instead of with the immortal, higher part of ourselves which is eternal, and one with all other beings.

The Sacred Task

Most human beings "identify" with their ego personality, the Khaibit and Ren. The task is to explore and consciously discover our other seven "parts". Even before death, we must have the other seven of these re-membered and permanently integrated into one so that at the time we leave the earth and leave the body and name behind, we are ready to fly in our spiritual body to join Asar (our divine self: GOD) and merge with that ultimate reality from which we not only come, but who is our innermost essence: "Asar (our individual soul) joins Asar (Supreme Soul)". Thus when we join God, we are really joining our higher selves. We are God as are all people and objects in the seen and unseen universe. It is our sacred task to "know" this to be true. This may be done through the practice of virtues and meditation.

If the KA part of our spirit identifies itself with the physical body and its erroneous subconscious ideas about reality, it will not operate correctly in the spiritual realm. Through wisdom, inner-experience and a meditative, peaceful mind, the Ka and the other bodies may be experienced, developed and integrated.

BKA

The Ba (soul) is connected to the Ka (body of emotions and desires), through the Ab (conscience). From here the Ba controls the Khaibit (shadow-dense subtle body) and the Khat (physical body).

In Egypt, the process of impregnating the female is called BKA. This is the process that must also occur in spiritual evolution. Our KA must be impregnated with the words of wisdom and intuition from the BA. This is the virgin birth of our spiritual life which leads to the birth of ourselves as transformed beings --- as Gods.

If we identify with our BA as being one with the Universal BA instead of our ego, the actions prescribed by our individual BA (soul) will be in harmony with the spirit world and nature. Therefore, following one's intuition is taking advice from

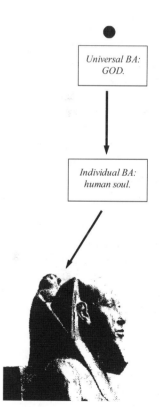

| Universal BA: GOD. |
| Individual BA: human soul. |

Statue of Pharaoh Chefren. The arrow points to a hawk situated *behind* *the head of the statue.*

The BA gives life to the body and all other parts of the spirit, Sahu, Khu, Khaibit, Ab, Sekhem, Ren, Ka, Khat.

*HERU (Horus) is shown as a Hawk or Falcon **BEHIND** the head, signifying the fact that the essence of what we are, is a spirit that is supposed to USE and CONTROL the body as an instrument, as one would control a car or an ox.*

one's BA. Through quiet contemplation and meditation, one's own BA offers insight into the truth and will lead one to prosperity and fulfillment.

Our true self is the consciousness DEEP WITHIN. Our physical nature is only a manifestation of our spirit. It is our spirit which gives life to the body, senses, mind processes, etc., and therefore, our body, intellect, mind and senses are a reflection of the degree of ignorance or wisdom, of the SELF, which we possess in our consciousness. In this light, all mental illnesses with the resultant physical illnesses, are due to one cause, which is "Ignorance of our divine and spiritual nature, our true SELF."

In order to find the ultimate truth, we must go beyond our mind, senses and body. We must go beyond all mental images of names and forms to which we are accustomed by developing our INTUITION.

Through intuition only will we discover who we really are and our purpose of existence. This is the messege above the Temples. To in effect:

"KNOW OURSELF."

The spirit is distinct from the body. If the Individual BA "identifies" with the other parts of the Spirit, it will forget it is connected to the Universal BA. If it forgets (overcome by worldly desires and ignorance), it will live a life of mortality, thinking it will die when the body dies. Heruhood is being connected to all parts of the spirit all the time by remembering that you are not only connected to the Universal BA (GOD, Cosmic Consciousness, Universal Soul), but that you ARE the Universal Soul deep inside. To attain this state of mind is to achieve: Christhood, Heruhood, Cosmic Consciousness, The Kingdom of Heaven, Moksha, Kaivalya, Nirvana, Enlightenment, etc.

The Universal BA and the Individual Bas form a circuit, where energy is given and then returned to the source in an endless cycle. To be consciously connected with this, our true essence, is the coveted goal, the epitome of our existence and the reason for it. Humans partake of both qualities of the spirit and those of matter. To master both is termed: The HIGHEST GOOD.

All humans can potentially become "Masters of The Universe" by becoming one with the universe.

In *The Egyptian Book Of Coming Forth By Day* and in other hieroglyphic texts, the individual Soul is depicted either as a human headed hawk (Heru) or as a ram (Amun). In this manner, we are led to understand that the individual soul is in reality a manifestation of the universal soul, the High GOD Amun, who is the soul of everything and is symbolized as a ram-headed man. In its highest aspect, the individual soul cleanses itself from its association with the mortal body-consciousness achieves identification with the Universal Ba-Amun. At this stage, the soul is said to have become *"glorified"* and is thus referred to as *"Sahu".* In the aspect of *Sahu,* the hieroglyph for soul is depicted as a ram with an Ankh necklace, symbolizing that it is endowed with "life".

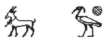

Sahu akhu (glorious, eternal, immortal spiritual body)

The Macrocosm and the Microcosm

Universal BA

Individual Ba

GOD, the universal BA (spirit) gives humans their individual BA so they may experience and grow in consciousness (wisdom) and achieve immortality. Just as the human being has "parts" so too the universe has parts. Thus, there is a Universal BA, Universal SAHU, Universal KHAIBIT, Universal KHU, Universal KA, Universal SEKHEM, Universal AB, Universal KHAT and a Universal REN. The universal is the macrocosm and the individual is a reflection of the universal, the microcosm. So the human being is a reflection of the Supreme Being in every way.

Above: A segment from a Tomb in Thebes Egypt showing a creation story in which the Goddess, represented as a cow, gives birth to the constellations and to humanity. This scene is called *The Meskhen or Birthplace*. It is similar in most respects to the centerpiece of the zodiac originally located in the ceiling of the temple of Hetheru at Denderah in Egypt.

For a more detailed study of the elements of the human personality see the book *EGYPTIAN YOGA VOLUME II: The Supreme Wisdom of Enlightenment*. By Dr. Muata Ashby

||||||||

CHAPTER 9: THE ASARIAN RESURRECTION AND THE STORY OF HERU AND SET

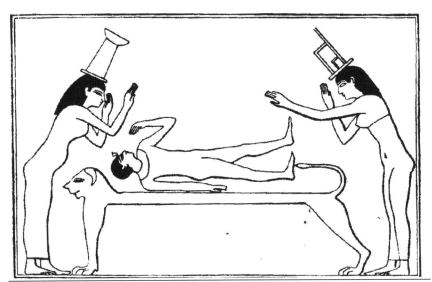

Aset and Nebethet bewailing over the dead body of Asar as they would later do over the dead body of Heru. From a bas relief at the temple of Aset in Philae.

"Whosoever knoweth these things, being attached to his place shall have his bread with Ra. Whosoever knoweth these things, being a Soul and Spirit... shall never enter into the place of destruction."

Egyptian Mystical Wisdom

HERU, RA AND PTAH

Heru is one of the most ancient representations of the *NETER NETERU*. Represented as a falcon headed deity (Neter), Heru encompasses all within his wingspan. Heru is also the soul which vivifies all life and existence. The ancient Sphinx is called: *"Heru in the Horizon"*. Ptah and Ra are forms of Heru, as stated in the scriptures, where Heru is referred to as: *"Great Heru"*. Heru is represented in all periods of Egyptian mythology in various forms.

The name of Ptah is written in hieroglyphic as a human form supporting heaven and earth. The name *Ptah* is composed of the following parts:

Pt = "heaven", ta = "earth", h = as in heh - "support"

Thus, Ptah (NETER, GOD, HERU) is the support of heaven and earth.

Know that there is one God who manifests in many ways; the Neters (cosmic forces) are within us and in all that is seen and unseen; as the children of God we have their powers; know that the same power in the Cosmos is also in MAN; therefore, as we learn about the cosmos, we learn about ourselves. The more we learn about others the more we learn about ourselves. In this manner, Heru is in reality: Ra, Ptah, Min, Anpu, and Asar. Like Asar he is androgynous, therefore Heru is also Hetheru, Aset, etc. Even more importantly, Heru is also the Hawk, the Ba, the symbol of the eternal human soul.

"Make your self the object of intense study and you will discover God."

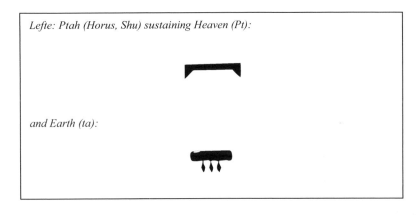

Lefte: Ptah (Horus, Shu) sustaining Heaven (Pt):

and Earth (ta):

THE OSIRIAN (AUSARIAN) RESURRECTION

As previously discussed, Ra represents COSMIC CONSCIOUSNESS, THE ALL, which manifests as the seen and unseen universe, the Cosmos. Asar is Ra in material form. HERU represents the way to reach the father, Ra; Asar and Heru both are aspects of the ONE GOD (NETER NETERU or NEBERTCHER). As previously stated, the visual forms and ideas presented in each of the Gods were created by the ancient Sages to help us understand the qualities and characteristics of GOD through the descriptions of the various Neters and deities.

"The birth of Asar is the birth of RA, and reciprocally."

The Passion of Asar

Asar (Asr) was the first King of Egypt. Asar taught the people agriculture and husbandman. He established a code of laws and bade all to worship the Gods.

One day, through his lack of vigilance, Asar became intoxicated and slept with Set's (his brother's) wife, Nebethet. Nebethet, as a result of this indiscretion on the part of Asar, begot Anpu. Asar' lack of vigilance implies that he allowed his passions to control him.

Set, who represents the personification of evil forces, plotted in jealousy and anger (the blinding passion that prevents forgiveness) to usurp the throne and conspired to kill Asar. Set secretly got the measurements of Asar and constructed a coffin. Through trickery, Set was able to get Asar to "try on" the coffin for size. While Asar was resting in the coffin, Set and his assistants locked it and then dumped it into the Nile river.

The coffin made its way to the coast of Syria where it became embedded in the earth and from it grew a tree with the most pleasant aroma in the form of a DJED. The DJED is the symbol of Asar' BACK. It has four horizontal lines in relation to a firmly established, straight column. The DJED column is symbolic of the upper energy centers (chakras) that relate to the levels of consciousness of the spirit (see The Scale of MAAT and The Chakras).

The *"Djed"* Pillar. The *"BACK"* of Ausar (Asar) symbolizes the upper steps of spiritual development, the higher energy centers or Chakras (4-7) located in the spine of the spiritual body.

The King of Syria was out walking and as he passed by the tree, he immediately fell in love with the pleasant aroma, so he had the tree cut down and brought to his palace. Aset (Auset, Ast), Asar' wife who is the personification of the life giving, mother force in creation and in all humans, went to Syria in search of Asar. Her search led her to the palace of the Syrian King where she took a job as the nurse of the King's son. Every evening, Aset would put the boy into the "fire" to consume his mortal parts, thereby transforming him to immortality. Fire is symbolic of both physical and mental purification. Most importantly, fire implies wisdom, the light of truth, illumination and energy. Aset, by virtue of her qualities, has the power to bestow immortality through the transformative power of her symbolic essence. Aset then told the king that Asar, her husband, is inside the pillar he made from the tree. He graciously gave her the pillar (DJED) and she returned with it to Kamit (Kmt, Egypt).

Upon her return to Kmt, Aset went to the papyrus swamps where she lay over Asar' dead body and conceived a son, Heru (Heru), with the assistance of the Gods Djehuti (Thoth) and Amun (Amon).

One evening, as Set was hunting in the papyrus swamps, he came upon Aset and Asar. In a rage of passion, he dismembered the body of Asar into several pieces and scattered the pieces throughout the land. In this way, it is Set, the brute force of our bodily impulses and desires that "dismembers" our higher intellect. Instead of oneness and unity, we see multiplicity and separateness which give rise to egoistic (selfish) and violent behavior. The Great Mother, Aset, once again set out to search, now for the pieces of Asar, with the help of Anpu and Nebethet.

After searching all over the world, they found all of the pieces of Asar body, except for his phallus which was eaten by a fish. In eastern Hindu-Tantra mythology, the God Shiva who is the equivalent of Asar also lost his phallus in one story. In Egyptian and Hindu-Tantra mythology, the loss represents seminal retention in order to channel the sexual energy to the higher spiritual centers, thereby transforming it into spiritual energy. Aset, Anpu, and Nebethet re-membered the pieces, all except the phallus which was eaten by a fish. Asar thus regained life in the realm of the dead.

Heru, therefore, was born from the union of the spirit of Asar and the life giving power of Aset (physical nature). Thus, Heru represents the union of spirit and matter, and the renewed life of Asar, his rebirth. When Heru became a young man, Asar encouraged him to take up arms (vitality, wisdom, courage, strength of will) and establish truth, justice and righteousness in the world by challenging Set, its current ruler.

Note: the concept of the virgin birth existed many thousands of years before recorded history and always signified the "second birth" which all human beings may achieve through spiritual advancement. This is a universal truth also evident in the "virgin births" of Jesus, Krishna, Buddha, Quetzalcoatle and many other male and female "saviors" in many cultures throughout the world. Therefore, the savior of our spirit is none other than ourselves.

The Battle of Heru and Set

The battle between Heru and Set took many twists, sometimes one seeming to get the upper hand and sometimes the other, yet neither one gaining a clear advantage in order to decisively win. At one point, Aset tried to help Heru by catching Set, but due to the pity and compassion she felt towards him, she set him free. In a passionate rage, Heru cut off her head (even Heru is susceptible to passion which leads to performing deeds that one later regrets) and went off by himself in a frustrated state. Set found Heru and gouged out Heru' eyes. During this time, Heru was overpowered by the evil of Set. He became blinded to truth (as signified by the loss of his eyes) and thus, was unable to do battle (act with MAAT) with Set . His power of sight was later restored by Hetheru (Goddess of passionate love, desire and fierce power), who also represents the left Eye of Ra. She is the fire spitting, destructive power of light, which dispels the darkness (blindness) of ignorance.

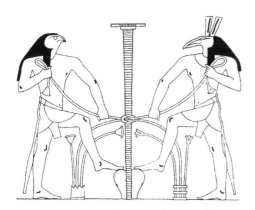

Left: Heru and Set join forces to tie up the symbol of Union (Sema). This symbol refers to the Union of Upper and Lower Egypt under one ruler, but also at a more subtle level, it refers to the union of one's higher and lower self (Heru and Set) as well as the control of one's breath (life) through the union (control) of the lungs (breathing organs).

When the conflict resumed, the two contendants went before the court of the Ennead Gods (company of the eight Gods who ruled over creation, headed by Ra). Set, promising to end the fight and to restore Heru to the throne invited Heru to spend the night at his house, but Heru soon found out that Set had evil intentions when he tried to have intercourse with him. The uncontrolled Set also symbolizes unrestricted sexual activity. Therefore, all sexual desires should be pursued in accordance with moral and intellectual principles which dictate rules of propriety that lead to health and personal, societal and spiritual order (MAAT). Juxtaposed against this aspect of Set (uncontrolled sexual potency and desire) is Heru in the form of ithyphallic (erect phallus) MIN, who represents not only control of sexual desire but its sublimation as well (see Min and Hetheru). Min symbolizes the power which comes from sexual energy sublimation.

So the battle ensued again, and this time after many fights, Heru took Set's phallus. In chapter 17 of the *"Egyptian Book of Coming Forth By Day,"* it is explained that *"the way to restore the Eye of Heru is to take away Set's testicles."* That is to say, mastering the sexual Life Force enables one to have the capacity to restore the eye of intuitive vision, the Eye of Heru.

Through more treachery and deceit, Set attempted to destroy Heru with the help of the Ennead, by tricking them into believing that Heru was not worthy of the throne.

Asar sent a letter pleading with the Ennead to do what is correct. Heru, as the son of Asar, should be the rightful heir to the throne. All but two of them (the Ennead) agreed because Heru, they said, was too young to rule. Asar then sent them a second letter (scroll of papyrus with a message).

Asar began the letter sarcastically:

> *"How good are the deeds of the Ennead! Justice has sunk into the netherworld. Now listen to me, the land of the dead is full of demons who fear no God or Goddess. If I send them out into the world of the living they will bring back the hearts of evildoers to the place of punishment. Who among you is more powerful than I? Even the Gods must come at last to the Beautiful West* (the final resting place and original source of all things including the Gods).*"*

This signifies that even the Gods cannot escape judgment for their deeds. Since all that exist is only a manifestation of the absolute reality which goes beyond time and space, that which is in the realm of time and space (humans, spirits, Gods, Angels, Neters) are all bound by its laws.

Following the receipt of Asar' scroll (letter), Heru was crowned King of Egypt. Set accepted the decision and made peace with Heru. All the Gods rejoiced.

Heru

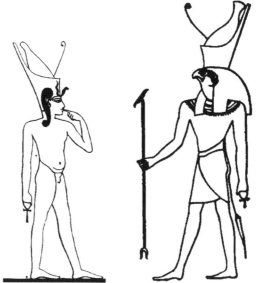

Left: Heru as the Divine Solar Child, Right: Heru as the King

HERU (Heru) is the God of Light. Before Heru is victorious, he is a symbol of the "Dual Nature of Humankind". Heru in this aspect represents the opposite forces that are within each of us, the animal nature (passionate behavior as demonstrated by, cutting off Aset' head) and the divine. Therefore, the real battle is within each of us.

The picture of Set-Heru shows us that the "enemy" or foe of truth *(MAAT)* is inside each of us. Set, the symbol of evil, is actually a part of Heru that must be conquered. In this aspect, Set represents the "Beasts" or "Demons" we must conquer: passions, desires, restlessness of the mind, temptation, lust, greed, depression, insecurity, fear and pain. Only this way can the "God of Light" inside us shine through.

Heru is the symbol of: *The resurrection and the life", "The anointed one", "The WORD made flesh", "The KRST (Christ)", "The WORD made TRUTH", "The one who comes to fulfill the LAW", "The destroyer of the enemies* of his father," "The one who walks upon the water of his Father"*

*ENEMIES: ignorance, lies, deception, too much talking, covetousness, depravity, selfishness, etc.

Heru says:

"I am the hawk in the tabernacle, and I pierce through the veil*."

*"Veil" refers to the veil of ASET, the material body and the desires for worldly objects which lead to mental agitation and prevents us from realizing our Godhood.

HERU is the innermost essence of every human being. To achieve "Heruhood" is the goal of every person on the spiritual path, that by the example of HERU and his like, WE may also live the WORD, and thus THE WORD OF GOD is made flesh in the heart of humans. Heru is the principle, the example, of the word of love and truth in a purified heart.

"HERU is the savior who was brought to birth. As light in heaven and sustenance on earth. Heru in spirit, verily divine, who came to turn the water into wine. Heru who gave his life, and sowed the seed for men to make the bread of life indeed. Heru the comforter who did descend in human fashion as the heavenly friend. Heru the word, the founder in youth. Heru the fulfiller of the word made truth. Heru the Lord and leader in the fight against the dark powers of the night. Heru the sufferer with cross bowed down, who rose at Easter with his double crown. Heru the pioneer, who paved the way of resurrection to the eternal day. Heru triumphant with the battle done, Lord of two worlds, united and made one."

The Forms of Horus

Left: Horus as the winged sundisk (Heaven).

Left: Heru is the hawk.

At right: Heru as the human headed Hawk in association with Set.

Above: Heru as Anubis.

Above: Heru as the Winged Uraeus.

left: Heru as the hawk ddesses Isis and Nephthys they watch over and ist Osiris to achieve irth.

low: Heru as the seated n, Ra-Harakte.

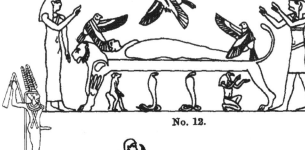

No. 12.

Above: Heru as Amun-Ra..

Above: Heru as Min.

Below: Heru in the form of MAAT.

Above: Heru in the form of

Above: Heru as The Moon God, the mind and wisdom, Djehuti

At left: The female initiate propitiates her Ba, the soul within all things, the true essence of every human being, while holding her heart in her left hand.

Below: Heru in the form of Winged Khepra.

Above: Heru in the form of Asar

The Goddess

During the pre-dynastic period (+10,000 B.C.E.-5,000 B.C.E.) in which the *Realm of Light* mythology was prominent, GOD was conceived of as being the cause of all existence but not as having any particular form*. In later predynastic times, GOD in the female form (female aspect of GOD) reigned supreme in Egypt as well as in the rest of Afrika (especially in Ethiopia), her power of fertility being identified with creation itself. GOD as the "Great Mother" (Hetheru-Hetheru), who gave birth to the elements, cosmic forces and life itself, was depicted in various zoomorphic (non-human) forms such as a hippopotamus, a cow, a cobra, a crocodile, and a lioness to emphasize specific female oriented forces in nature and her life giving qualities. In early dynastic times, the Divine Cow (Hetheru-Hetheru), the Cobra Goddess (Buto), Nekhebet the Vulture, and Sekhmet the Lioness were major forms representing the Goddess. In later times, the Goddess in the anthropomorphic forms of Aset, Nut and Nebethet became prominent, although never supplanting the previous zoomorphic depictions or mythologies.

A striking example of the integration of the female principle into Egyptian mythology is to be found in Chapter 78, Line 47 of the Egyptian *Book of Coming Forth By Day* where it is stated to the initiate:

> "...*To the son* (initiate), *the Gods have given the crown of millions of years, and for millions of years it allows him to live in the Eye* (Eye of Heru), *which is the single eye of GOD who is called Nebertcher, the queen of the Gods."*

The previous passage is of paramount significance since it states that the primary Trinity, *Nebertcher,* the High GOD of Egypt, which is elsewhere primarily associated with male names, *Amun-Ra-Ptah,* is also *"the queen of the Gods."* Therefore, the primary *"Godhead"* or *Supreme Being* is both <u>male and female.</u> As we will see in the next section, even in dynastic times, the Goddess is attributed equal status and importance for the salvation of humanity. Further, as we will see in the next section, the name Auset (Aset) signifies the very foundation (seat) of the rulership of Egypt.

The Female Savior of Mankind

Left: *Apt* (Hetheru-Aset), the Ethiopian and Egyptian Goddess in the composite form representing the forces of nature (creation).

In a text from the Temple at Dier al-Medina, Hetheru is referred to as having the same divine attributes as Heru. She is described as *"The Golden One"* and *"The Queen of the Gods".* Her shrines being even more numerous than those of Heru, Hetheru or *Het-Heru,* meaning *"The House of Heru"* and *"The House Above* (sky),*"* became identified, like Heru, with the salvation of the initiate. In the *Egyptian Book of Coming Forth By Day,* she is the one who urges the initiate to do battle with the monster Apep so as not to lose his / her heart as she cries out: *"Take your armor".* In a separate papyrus, the initiate is told that she (Hetheru) is the one who: *"will make your face perfect among the Gods; she will open your eye* (see Eye of Heru) *so that you may see every day... she will make your legs able to walk with ease in the Netherworld, Her name is Hetheru, Lady of Amenta."*

In chapter 81- utterance 1, the role of Hetheru in the process of salvation is specified as the initiate speaks the words which will help him / her become as a lotus:

"I am the lotus pure coming forth from the god of light, the guardian of the nostril of Ra, the guardian of the nose of Hetheru; I make my journey; I run after him who is Heru. I am the pure one coming forth from the."

In this manner, Hetheru and Heru form a composite archetype, a savior with all of the complementary qualities of the male and female principles, inseparable, complete and androgynous.

AUSET (ASET) is the anthropomorphic (depicted in human form) version of the Egyptian Goddess-Savior (Hetheru). She is the personification of motherhood and the life giving principle who is often portrayed breast-feeding Heru on her lap. She is the nurturer. She is the Madonna who gives birth to a Christ (Anointed one).

ASET is the one who finds the pieces of Asar' dismembered body, reassembles it except for the lost penis and conceives his son, thereby giving the spirit of Asar rebirth through Heru. This is the second birth that can occur in all humans. It is the birth of the spiritual life. Out of a mind which is concerned with materialism and pleasures of the body comes a new consciousness. This is the concept of Heru and Christ.

> *"Moved by your prayer I come to you - I, the natural mother of all life, mistress of the elements, first child of time, Supreme Divinity, Queen of those in Hell, First of those in Heaven.... I, whose single Godhead is venerated over all the Earth under manifold forms, varying and changing names. Only remember me, fast in your heart's deep core, if you are found to merit My love by your dedicated obedience, religious devotion, and constant chastity, you will discover that it is within My power to prolong your life beyond the limits set to it by Fate; and after death live on praising Me in the Fields of Reeds."*

The idea of a "savior" is not to be considered a high philosophical concept but it is useful in helping us to understand early on in our spiritual quest that there is a higher power which we can call upon to assist and guide us through our lives. Thus from a more advanced perspective, the main Gods and Goddesses of Egyptian mythology such as Heru and Hetheru should be viewed as guides or teachers, rather than as "saviors" in the western religious sense of the word which suggests that it is through the efforts of someone "outside of ourselves" (i.e. Jesus Christ, Gods, Angels, Saints, etc.) that we will be liberated. It is we who must do the work of saving ourselves through the application of the teachings. Thus, when discussing the idea of a savior we must consider that it is our own higher self who is being described therefore, we must strive to acquire those qualities which will lead to our own liberation.

Ausar (Asar) is

"The Lord of the PERFECT BLACK."

The Egyptian God AUSAR (ASAR) (+10,000 B.C) referred to as **"The Lord of the Perfect Black",** symbolic of the "Blackness" from which light comes. This is the "Blackness" deep in our mind which we must explore and master in order to find ourselves. The erect phallus signifies the power of that "Blackness" (sexual energy), to create and give life. This power which is behind all life, pushes it forth in an inexorable movement to live, die and be reborn again.

It was said to Egyptian initiates:

"Asar is a dark God... A dark God because no man could know him and also, because light is born out of Darkness."

Asar represents the Principle of DEATH and RESURRECTION who was destroyed by evil but who came back to life as *HERU*. To die is to be defeated by evil. To resurrect is to have a *"SECOND"* Spiritual, Mental, Psychological birth in the form of a new consciousness which is termed HERU.

*A*usar is the symbol of all humans. His journey is our journey. His struggle is our struggle. His reward is our reward. His victory is our victory. Each one of us is Asar.

Asar' color is sometimes represented as green. Green is the color of the fourth energy center, the Anahata (heart) chakra in Indian Kundalini Yoga philosophy. Green is also the color of nature, the relentless life force of vegetation. Vegetation, nature itself, is Asar as it grows in countless varieties and dies only to decay and become a source of nutrients for new vegetation. The Life Force (sexual energy) within us is the same as that which is in vegetation (Asar). As Asar, men and women exist in an endless cycle of birth, death and rebirth in which the Life Force is engaged in an inexorable movement forward. The movement of the force keeps the grass growing regardless of how many times it is cut. In the same manner, our soul (Asar) will be reborn in many different times, places and forms. Each time our soul lends itself to a clump of matter (body), it experiences life among the living only to someday shed it again. As the cut grass decomposes to produce food for the new grass, so too our used up and decayed body provides the experiences (pleasure and pain) that the soul requires in order to achieve another level of life.

Krishna (+1000 B.C.E.)

Above: Krishna playing divine music.

Lord Krishna is a God form or symbol in the Indian Hindu Mythological system. Literally translated, the name "Krishna" means "Black" or "The Black One." Therefore, Lord Krishna and Asar both were known as "The Black One." Krishna of India and Heru of Egypt have equivalent symbolism in that they show, through their myths, what is correct action that leads the way to salvation.

Like Heru, Krishna was viciously pursued by his evil Uncle from the time of his birth. The evil King Kamsa, Krishna's Uncle, foresaw that Krishna would assume the kingship and defeat him so Kamsa ordered that all male children born around the same time as Krishna be killed (this part also parallels the story of Jesus c.1 A.C.E.).

Like Heru, the eyes of Krishna represent the Sun and the Moon, duality unified into one whole. Krishna was born immaculately as were Heru and Jesus, to fight the forces of evil on earth. As with Heru, he contained the entire Universe in his essence, as do all humans.

Heru, Jesus and Krishna are symbols of the Christ in each of our spirits which are entombed in bodies and engaged in a battle of opposites (duality): good-evil, light-dark, ying-yang, positive-negative, prosperity-adversity, etc. This is the endless battle which goes on in the realm of time and space, the earth, dwat and heavenly realms (physical, astral and causal worlds). They represent symbols, principles and examples of how we can attain our highest potential (self-realization, enlightenment, Heruhood), which is the purpose of life.

In the Bhagavad Gita Chapter 5 Line 16, Lord Krishna says:

"For those whose ignorance has been destroyed by the knowledge (Yoga of Wisdom) of the Self, wisdom shines forth like the sun, revealing the Reality of the Transcendental Self."

Left: *Aset nurses baby Heru: The Egyptian version of the mother and child (The Madonna).* Above right: The image of The Madonna from India, c. 16th century A.C.E. *Yasoda nurses the child Krishna.*

The Story of the Uncle who tried to kill the Newborn

The story of an uncle who tries to kill the newborn child (parallels the story of Heru and Set) appears in the *Jaiminiya Brahmana* (900 B.C.E.) and also in the *Mahabharata* (500 B.C.E.) scriptures of India. In the Jaiminiya the story is as follows:

> *When the child Vyasa, son of Sakamasva was still in the womb of his mother, his uncle, Gaya, understood that Vyasa would some day become a great sage. At his birth, Gaya ordered that he should be thrown out and that it would be said that he was born dead. This was done but Vyasa's shadow did not leave him and so his two thumbs gave him milk for nourishment. Then Gaya was told: "The child which you ordered to be thrown out is still alive." Gaya then took a club and went out to kill Vyasa. Knowing what Gaya wanted to do, Vyasa prayed thus: "Let me out of this, let me find help and a way out of this predicament." Vyasa realized this chant and then sang it over Gaya and then Gaya's club hit Gaya and split open Gaya's own head.*

The theme of the birth of the hero (in this case *Vyasa*) once again signifies the struggle of every soul to have worldly experience and to succeed in realizing its potential. The shadow of Vyasa brings to mind the idea that the soul has vast resources to deal with physical privation and hardship. Once again, the "evil" uncle, symbolizing the egoistic aspect of each person which, intoxicated by worldly pleasure and body identification, refuses to relinquish its position and power to the rightful heir (a new generation, a new expression of the spirit), and thus, threatens the new life. It also reminds us that the most effective defense against evil is faith, the faith which comes from self-knowledge and trust in our higher self and not just our ego-self.

For a complete rendering of the Ausarian Resurrection Myth and the mystical teachings and practices of Shetaut Asar (The religious path of Asar, Aset and Heru) see the books: *THE AUSARIAN RESURRECTION: The Ancient Egyptian Bible, THE MYSTICAL TEACHINGS OF THE AUSARIAN RESURRECTION: Initiation Into The Third Level of Shetaut Asar* **and** *MYSTICISM OF USHET REKHAT: Worship of the Divine Mother* by Dr. Muata Abhaya Ashby

∩

MAAT

CHAPTER 10: Virtue and Order

"Performing MAAT is breath to the nostrils."

"Do Maat, that your years upon the earth may be long."

Egyptian Mystical Wisdom

MORE INSIGHTS INTO MAAT PHILOSOPHY

How did Heru succeed in restoring righteousness, peace and harmony in the world and how does this apply to the spiritual evolution of every human being? This is the path of Maat or the path of righteous action. But what is Maat and what are its teachings? Now we will expand on some themes introduced in chapter five.

The Judgment:

"The Conscience (HEART) of a Human is his and her own GOD."

From *the "Book of Coming Forth by Day".*

The Egyptian *"Book of Coming Forth by Day and Night"* is one of the oldest philosophical and spiritual texts. It describes the journey of the human soul in the realm of the after life and describes what each man and woman must do to survive death and *"Come Forth"* into the light of *"Day"* (life, illumination, eternal happiness).

At the time of death or prior to death, the heart (consciousness, symbolized by the AB) of the being is weighed against TRUTH, symbolized by the feather of MAAT. Here our godly faculties, symbolized by Anpu and Djehuti (Thoth) and our ability to use them while on earth are judged.

"I HAVE N0T DONE INIQUITY. I AM PURE OF HEART AND WORTHY OF IMMORTALITY."

Above: Precept #1 from the 42 Precepts of MAAT (10,000 B.C.E.-5,000 B.C.E). (See page 110).

In the Hall of MAAT, the heart and internal organs of the deceased are judged by 42 judges who are each in charge of one regulation. All 42 regulations or virtuous guidelines for living make up the basis for the 42 "negative confessions." If one lives righteously, one will be able to say that one has <u>NOT</u> committed any offence.

Upon uttering these words, the deceased takes on a new name. Instead of Cathy Jones, it is now Asar Cathy Jones.

If the heart of Asar Cathy Jones is found to be heavier than the feather, instead of joining with Asar, she is sent back to the realm of mental illusion (the world) in the form of an animal or beast to be eaten by the monsters (evil spirits) who feed on sin, greed, un-righteousness, etc.

If the heart of Asar Cathy Jones is found to be lighter than the feather or of equal weight, it signifies that she had lead a virtuous life and had mastered the knowledge and wisdom of every God (all of which are aspects of the one GOD) and that she is fit for a new life. Asar Cathy Jones is ready to transcend this world onto the next realm of existence. She is ready to journey back to meet Cosmic Asar who represents Cosmic Consciousness or Ra.

Asar Cathy Jones, through her own virtuous life, is allowed to take or fashion a new, GLORIOUS body, to live in eternity with Asar.

<u>Thus, Asar Jones, the individual human soul, meets and joins with Asar, the Supreme Being.</u>

This signifies that our own nature is that of universal consciousness. What was separated only by ignorance is now re-united, re-membered. It is only due to ignorance and to distraction in the world of desirable objects that we think we are individual human beings with bodies which are mortal. In reality, we are immortal and eternal beings who are one with the universe and each other.

To realize this even before death, it is necessary to live in a virtuous manner, learning the lessons of human existence and uncovering the veil of ignorance which blinds us from the realization of our essential nature. We must therefore master the knowledge and wisdom of "EVERY" God.

Anpu (God of discernment between reality and illusion) and DJEHUTI (God of Wisdom, experiencing truth) oversee the scales of MAAT. These judge the condition of the Heart (AB) and determine its level of spiritual achievement.

This is also symbolized by the Ammit monster, devourer of hearts, who according to the Greenfield papyrus, determines those who are the advanced spirits and worthy of salvation (those who have developed their higher consciousness centers symbolized by the fourth through seventh rings or levels of consciousness) and those who have not progressed beyond their base animal natures (lower consciousness centers symbolized by the lower three rings). The un-righteous are symbolically devoured by the monsters and evil spirits.

As in the Chakra system of India, those who achieve no higher than the level of the third Chakra are considered to be people on the same level of consciousness as animals. They will have to reincarnate in order to further evolve beyond this stage. Upon reincarnating, they will once again have the possibility of confronting situations which will afford them the opportunity to performing correct action.

Correct action leads to correct feeling and thinking.

Correct feeling and correct thinking lead to "Correct Being" which is the goal --- to "BE" what we really are: ONE WITH GOD.

The Science Of Virtues

"The Soul is a Prisoner of its own ignorance. In this condition it is fettered with the chains of ignorance to an existence where it has no control over its fate in life. The Purpose of Each Virtue is to Remove One Fetter."

Egyptian Proverb

Virtues are practiced to promote peace of mind and body: *Hetep*

Peace of mind promotes study and listening.

Study and listening promotes reflection.

Reflection on life and the teachings allows the mind to be concentrated:

"making the mind and body still."

Concentration of mind allows meditation to occur.

135

Meditation allows the experiencing of increasing levels of awareness beyond the regular state of waking consciousness leading to the experiencing of cosmic consciousness: complete freedom.

PRACTICING VIRTUES AND MAINTAINING A LIFE OF SIMPLICITY opens the way for spiritual growth by decreasing mental agitation from worries or inordinate worldly concerns. If one maintains balance in all conditions, there will be no situation that will interfere with one's intuition of truth and righteousness, or in achieving mental calmness for meditation. This is the way to the top of the Pyramid.

"Feelings, emotions and passions are good servants but poor masters."

Giving into hate and vengeance will lead to the undoing of the body and spirit. To control one's passions is to master one's own fate. Study the teachings and practice self control, silence and meditation.

Never go to extremes with anything, for one extreme leads to another. Always strive for balance in all things. Moderation and equanimity in all events and situations are the deeper implications of the scales of *MAAT*. In this manner, the inner peace that allows for the quieting of the mind occurs. In this quiet, it is possible to discover our deeper self. This is the meaning of the ancient admonition:

"Now, make thy body still. Meditate that you may know truth."

Ancient Egyptian Proverb, also found in the Bible

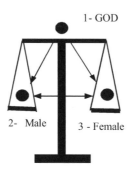

Maat: Achieving Harmony (Enlightenment) through the Union of Opposites, Male and Female.

MAAT IS THE PHILOSOPHICAL CONCEPT OF LIVING A LIFE OF TRUTH AND RIGHTEOUSNESS. MAAT REPRESENTS AN EXPOSITION OF VIRTUOUS RULES OF LIVING BY WHICH ONE MAY EXIST IN HARMONY WITH FELLOW HUMANS AND ALL CREATION: THEY WHO ARE ABLE TO UTTER THESE CONFESSIONS IN THE AFFIRMATIVE AT THE END OF THEIR EARTHLY LIFE MAY LOOK FORWARD TO THE HELP OF GOD AND GOD'S ASSISTANTS (ANGELS, NETERS, DAEMONS, SAINTS, ETC.) IN RE-MEMBERING AND RECOVERING THEIR TRUE ESSENCE, WITH THE RAISED CONSCIOUSNESS OF A DEVELOPED AND CONTROLLED PERSONALITY (MIND).

The scales of Maat imply balance, but balance decreed by whom and for what reason?

From the one: Pure Consciousness, GOD, comes the other two, male and female, so now there can be interaction between the three, which are really one. This principle of duality (male and female) is present throughout all manifestations in the phenomenal world (nature) including the human body. In each of us, there is a male and female aspect of consciousness. Chakras 5 - 7 represent the feminine aspect of consciousness energy centers while Chakras 1-3 represent the masculine aspect.

Therefore, in order for creation to exist, the ONE TRUTH must appear to be more than one. Maat is therefore composed of two aspects or two truths, which are really two sides of the same reality. This concept is termed *"MAATI."*

The task of all religious or mystical systems is to BALANCE the interplay between Male and Female (considered together: MAATI). That is, to achieve an internal mode of consciousness which is rooted in the one instead of being caught in the interplay between 2 and 3. In other words, *"To keep the balance."*

Evidence from prehistoric times suggests that an imbalance existed between male and female humans such that females controlled the knowledge of birth and therefore controlled men by keeping them ignorant as to their participation in childbirth. Some historians believe that women were able to maintain an illusion of superiority which caused men to hold women in awe. Therefore, women were able to control men and abuse them not unlike the modern day abuse of women by men in our society. As the men gradually became knowledgeable about their participation in conception, they reacted in a vengeful manner. Thus, civilization plunged into the other extreme which eventually led to the witch hunts and other such atrocities.

The imbalance now is still on the side of males who control women and seemingly, all else. The imbalance on either side is a reflection of our individual consciousness. As a result, there is an imbalance created in whatever is manifest in the world of physical reality resulting in: wars, sexism, racism, capitalism, sense of individuality (egoism), mental disease, physical disease, etc. Therefore, anything that promotes the "balance" of the apparent opposites in creation constitutes the following of MAAT, upholding the cosmic order, supreme mental balance and supreme peace.

"Harmony is the Union of Opposites."

Egyptian Proverb

From a deeper perspective, by having an intuitive understanding of the union underlying creation and of its appearance of duality, one can identify with the Union, the Oneness, and therefore cultivate this unity within one's self. This is the basis of Tantra Yoga --- seeking union with GOD through the worship and understanding of Nature (Female) as a projection of GOD (Male).

"As above, So Below."

"We are created in the IMAGE of GOD."

Egyptian Proverbs

If we understand that which is below (the physical, manifesting world), then we will understand that which is above (the spiritual world: GOD, who causes the physical world to exist). If we understand the human constitution, we will understand the cosmic constitution because the manifestation is an exact image of the source. For every function of an organ in the human body and in the objects of the universe, there are likewise cosmic functions and organs which cause them to manifest. Therefore, in order to pursue union with GOD, one must seek to uphold the Cosmic Laws with respect to the balance of the opposites in all areas, through perfect justice and righteousness and with the greatest wisdom which comes not from our mental process, but from our soul (BA). The wisdom of the BA can be accessed through seeking purity of heart and meditation. As we pursue *"the union of opposites"*, we will discover that there are no opposites, only the projected appearance of them. We will discover that underlying the names and forms projected by the Neters (causal powers from GOD), the only reality is GOD. The Cause is GOD, the Causing Neters are GOD, "We are God," All is God. Therefore, from an advanced standpoint we begin to see that there is no cause for the creation of the world, there is no past and no future but only an eternal present. By practicing the 42 precepts of Maat which are further explained in the "Precepts of Ptahotep" and "The Instruction to Merikare", mental peace and subtlety of intellect (purity of heart) arise.

NOTE: The Precepts of Maat vary slightly in different papyruses. However, the themes are the same and we have included representative precepts from various Ancient Egyptian sources.

(1) "I have not done iniquity." Variant: Acting with falsehood.

(2) "I have not robbed with violence."

(3) "I have not done violence (To anyone or anything)." Variant: Rapacious (Taking by force; plundering.)

(4) "I have not committed theft." Variant: Coveted.

(5) "I have not murdered man or woman." Variant: Or ordered someone else to commit murder.

(6) "I have not defrauded offerings." Variant: or destroyed food supplies or increased or decreased the measures to profit.

(7) "I have not acted deceitfully." Variant: With crookedness.

(8) "I have not robbed the things that belong to God."

(9) "I have told no lies."

(10) "I have not snatched away food."

(11) "I have not uttered evil words." Variant: Or allowed myself to become sullen, to sulk or become depressed.

(12) "I have attacked no one."

(13) "I have not slaughtered the cattle that are set apart for the Gods." Variant: The Sacred bull – (Apis)

(14) "I have not eaten my heart" (overcome with anguish and distraught). Variant: Committed perjury.

(15) "I have not laid waste the ploughed lands."

(16) "I have not been an eavesdropper or pried into matters to make mischief." Variant: Spy.

(17) "I have not spoken against anyone." Variant: Babbled, gossiped.

(18) "I have not allowed myself to become angry without cause."

(19) "I have not committed adultery." Variant: And homosexuality.

(20) "I have not committed any sin against my own purity."

(21) "I have not violated sacred times and seasons."

(22) "I have not done that which is abominable."

(23) "I have not uttered fiery words. I have not been a man or woman of anger."

(24) "I have not stopped my ears against the words of right and wrong (Maat)."

(25) "I have not stirred up strife (disturbance)." "I have not caused terror." "I have not struck fear into any man."

(26) "I have not caused any one to weep." Variant: Hoodwinked.

(27) "I have not lusted or committed fornication nor have I lain with others of my same sex." Variant: or sex with a boy.

(28) "I have not avenged myself." Variant: Resentment.

(29) "I have not worked grief, I have not abused anyone." Variant: Quarrelsome nature.

(30) "I have not acted insolently or with violence."

(31) "I have not judged hastily." Variant: or been impatient.

(32) "I have not transgressed or angered God."

(33) "I have not multiplied my speech overmuch (talk too much)."

(34) "I have not done harm or evil." Variant: Thought evil.

(35) "I have not worked treason or curses on the King."

(36) "I have never befouled the water." Variant: held back the water from flowing in its season.

(37) "I have not spoken scornfully." Variant: Or yelled unnecessarily or raised my voice.

(38) "I have not cursed The God."

(39) "I have not behaved with arrogance." Variant: Boastful.

(40) "I have not been overwhelmingly proud or sought for distinctions for myself (Selfishness)."

(41) "I have never magnified my condition beyond what was fitting or increased my wealth, except with such things as are (justly) mine own possessions by means of Maat." Variant: I have not disputed over possessions except when they concern my own rightful possessions. Variant: I have not desired more than what is rightfully mine.

(42) "I have never thought evil (blasphemed) or slighted The God in my native town."

As ONE lives according to one's MAAT faculty, one will be able to triumphantly say:

"I ascribe praise to thee, O Lord of the Gods, thou GOD one, who lives upon righteousness and truth, behold I, thy son Heru, come unto thee; I have avenged thee and I have brought thee MAAT - even to the place where is the company of the Gods. Grant thou that I may have my being among those who are in thy following, for I have overthrown all thy foes, and have established all those who are of thy substance upon the earth forever and ever."

*From *"The Egyptian Book of Coming Forth By Day."*

Your name will become Asar and even while still alive, you will ever be established in the knowledge that whatever you do, say, think or feel, you are one with the Supreme Being; you will have attained cosmic consciousness. You will be a sage, saint, initiate, guru, master or spiritual preceptor. You will be able to say:

"I am the divine Soul which dwells in the divine Twin Gods."

During life or at the time of your death, you will tell the 42 judges (your own mental wisdom capacity, Djehuti) the 42 utterances (negative confessions). Your mind being fearless, clear of desire and agitation will be lighter than the feather of MAAT. Since you led a life of peace and purity, YOU will allow **YOURSELF** to travel to join <u>ASAR,</u> the symbol of cosmic consciousness, WHO IS YOUR VERY OWN SELF, YOUR TRUE NATURE.

YOUR NATIONALITY OR RELIGION IS SECONDARY TO YOUR UNDERSTANDING OF GOD, THE SUPREME BEING, FATHER AND MOTHER OF ALL THINGS, TRANSCENDING THE UNIVERSE OF DUALITY.

In the Ancient Egyptian Temple and Pyramid carvings, Egyptian Kings are depicted as making offerings to another figure of their very own likeness. They are paying homage to their divine nature. In this same manner, we must learn to pay homage ("make offering") to our higher self for its divine grace by listening to the words of truth and wisdom, reflecting on those words, meditating on those words and finally, acting on those words (the most difficult part).

"Knowledge without action is like hoarding precious metals, a vain and foolish thing. Knowledge is like wealth, intended for use; those who violate the universal law of USE conflict with natural forces."

"Morals are judged by deeds."

One must develop the virtues and assimilate all of the qualities of the Gods that one may put together your eternal soul. The righteous person can say:

"Behold me, I come to you, and have carried off and put together my forms."

"I am Asar."

*"*My heart* (mind-memory) *is with me and it shall not be taken away, for... I live by truth, in which I exist; I am Heru who is in the heart, that which is in the middle of the body. I live by saying what is in my heart...I have committed no sin against the Gods."*

*"*I AM the Soul of Asar, and I rest in HIM.*"*

*"*All things which exist are in my grasp, and those which are not yet in being, depend on me. I have received increase of length and depth and* <u>fullness</u> *of breathing within the domain of my parent, the great one, which is all that exists."*

*From: *"The Egyptian Book of Coming Forth By Day."*

The <u>fullness</u> of breathing in the statement above refers to the feeling of fullness which comes from knowing and living within one's true nature. As individuals, we are bound to feel something missing regardless of our efforts on the physical level because through ignorance we are separated from the feeling of fullness, of oneness with all things, the absolute reality. This concept of <u>FULLNESS</u> is also expressed in the following prayer from the Indian Upanishads (ancient philosophical scripture):

"Om Purnamadah Purnamidam Purnat
Purnamudachyate Purnasya
Purnamadaya Purnamevavashisyate.
Om Shantih, Shantih, Shantih!"

"Om, The Absolute, is <u>full</u>,
This (world, being a manifestation of The Absolute) *is also full.*
When this (world process) *is taken away,*
what remains is <u>Fullness</u> (The Absolute).
May there be Peace, Peace overwhelming Peace!"

Reincarnation and Transmigration of the Soul

"The Egyptians were the first to maintain that the soul of man is immortal, that after the death of the body, it always enters into that of some other animal which is born, and when it has passed through all those (animal incarnations) of the earth, water, and air, it again enters that of a man, a circuit which it accomplishes in 3000 years."

Herodotus, Greek Historian

Sebi (Bondage)

Within our context in the present work, bondage signifies the condition of the soul which is bound to its agitated mind. Mental agitation, caused by unfulfilled desires, causes the soul to seek rebirth in search of fulfillment of those desires. As mentioned repeatedly throughout this text, the primary cause of the soul's search for fulfillment in transient, worldly experience is <u>ignorance of the truth.</u>

The most important teachings relating to the concept of Karma and Reincarnation were given in chapter 125 of the *Ancient Egyptian Book of Coming Forth By Day.* These will be discussed later in this text and more extensively in *EGYPTIAN YOGA VOLUME II: The Supreme Wisdom of Enlightenment.*

Smai Heru-Set

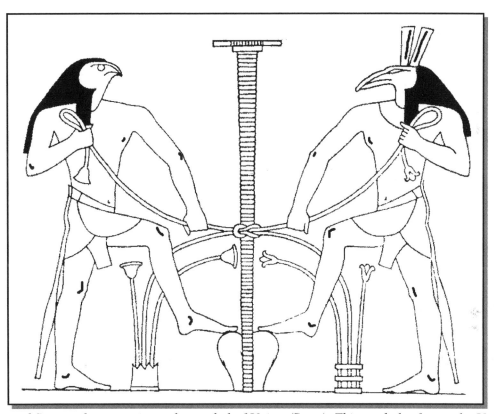

Above: Heru and Set join forces to tie up the symbol of Union (Sema). This symbol refers to the Union of Upper and Lower Egypt under one ruler, but also at a more subtle level, it refers to the union of one's higher and lower self (Heru and Set) as well as the control of one's breath (life) through the union (control) of the lungs (breathing organs). Further, it refers to the practice and understanding of the mysteries of the mind. By developing intuitive vision, the dualistic understanding of oneself and creation is transformed into the vision of union (Sema).

For more on the Ancient Egyptian path of spiritual enlightenment through righteous action see the books: *HEALING THE CRIMINAL HEART: Introduction to Maat Philosophy, Yoga and Spiritual Redemption Through the Path of Virtue, EGYPTIAN PROVERBS* and *INTRODUCTION TO MAAT PHILOSOPHY: Spiritual Enlightenment Through the Path of Virtue* by Dr. Muata Ashby.

CHAPTER 11: The Scale Of Maat And the Souls of Ra:

"Master the fire of the back....
the life giving fire"

Egyptian Mystical Wisdom

*For more on the Ancient Egyptian path of spiritual enlightenment through the developing the internal Life Force see the book: *THE SERPENT POWER: The Ancient Egyptian Mystical Wisdom of the Inner Life Force* by Dr. Muata Ashby.

The Seven POWERS anD EnERgy centers

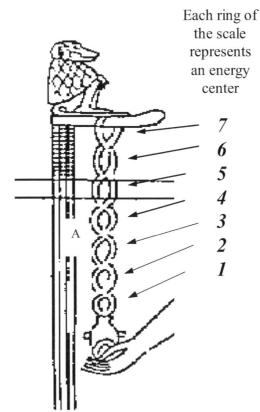

Each ring of the scale represents an energy center

7
6
5
4
3
2
1

The weighing of the heart of the deceased against the Feather of Maat.

Goddess Maat (F) presides over the judgment. Each rung (Fig. A.) represents a level (chakras, energy centers) of evolution of the heart (consciousness) (Fig. B.) of the deceased (initiate) against the Feather of Maat (D). The judgment is presided over by Djehuti (wisdom faculty of the deceased) in the form of a Baboon (C) and Anubis (E).

(From the Greenfield Papyrus)

In Ancient Egypt there existed a concept of seven vortices of energy in the subtle spine called Sephek Ba Ra (Seven Souls of Ra). In India they are called Chakras. In the beginning, NETER was one, and then through the power of thought, became three (Holy Trinity); from these three came the uncountable number of Neters which through the extension of their consciousness (mental-thought power), created the projection (illusion) which we call creation. These are the Souls of Ra (Heru). The Neters sustain and govern creation with their thought-power. There are seven levels of creation (with many sub-levels in each), and there are a total of seven levels of consciousness. The task is then to attune the seven individual energy-consciousness centers in the human being with the seven powers of the universe (GOD) through wisdom and virtue. The knowledge of the attainment of wisdom and virtue are encompassed in the 42 precepts of MAAT which are a multiple of 7, and in the 42 books of Hermes (Djehuti) which contain the knowledge of the nature of the universe which is also the subject of this volume.

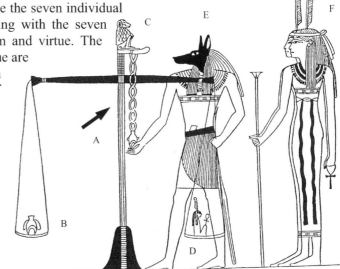

The Psychic Energy Centers are located in the spiritual body and runs parallel to the spinal column. The energy centers are 7 centers of expanding levels of consciousness from the base of the spine (physical - animal consciousness -**Apophis)** to the top (spiritual consciousness) at the Crown of the head:

Uraeus - Buto. As in the Indian Chakra System, The Egyptian Seven Powers are related to the seven energy centers of the spine and are linked to the awakening of one's spiritual powers. As one progresses on their spiritual path of evolution, while either purposely employing a spiritual discipline (study and application of spiritual and philosophic scriptures, reflection and meditation) or learning through the process of trial and error, these centers will automatically open, allowing one to experience increasing communion with the higher self: GOD. The process of raising one's spiritual power may be accomplished by concentration, proper breathing, meditation on the meanings of the symbols and surrendering to the will of the Higher Self (GOD). These techniques allow one to transform one's waking personality so that one may discover their innermost self: GOD. This should be done under the guidance of a qualified teacher (spiritual master, guru, etc.).

Sefekh Ba Ra (The Seven Souls of Ra) or Sefekh Uadjit (The Seven Serpent Goddesses)

The Subtle Body and The Energy Centers of the Human Body

The 7 Energy Centers

The Psychic Energy Centers in the spiritual body are distributed throughout the spine going up from the base to the Crown of the head: The Uraeus.

SEFEKHT
CORRESPONDS TO THE FIRST ENERGY-CONSCIOUSNESS CENTER (INDIAN - SANSKRIT - "MULADHARA CHAKRA")

Also known as Sheshat, it is the root center (chakra) which is located at the base of the spine. It is the level of energy-consciousness we use to manifest (project) our "body" on the physical plane of existence, so that our spirit may be able to have experience in the physical realm. The energies here are concerned with survival issues and in the unbalanced state, manifest as fear, selfishness, possessiveness, etc. It represents dormant (coiled up as a serpent) and uncontrolled sexual energy as represented by Apopis, the enemy of Ra. Our "task" is to convert this sexual energy into spiritual energy, thereby achieving expanded consciousness in the realms above and beyond the physical. We must develop, raise and master this energy to the 7th energy center, thus becoming one with the universe: GOD. The mastery of the primal energies is represented by the Goddess Buto of Egypt and Goddess Kundalini of India.

TEKH
CORRESPONDS TO THE SECOND ENERGY-CONSCIOUSNESS CENTER (CHAKRA - INDIAN SANSKRIT: "SWADHISHTAN CHAKRA")

It is in the area of the organs of procreation where, if controlled by the higher centers, cosmic energy may be absorbed and transmuted to create more than just physical offspring; one may give birth to their untapped creative talents. However, if the individual is psychologically developed to this level only, he or she will be preoccupied with sexual matters.

AB (OB)
CORRESPONDS TO THE THIRD ENERGY-CONSCIOUSNESS CENTER (INDIAN SANSKRIT: "MANIPURA CHAKRA")

Its location is in the solar plexus. The vital fire which sustains the physical body is located here. This energy center gives one a sense of power and will. Meditation on this spot sends SEKHEM or vital energy (Prana, Chi) to this center which promotes health by increased digestion and equal distribution of energy throughout the body; the effect is physical and emotional balance. This is a prerequisite for higher spiritual advancement.

Imbalance or obstruction in this energy center manifests as feelings of inadequacy and powerlessness; one feels incapable of expressing their willpower.

The fourth to the seventh energy-consciousness centers (chakras) represent the evolution of spiritual life, the divine nature which is latent in every one. The lower energy centers (3 - 1) represent the life of the lower nature, the animal nature which seeks survival and supremacy over others and gratification of the senses. Moving from the lower to the higher consciousness represents the second birth, the birth of the spirit.

KHEPER
CORRESPONDS TO THE FOURTH ENERGY-CONSCIOUSNESS CENTER (INDIAN - SANSKRIT - "ANAHATA CHAKRA")

Its location is at the heart. This center opens up the possibility of the *"virgin birth"* which is the spiritual consciousness as opposed to the lower animal consciousness. At this level, your spiritual essence becomes revealed in the caring (expressing love) for others.

The Kheper or Anahata chakra is related to a gland in the body known as the thymus. Being very large in babies, the thymus shrinks as we mature. The thymus is intricately related to the immune system, producing antibodies to ward off infections. It is not surprising then, that when we are stressed, our immune system weakens and we become ill. If we evaluate ourselves when we become ill, we will find that we usually are involved with self-defeating and self-destructive attitudes and behaviors---overworking, frustration, drugs, alcohol, bad relationships---and are not in a situation to freely give love to our very selves, much less to all humanity. If we are not cautious, we become trapped in this negative way of existence which becomes a vicious cycle. How do we break this cycle? By performing self-less service to others, a very difficult task when we feel as though we are the ones who need to be served. However, we must remember the divine rule (Cosmic Law): To give is to receive.

SEKHEM
CORRESPONDS TO THE FIFTH ENERGY-CONSCIOUSNESS CENTER (INDIAN - SANSKRIT - "VISHUDHI CHAKRA")

It is the throat chakra, the Chakra of *Medu Neter* (divine speech). This center is involved with our ability to receive love from others---our self-value. Imbalance in this energy center may be expressed as the inability to communicate our needs to people around us and the world at large. Thus, it is linked to illnesses such as hoarseness and sore throats, which usually occur as a result of communication difficulties such as shouting and screaming in an attempt to be heard.

MER
CORRESPONDS TO THE SIXTH ENERGY-CONSCIOUSNESS CENTER (INDIAN - SANSKRIT - "AJNA CHAKRA")

It is the third eye, the level of intuitive wisdom that does not require "thinking or the mind processes." This is the Eye of Heru, the light of intuitive vision. It is the level of "knowing" something instead of "thinking" we know something. Herein lies the ability to perceive the spirit as well as matter, and to live in both equally.

IKH
CORRESPONDS TO THE SEVENTH ENERGY-CONSCIOUSNESS CENTER (INDIAN - SANSKRIT - "SAHASRARA CHAKRA")

This is the energy-consciousness level where the dualistic mind symbolized by Apopis and the *"life giving fire"* (primal energies), becomes united into one whole. This is where Apopis is transformed into the Uraeus (Buto), the highest achievement of all spiritual movement. This consciousness level represents the level of transcendence, where the Christ anointing occurs. It is here where the merging of the individual BA (soul) with the Absolute reality (The Universal BA, Heru, Ra, Asar, Ptah, etc.) occurs. The same symbolism is expressed in the idea of the Sphinx wherein the lion body (lower self) of the Sphinx merges with the human head (higher self, GOD). The Sphinx is also a symbol of Heru.

Below: From the *Book of Coming Forth By Day* of Kenna*. Ammit- Devourer of sinful souls shows the difference between animals (centers 1-3) and those born of the spirit (centers 4-7) by biting the staff of the Scale of Maat at the point between the third and fourth circles which symbolize the energy centers of the body. Maat holds out her left hand which is holding the Menat, symbol of union of the male-female organs.

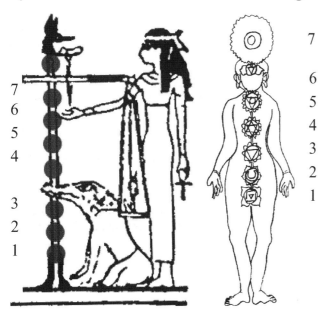

The seven energy centers are also called *"The Seven Uraeuses"*. At right: A drawing from Indian Kundalini Yoga showing showing the location of the energy centers of the body.

*This particular version of the *"Egyptian Book of Coming Forth By Day"* was prepared for initiate *Kenna.*

The !Kung People of Afrika

The knowledge of the *"Life Force"* inherent in the human body which was known as *Ra-Buto* in Egypt, *Kundalini* in India, *Chi* in China, and *Qi or Ki in Japan,* existed in various traditions around the world. The *!Kung Nation of Africa* who reside in the *Kalahari Desert* are one of the societies referred to as *"Bushmen."* They possess the knowledge of the inner Life Force, and from ancient times, practiced the disciplines to arouse it for the purpose of attaining spiritual evolution.

The *!Kung* practitioners describe the classical Life Force arousal which begins at the pelvic region, moves up the back and rises to the brain, there causing ecstatic and mystical experiences which allow the practitioners to attain expanded states of consciousness known to them as: *!Kia*. This* allows them to better serve their society. As in other nations of Africa, the *!Kung* begin by engaging in hours long rituals of dancing (see also The Whirling Dervishes). The goal is to arouse *n/um* (Life Force) which is said to reside in the pit of the stomach (see also *Lower Dan Tien, Energy Centers in the Body: Chakra #3*), and when *"warmed"*** (aroused), rises from the base of the spine. As with other accounts from around the world, the initial onset of the arousal may be painless or may be attended by the painful movement of energy (not unlike the birth of a child) with such a force that it may challenge the sanity of the individual (see also Altered States of Consciousness) . This occurrence can understandably cause intense fear (of bodily injury or loss of sanity) which when overcome, allows the release of the spirit into new realms of consciousness (the *!Kia State).*

The state of *!Kia* is equal to the state of *Samadhi* in Indian Yoga and *Satori* in Zen Meditation.

*Kiai is also a word of power in China and Japan describing the Life Force which resides in the solar plexus or *"Lower Dan Tien"* region of the body.

**See also: "The Secret of The Philosopher's Stone."

The Nervous System.

Through the mind and the nervous system, the soul is able to experience interaction with the physical world. The mind formulates the thoughts which are carried out by directing the nervous system to act in various ways.

Therefore, maintaining healthy mental and nervous systems is one of the most important tasks on the spiritual path.

The spiritual body is composed of subtle (cannot be seen) channels which act as transformers of spiritual energies. This process allows the Ba or soul to have a "form" which it can use to physically interact with the physical universe. There are many subtle channels in the subtle (spiritual) body. The three main ones are symbolized by the stale of SHU and the Caduceus of Djehuti-Hermes. These subtle channels are said to be located alongside the physical spinal cord and control the distribution of energy throughout the physical body. There is a primary channel in the center of the back. The other two channels, represented as the serpents in the caduceus of Djehuti-Hermes, are coiled around the central channel.

Hermes is the name that the Greeks gave to the Egyptian God Thoth or Djehuti. This symbol has many esoteric meanings. This *"Magic Wand"* of Djehuti is one of the most sacred symbols. The *"CADUCEUS"* (see page 122) represents the two opposite forces in nature which, when brought into balance, bring about physical and spiritual health. It is a variation of this same symbol which is used by the medical professions today. The center, vertical pole, represents the center of the etheric spine (spine in the etheric body) and the two snakes represent the male and female Life Force in all things, including the human body. The wings symbolize the power that can be achieved by raising the sexual energy (Life Force) to the top energy center and mastering it, one can unfurl one's spiritual wings with un-imagined power. This system of subtle channels comprises the *"Back of Asar."* In balancing the positive and negative forces, it is possible to experience the singularity of all things in the universe including one's own being.

In the Indian Yoga system, the subtle channels are known as *"Nadis".* The main subtle channel is known as *"SUSHUMNA"* and the two smaller subtle channels corresponding to the left and right sympathetic systems are called *"IDA AND PINGALA",* respectively.

As the serpents are controlled, so too the psychic force Sekhem or Kundalini will be aroused. This is the association with the *"BACK OF ASAR."*

When the dormant energy is awakened, it flows up through the spine passing through the energy centers. Upon reaching the seventh center, anointing or contact with the Cosmic Consciousness (Universal BA, GOD) occurs.

SHU, the God of Air, the breath of Ra (NETER), gives a clue as to a method of controlling these vital forces. Shu is said to possess power over serpents (serpents were a symbol of *"physical and moral evil"*) and in the Egyptian Coffin Texts, Shu tells us where GOD (the SUPREME BEING) is:

"I am indwelling in the millions (of creatures) who is heard in a million words. I am he who brings the words of the Self-Creator to his multiplicity...I am the strongest and most vigorous of the Divine Band... I came into being in the limbs of the Self-Creator."

Egyptian Proverb

Shu tells us he was created in the "limbs of the Self-Creator" and that he (air) is the messenger of GOD, and the strongest of all other Gods created by the Supreme Being. Further, Shu tells us that GOD is indwelling in the millions of creatures. GOD is inside each of us and through the control of breath (air), the link between Creator and that which is "Created" may be established.

In Chapter 23 of the *"Egyptian Book of Coming Forth By Day,"* the initiate is told to pray that Shu will open the mouth of the initiate as he had opened the mouth of the Gods. Later, the initiate is nourished with the food of Shu who lives on light (Ra). Light is spiritual energy, gained by the accumulation of the Life Force of Ra (sunlight) and by the sublimation of sexual energy, which the initiate uses to reach heaven. Sunlight (the rays of the sun) is described as being *"The Ladder of Heaven."* The same description of the importance of sun rays is also indicated in *Mundaka Upanishad* (Sacred Sanskrit Indian Vedanta philosophy Texts) where it is stated that *"sun rays are a ladder to the divine"*.

It is important to understand that the vital energy, *"Sekhem,"* which runs through the subtle channels, is controlled by the mind. *"The Universe is Mental"* says Djehuti-Hermes, the God of Wisdom. Controlling the mind is therefore, the way to gain control over the vital forces of the larger universe (cosmos) and the inner universe (human being), for when the individual human mind gives up its individuality and becomes one with the mind of the cosmos (GOD), it discovers that there is only one mind that exists. It discovers that it is not limited to a physical body but that it is one with all that exists, since all that exists is a projection from the mind of GOD. This state of attunement between the human mind and the cosmic mind leads to health and peace. To the extent that the human mind is out of attunement with the cosmic mind, there will be varying levels of dis-ease and emotional-psychological-spiritual unrest.

By breathing *"rhythmically and deeply"*, remaining calm in concentration or meditation, the Sekhem (Life Force) is harmonized and increased. Healthy living, (active life), vegetarian meals and healthy thinking (following the Laws of Maat) and certain poses or exercises purify and awaken the serpents and allow the Sekhem to flow.

> *"Develop the life giving fire; few know how to use it and fewer how to master it."*
> *"Master the fire of the back."*

In Kundalini and Tantra Yoga, sexual energy is seen as the force which transforms the energy centers and their corresponding nerves in the physical body in order that the entire nervous system may be attuned to the all pervasive cosmic consciousness. Through the increasing wisdom, force of will (self discipline) and purification of the mind and body of the aspirant, the essence which makes up the cells of their human body is changed (mutates).*

Left: The Caduceus of Djehuti-Hermes.

Throughout the last 5,000 years of Egyptian history, severe moral and social decay led to the end of Egyptian civilization. This decay resulted in a division of Egypt into two lands, (upper and lower Egypt).

From the earliest times of the dynastic period (5,000 B.C.E. to 600 A.D.), the ancient Egyptian texts speak of "rejoining the two lands." The double Uraeus also symbolizes this separation between upper and lower Egypt. There is also a deeper mystical implication to this symbol. The double Uraeus, representing the serpents of the caduceus (wand) of Djehuti, is leading us to understand that we must re-unite the two levels of our consciousness (lower self and higher self).

Center: The double Uraeus. Right: Djehuti (God of wisdom and intellect) holding the double Uraeus scepter (Caduceus).

Left: The God of air, Shu (Heh), holding the serpents in control (sublimation). Air is what separates heaven and earth. We must control air in order to re-unite heaven and earth.

CHAPTER 12: Min and Hetheru

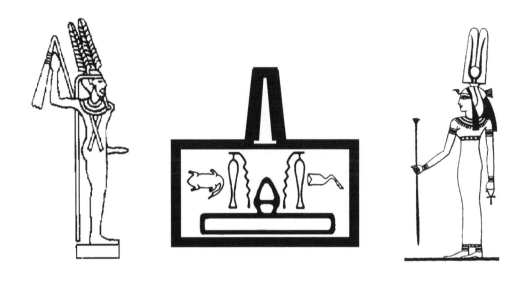

"To free the spirit, control the senses; the reward will be a clear insight."

"Be circumspect in matters of sexual relations."

<u>Egyptian Mystical Wisdom</u>

Min and Hetheru

The God and Goddess Neters (principles) represented by Min and Hetheru (Hetheru) are of paramount importance in the process of human evolution (Yoga) with respect to the Life Force which lies dormant inside every human being.

MIN The Aspect of Heru as Sublimated Male Sexual Power

The Egyptian God MIN is the aspect of Heru representing *"the victorious one over the enemies of his father,"* the enemies being: ignorance, passion, greed, anger, lust, etc. Min is also called *"Amsu-Amen"* which means "Min the Hidden One." The title "Hidden" relates to the underlying nature of all things, consciousness, and the erectile power of generation which comes from sexual energy, the power that makes life exist and causes it to strive, to move on in search of fulfillment and happiness. Heru in the form of Min symbolizes that stage in spiritual development when sexual energy is controlled and transformed into spiritual energy. Amen is also related to the "God of Gods", *Amen-Ra,* who is in-turn known as *"the hidden one"*, *"the lord of the phallus"*, *"the one whose skins (complexions and bodies) are manifold"*. Min is also known as Khem (heat, burnt, black, dry, hidden). Min is the operating Neter (active principle) during the new moon, the fifth month of the year and in the dream state of sleep when penile erection occurs in the male and clitoral erection occurs in the female.

Above: The God Min (Horus) in the aspect of "He Who Avenges His Father". Below: the flail, symbol of Min's sublimation.

The God Min is usually depicted with an erect phallus, holding a flail in his right arm. MIN represents the erectile, creative force of the universe that is latent in every human being (female and male), from which life springs. This is the blackness represented by the point in the center of the Sundisk, $\odot$, the origin from which all comes:

NETER NETERU, the Life Force which comes from the blackness of consciousness.

If controlled and sublimated, this creative, generative force could transform one into the heights of creation, but if misused such as in overindulgence of physical sexual activity, either in thought or action, it will erode the higher spiritual capacity. For reasons of physical health and spiritual strength, it is important to acquire the proper amount of sleep, nutrition and to observe the practices of sexual energy sublimation.

The hieroglyphs of Min show the attributes of Min. One of the hieroglyphs is a bed of lettuce. Lettuce is the food of Min. Lettuce is viewed as an aphrodisiac and also symbolizes the purity of a vegetarian diet. Another important point about lettuce is that it is also the favorite food of Set. Thus, our higher self (Min) as well as our lower self (Set) are equally nourished, since in order to achieve balance (MAAT), both natures should be equally mastered and sublimated, both must be subject to the command of the BA.

The "CROOK" and "FLAIL" are symbols of leadership. The crook symbolizes the ability to control (lead) one's forces and the flail signifies the self discipline needed to correct one's mistakes and to institute the proper "punishment" to one's self for not carrying out one's duty. Self punishment here does not mean masochism. Masochism is an extreme behavior which is in contravention to Maat (balance). Discipline can be as simple as an act of not allowing oneself to have dessert at dinner because you smoked that cigarette.

Sexual fire is one of the strongest forces that ground us to the earth. Overindulgence leaves subconscious impressions which make us believe that true pleasure (happiness) may be found only through some activity of the body. In reality, these erroneous impressions are setting us up for a disappointment since at the very least, sexual activity cannot go on indefinitely. These impressions subconsciously impel us to continuously search for more "carnal" gratification (pleasure at the level of the senses). This pressure to reenact the pleasurable occasion through physical means leads to mental agitation which inhibits higher spiritual achievement. Furthermore, since the world is set up in such a way that we cannot have everything we want whenever we want it, we are liable to become disappointed repeatedly and further become more mentally agitated. Nature is trying to show us that sexual pleasure is only a glimpse of the true bliss which can be found by "knowing oneself", through the initiatic science of Yoga. If through developing wisdom, one learns to transform the energy developed from the disappointment into spiritual energy, one will discover that there is a higher level of consciousness where instead of disappointment, one can experience boundless fulfillment, ecstasy and peace.

The *Lingam-Yoni* from India is used in ritual. It symbolizes the union of the male and female sex organs.

By directing that sexual energy inward instead of outward, the power to discover who we are becomes potent. Maintaining a moderate sex life or practicing total or partial celibacy (not for all people) is important so as to not waste this vital cosmic energy which is stored in the base of the spine. Also, the psychological process of directing one's energies (thoughts) to the sexual area prevents those energies from being directed and used elsewhere. Working with one's conscious will to direct the sexual energies to the higher energy centers, one can experience the ecstasy of union and seventh energy center, "orgasm." This holds true for males as well as for females. This is not to be seen as masturbation. Orgasms at the highest levels of consciousness, the Uraeus, are experienced due to union of one's self (Ba) with the Divine Self (Universal Ba - Neter Neteru). Through training, practice and will, the ecstatic feelings and energies developed at the higher energy centers can be experienced at the physical level with a partner as well (see Egyptian Tantra Yoga).

Above: the Menat necklace.

Below: Hetheru offering the Menat to the King

As previously stated, there are many roads in Yoga, and anything in the universe may be utilized with the correct knowledge, attitude and instruction. Sex may be used as a vehicle to unite with GOD, but only if used in a disciplined, spiritual manner.

During intercourse, one should keep the TEACHINGS in mind, always realizing that it is the Ba-soul who is using the body and not the perishable ego-personality.

In this manner, all activities including sexual relations, are performed with this mental attitude of dispassion and detachment, thereby developing the witnessing, Ba aspect of our spirit. Gradually, it will be realized that while making love with a partner, one is actually making love to one self.

HETHERU Goddess of Passionate Love and Sexual Desire.

The hieroglyphs of Hetheru, as with Min, show various attributes of this Neter. Her bull horns are an ancient symbol of the procreative, generative principle as well as the abundant fertility as represented by the cow.

Hetheru represents life, potency, fertility, birth, renewal, passion and sexual desire. Hetheru is an aspect of the female principle which comes from the Androgynous (male - female) GOD, NETER, as are all female Goddesses. Hetheru is "full of life" and therefore wears the head piece of cow horns sometimes containing the Sundisk, symbolizing the fullness of her "sun-power."

Hetheru symbolizes female sexual energy and as previously discussed, she is also the Eye of Ra. The Eye (Hetheru) has the power (fire) to destroy evil and unrighteousness. Much like the Hindu Goddess Kali, Hetheru is both sexually potent and fierce at the same time. Hetheru is also known as *"Het-Heru"* meaning *"The House of Heru,"* and *"The House Above"* the implication being that Hetheru is Min's (Heru') "sanctuary" and his counterpart *"Above"*. She was the spark which urged Heru to fight on in the battle against the evil Set in the struggle of Life. In order to succeed in the struggle of life, Heru (Min) must "live" in Hetheru's qualities (sanctuary). All humans must find Hetheru within themselves in order to succeed in the struggle of existence.

Above: The headpiece of Hathor (also worn by Isis) at once depicts both of the complementary opposite principals which run throughout Egyptian and Ethiopian mythology, that of male and female. The sundisk in the center representing the male (giving) aspect and the cow horns representing the female aspects of fertility and life giving strength. Hathor, being the sensual, fiery aspect of Isis unites the power of the sun (phallic, generative) within herself (horns).

In the Chester Beatty Papyrus a story is told of how Ra, the King of the Gods and Hetheru's Father, was depressed one day and how Hetheru improved his disposition through her charms, showing how properly channeled sexual energy can change one's negative mental vibrations into creative vitality:

> *"The Great God (Ra) passed the day on his back in his arbor, and his heart was very sad, and he was alone. After a long time, Hetheru, lady of the southern sycamore, came and stood before her father, the master of the universe. She uncovered her vulva for his face, and the great God smiled at her...."*

From the Chester Beatty Papyrus.

This hieroglyph is therefore related to the other major symbol of Hathor, the Menat, as well as to the Ankh, and the Lingam-Yoni of India.

One of Hetheru's instruments is the *"Menat";* it is equal to the *"lingam-yoni"* (phallus-vulva) of Indian - Hindu and Tantra Yoga.

 The Menat

The Menat and the Ankh of Egypt as with the Indian Lingam-Yoni symbols or amulets, represent the united male and female sexual organs. When these opposite and complementary energies combine, the result is life, in this case referring to the birth of the spiritual life of the individual. Hetheru is known as *"The Great Menat."* She and her priestesses wear the menat as a necklace and use it to pass their power to others. In joining the powers of Min and Hetheru, the innate and dormant powers inside every human are awakened and perfected.

Above: An Egyptian ***"Hetep Offering Table",*** *(this one now located at the Louvre museum.) The Hetep Offering Table-Slab is an article equal in use to the Indian Lingam Yoni. It displays the male and female symbols, a Hetep symbol, two water jars, symbolizing the male and female fluids (essence) which are to flow down the central canal of oneness to achieve the union (yoga) which brings Supreme Peace (Hetep).*

In order to develop Min's and Hetheru's qualities within one's self, a healthy and honest attitude towards one's body and mind must be cultivated. These principles are to be viewed as tools to assist us in learning how to master the art of living. They are not life itself nor are they the purpose of living. Abstinence and overindulgence are two extreme sides of the same coin. Both lead to imbalance. The middle path (Maat) of progressing at one's own pace is the preferred strategy.

From the practice of sexual sublimation and virtue, spiritual powers or "Siddhis," as they are called in India, will come in the form of understanding, being able to control one's temper, patience and tolerance in adverse situations. As one advances, greater powers will develop when one is ready to understand and use them properly.

Psychic Powers

Psychic powers are any form of mental achievement and they may or may not be related to spiritual achievement. The attainment of a college degree, for example, is a psychic power but it is done for worldly achievement (magic). The development of psychic powers for spiritual attainment require purity of heart (a mind which is free from passionate desire for worldly objects or achievements). All psychic powers, however, require some level of mental concentration in order to attain them. The ability to concentrate may be improved through practice of mental concentration exercises, meditation and practicing the virtues.

Forgiveness is a most important psychic power. The ability to forgive one's self and others for one's mistakes is essential. There will be many "failures" on the spiritual path. These are merely tests to help strengthen one's resolve and to raise consciousness and wisdom. If we take life (relative reality) so hard and forget the greater picture (absolute reality), we become preoccupied and un-forgiving. Bitterness and mental unrest become constant companions and higher spiritual evolution becomes impaired. Life becomes a constantly miserable experience in which there is always fault with something, therefore mental peace is seldom, if ever, possible.

Introspection and self analysis are good ways to discern one's motives and actions. Only you can decide if you acted on the basis of the lower self (SET, emotion, ego, body desires, guilt and fear) or if you acted out of the BA, the higher self (HERU, Maat, purity, light, righteousness).

One of the greatest psychic powers is to be able to control one's emotions. It is said that emotions are great servants but poor masters because intense emotions cloud the thinking process. Emotionally based actions usually promote detrimental results in which one becomes further embroiled in unwanted situations. These unwanted situations, when dealt with again in an emotional manner, will lead to further entanglements in the world of relative reality. Most people live in this way, acting and reacting based on their uncontrolled mental state which produces a cycle of alternating pleasurable or painful situations, both of which lead to mental agitation (unrest).

Patience is another important psychic power to develop. Patience is necessary for the task of spiritual growth, since it may take years to correct negative subconscious thought patterns learned in this life this or previous lives.

The Highest Psychic Power

Proper sublimation of the Life Force which is developed from the sexual energy center can increase the creative power if used for *MAAT*. When directed to the divine, psychic power can lead to union with the divine, NETER. This union may be seen in the Egyptian principles of: Heru and Set, Asar and Aset, Min and Hetheru, the Sun and Moon as well as the East Indian deities: Krishna and Radha, Shiva and Shakti (Parvati), Ganesha and Siddhi. This union also represents the marriage of cosmic energy and earth energy (Spirit and Body). Both energies are of the same nature and differ only in their polarity. Thus, when they are united, they revert to their primordial state which is beyond polarity. The earth energy (Geb) rises from the base of the spine and reunites with heaven (Nut). When this occurs, the energy consciousness center at the crown of the head opens and one becomes anointed with the Life Force energy

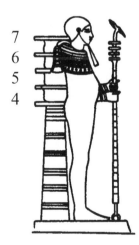

The *Djed* pillar of Asar representing the "back" of Asar. The Djed is related to the top chakras or energy c e n t e r s   o f consciousness that are developed by all who are on the spiritual path. This is what is referred to as: *"Master the fire of the back"* and *"the life giving fire."*

produced from the union of the male principle and the female principle. This is the highest psychic power, where one becomes a Christ (anointed one).

The elephant deity and faculty, *"Ganesha"*, of Indian Hindu mythology symbolizes the awakening of sexual fire (the fire that urges us on to live and endure) and spiritual ideals, and also, the opening of of the way, creating auspiciousness in one's spiritual discipline. Invoking Ganesha enables one to attain peace of mind for meditation. The attainment of what Ganesha symbolizes are Siddhis or supernatural powers. Ganesha is one of the presiding deities at tantric rituals and is invoked before any spiritual or worldly undertaking. In the Egyptian system, the deity Anpu fills the role of "Opener of the Way." Geb, Min, and Asar are usually represented as the symbols of fertility and erectile power.

The Indian God *Ganesha,* with an erect phallus and his consort, *Siddhi* who holds his penis with her right hand. Psychic powers are "given" through the sexual organs through the development of sexual energy.

CHAPTER 13: Introduction to Egyptian Tantra Yoga

"Develop the life giving fire; few know how to use it and fewer how to master it."

<u>Egyptian Mystical Wisdom</u>

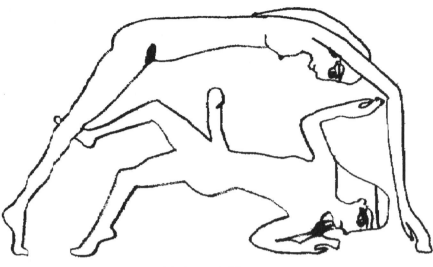

NUT and GEB

Egyptian Tantra Yoga

Tantra Yoga is purported to be the oldest system of Yoga. Tantra Yoga is a system of Yoga which seeks to promote the re-union between the individual and the Absolute Reality, *"NETER"* (GOD), through the worship of nature. Since nature is an expression of GOD, it gives clues as to the underlying reality that sustains it and the way to achieve wisdom. The most obvious and important teaching that nature holds is the idea that creation is made up of pairs of opposites: Up-down, here-there, you-me, us-them, hot-cold, male-female, Ying-Yang, etc. The interaction, of these two complementary opposites, we call life and movement.

Insight (wisdom) into the true nature of reality gives us a clue as to the way to realize the oneness of creation within ourselves. By re-uniting the male and female principles in our own bodies and minds, we may reach the oneness that underlies our apparent manifestation as a man or woman. The union of the male and female principles may be effected by two individuals who worship GOD through GOD's manifestation in each other or by an individual who seeks union with GOD through uniting with his or her male or female spiritual half. All men and women have both female and male principles within themselves.

In the Egyptian philosophical system, all Neters or God principles emanate from the one GOD. When these principles are created, they are depicted as having a *male and female* principle. All objects and life forms appear in creation as either male or female, but underlying this apparent duality, there is a unity which is rooted in the pure consciousness of oneness, the consciousness of GOD, which underlies and supports all things. To realize this oneness consciously deep inside is the supreme goal.

"NETER" (Supreme Being) created the Goddess *NUT* (Sky-Heaven-Fire) and the God *GEB* (Earth-Solid). The God *GEB* and the Goddess *NUT* represent the male and female principles of creation, respectively. Then the Supreme "nameless" GOD created *SHU* (air) to separate heaven and earth, making a physical world and a heavenly world. Thus it is through the separation of Heaven and Earth by the God *SHU* (air) that the universe was created.

The *"Obelisk"*, a tall tapering tower with a pyramid at the top, represents the erectile power of the physical human body as personified by the God of the earth principle, Geb (also Min as previously discussed). Our physical nature, though susceptible to the temptations of the flesh, is capable of great energy. In viewing any Obelisk, it should be noted that it represents a phallus uniting "Heaven and Earth" as it reaches up out of the earth *(Geb)*, through the air *(Shu),* towards Heaven *(Nut)*. Thus, symbolically, an obelisk represents the unity of the female and male powers (Heaven and Earth).

Love (The "Hoe")

The ritual of *"Hoeing of the Earth"*, relates to the preparation of the human body, cultivating physical health, in order to allow higher spiritual growth. The "Hoe" is the symbol of *"Love,"* therefore, the earth (Geb-physical human body) must be carefully "cultivated" (prepared to receive spirituality), through the practice of Love.

As it is the God Shu (air) who is responsible for keeping Geb and Nut (earth-male and heaven-female) apart, it is also Shu (air) who perpetuates the appearance of a world of duality, separation, with many male and female forms. Therefore, it is Shu (air) to whom we must turn to reunite the illusion of separation in our consciousness in order to end the appearance of duality.

"Builder must Obtain Secrets, it's Difficult to KNOW
the Movement of the Nostrils to Restore Life."

Egyptian Proverb

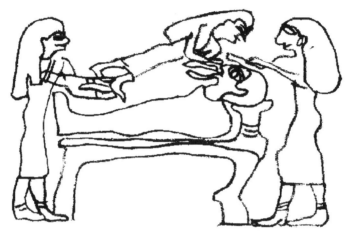

Aset (representing the physical body-creation) and the dead body of Asar (representing the spirit, that essence which vivifies matter) are shown in symbolic immaculate union (compare to the "Kali Position" on the following page) begetting Heru, symbolizing to the immaculate conception which takes place at the birth of the spiritual life in every human: the birth of the soul (Ba) in a human is the birth of Heru. From a Stele at the British Museum 1372. 13th Dyn.

SHU: The breathing process is the only autonomic body system that can be consciously controlled. Therefore, through breath control (control of air which contains within it the Life Force, Sekhem, Prana that sustains all life), we may have an effect on our own consciousness and thereby effect a reunification of *NUT* and *GEB* within our own consciousness. That is to say, we may unite our human consciousness, female principle-receiver of life, with the cosmic consciousness GOD, male principle-giver of life. An individual can thus re-unite the *Geb-Nut* principles within him or herself through the *SHU* principle. In Egyptian philosophy, this process is called *"The weaving of Heru"* and it encompasses the climbing of increasing levels of consciousness upon *"The Ladder of NUT"* (any process which brings one closer to one's heavenly nature-Yoga). In general, this explains the fact that females are usually more receptive and intuitive.

Above left: "The Spinning Top" position from Indian Tantra Yoga. Similar to the Geb and Nut pose, "The Spinning Top" pose is performed in the following manner: The female remains above while slowly spinning around while united to the male. It is clear to see that mental concentration is needed to perform these poses along with physical stamina. The effort in this direction allows time for the practitioners to develop Sexual Life Force energy and it's sublimation into spiritual energy.

During Tantric training, each individual is instructed to regard the other as a divinity (which all humans are innately) and to worship each other as such and to alternate roles (each partner sees themselves as male or female) as they visualize the Life Force growing. During "physical" sexual intercourse between a man and a woman, it is the male who "gives" and the female who "receives". Sexual intercourse is used to heighten the ecstatic feelings and to develop psychic energy for spiritual attainment. Due to the power of the sexual force and the danger of one's inability to control one's mind and direct it to GOD while in practice, Tantra Yoga involving sexual intercourse is not advised except for those aspirants who undergo the rigorous psychological training which may take months or years. It is possible that a misdirected practitioner may fall deeper into the earthly desires rather than using them to transcend the earth bound existence. Breathing exercises, physical and mental purification are necessary before pursuing Tantra Yoga.

Thus, the participants are not allowed to reach climax (physical sexual orgasm) in order to channel all energies towards concentrating on the goal: development of their Life Force and its union with the Transcendental - Absolute divine through ever increasing ecstasy and devotion (Uraeus). Through repeated stimulation and concentration of the energies to the higher energy centers, the sublimation of the primal sexual and mental energy, symbolized by the serpent Apophis, is possible. Apophis is thus transformed into the divine eye symbolized by Goddess Buto (Uraeus).

Left: The Obelisk represents the penis of Geb (earth). The skyline around it is Nut (heavens-cosmos). Thus, by directing sexual energy toward heaven, the unification of heaven and earth within oneself may be effected.

The Indian Kundalini Yoga system which teaches the development of sexual energy through the development of the seven energy-consciousness centers in the spiritual body is viewed as an outgrowth of the Tantra Yoga system. It seeks to unite the Life Force energy, Goddess Kundalini Shakti (Egyptian Goddess Buto-ASET-Nut), the female principle, with the male God principle, Shiva (Egyptian Ra-ASAR-Geb).

The Egyptian system of Yoga philosophy does not condemn sexual activity in the pursuit of spirituality. Rather, as it espouses responsibility and balance (MAAT) in all areas of activity including sex, it promotes wisdom as to the true nature and purpose of sexuality. *"Keeping the balance"* is the deeper implication of the scales of MAAT and the Egyptian scriptures advise one not to indulge in extremes because: *"one extreme leads to another."* Balance, consistency and equanimity are keys to sanity, success and sustained progress in any endeavor.

Tantra Yoga was also practiced by the early Indus Valley civilizations and met with opposition from the invading Aryans from Eurasia who tried to suppress it and to install a system which included many Gods. This was later called Hinduism and Vedanta. Archeological and historical evidence supports the idea that the Tantric philosophical teachings were carried on in the writings called the Upanishads which are said to be part of the Vedas (religious teachings of the invading Aryans) but which are viewed by some scholars as an attempt of the Tantric masters to re-establish and preserve the Tantric teachings.

Above Left: *The "Kali position": Shiva and Shakti (Kundalini-Prakriti) in divine union (India). As with Asar and Aset of Egypt, Shiva is the passive aspect who "gives" the life essence (spirit) and creative impetus and Shakti is energy, creation, the active aspect of GOD.*

Thus Creation is akin to the idea of GOD making love with him/herself. Shiva and Shakti are the true essence of the human being, composed of spirit and matter (body). In the active aspect, the female is in the "active" position while the male is in the "passive" position.

Above right: Tibetan Buddhist representation of The Dharmakaya, the cosmic father-mother. expressing the idea of the Supreme Being as a union of both male and female principals In reference to sexuality, Buddha is held to have said: **"Women are the Gods, women are life...Be ever among women in your thought".**

The Life Force energy (Ra-Sekhem, Prana, Chi) is a part of any undertaking and is increased normally as one progresses along any path of spiritual development, regardless of whether it is affected consciously or unconsciously. It might be said that no undertaking is possible without this force. Indeed, life would not exist without it. It is important to understand that nothing is to be "given up." That is to say, when it is stated that one refrains from physical orgasm, it is meant that this is not practiced in order to experience "orgasm" on a higher level of consciousness. If there is a feeling of "giving anything up", then the subject is not ready to practice this discipline. There are many roads to spiritual evolution, however, some control of the bodily urges and desires must be exerted to channel energies to any desired goal in life. There have been many married and fully active people (male and female) throughout history who became enlightened beings. Since all souls have accumulated different experiences and are at different levels of evolution, each must choose their own method of spiritual discipline. Total or partial celibacy can only be effective if the subject is ready to willingly and freely choose that path, otherwise the discipline would not work and might even be harmful since the subject's consciousness is still very much attached to his / her physical nature. Depriving oneself from natural needs and desires is neither wise nor healthy. However, "natural needs and desires" change according to one's level of evolution. All the philosophical and religious systems now in existence are at best merely guidelines or general outlines of the way. A map is not the land.

The statues and depictions of the God Min suggest to the initiate that the way to achieve higher mental and spiritual power is by sublimating one's sexual energy. In one statue, Min is shown holding his erect penis with his left (magnetic) hand signifying that the sexual energy is being drawn back into the body and up to the higher energy centers instead of being allowed to go out of the body. In this manner, the human body becomes a crucible for the creation of a higher physical, mental and spiritual state of being and consciousness.

As stated earlier, the principles represented by the God Set include physical strength, sexual promiscuity, passion and brute force. Set has one more important meaning with regard to sexual intercourse. The derivative word *SETI* which comes from Set also means "to shoot", as in shooting an arrow or as in ejaculation. From several mythological stories, it is clear that Set cannot control his sexual desires nor does he have the ability to contain his semen. In one episode of the battle between Heru and Set, Set tried to catch Aset in order to have intercourse with her. Unable to do so, he ejaculated on the ground, frustrated. Thus, Set represents the animal tendency to direct energy out of the body without control and to think passionately, reacting to life events without thinking. Min is the aspect of Heru who restores justice after the brutal murder of Asar. As *"The victorious one over the enemies of his father"*, Min is victorious over the primal animal tendencies to passionate behavior and ejaculation. Min's victory is not one of destruction over the primal forces, but one of mastery, control and sublimation.

Above left: In Anciewnt Egypt the cultivation of the physical aspect and its development into the obelisk was an important discipline. The Egyptian ritual of *"Hoeing of the Earth."* Similarly, in the *Bhagavad Gita* scripture from India, Krishna teaches Arjuna the same wisdom in reference to the spiritual discipline of the body, that the earth (body) is the field of battle between spirit and matter. Thus, as good farmers we must sow the proper virtues and spiritual discipline in order to reap the fruit of enlightenment.

The images of Min and Hetheru.

The Secret of the Philosopher's Stone, sexual sublimation, is the very messege that is conveyed in the images of Min (left) and Hetheru (right). Above: Hetheru offers the Menat necklace to a King.

The very image of Min symbolizes the Philosopher's Stone, however, more literal interpretations and explanations of the idea exist in other ancient texts.

Legend holds that the *"The Emerald Tablet of Hermes"* (Egyptian God: Djehuti) was found in the King's chamber of the Great Pyramid at Giza. It has long been studied as a possible means to transmute matter and energy. The hieroglyphic texts which were found as pyramid inscriptions* were called pyramid texts. These texts later formed the basis of the writings which the Greek called *"Hermetic"**,* since their origin was ascribed to the Egyptian God *Thoth (Djehuti)* whom they called *"Hermes".* It is known as the Philosopher's Stone. It discusses the basis by which all creation and transmutation may be effected:

"Truth is one. What is below corresponds to what is above and what is above corresponds to what is below in the creation of one thing. As all things have come forth from the one thing, so all things come from the one through meditation. The father is the Sun and the mother is the Moon. The wind has carried it in its belly. The Earth is its nourishment. It is the Father of all things in the Universe. If it is turned toward the earth, its strength is intact. The Earth is separated by Fire: with great skill and gentleness the fine is separated from the gross. Rising from the Earth to Heaven, it then descends to Earth, receiving the power of powers from both Above and Below. In this way one attains the grace of the whole Universe. All mysteries are revealed. This power overcomes the finest thing and penetrates every solid. In this manner, the Universe was created. From this formula there are amazing adaptations and applications since this is the basis of them. Thus I am called Hermes Trismegistus since I have the three parts of the knowledge of the Universe. I have explained completely the Operation of the Sun."

Pre-dynastic
Colossal Statue Of

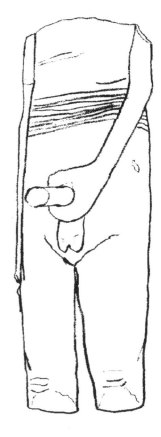

Form the earliest times, the students of mysticism have searched for the alchemical ingredients to construct the most powerful magical instrument that bestows wisdom, immortality and supreme power. For those whose search has remained externalized (i.e. in the world of objects), such an instrument has never been found because the alchemical elements can only be found and developed within the human consciousness and the human body. For this reason, human embodiment, although seen as a fall from heaven, is viewed by initiates as a blessed opportunity to achieve the heights of one's potential in terms of one's evolution. Sexual energy is the driving force of Creation. When sexual energy is sublimated and the mind controlled, the androgynous spirit which is the true self, emerges. The Sage no longer identifies with the sex of his or her particular body. Given that the search is to find the absolute truth which is universal, it is not surprising that the alchemical formulas and teachings expounded by mystical orders from around the world with direct or indirect lineage to the mystery schools of Egypt are similar, if not identical.

A Sage creates a Philosophers Stone by planting his/her Tree of Life in a tub filled with the elixir of life. Through constant heating with the fire of the Dragon, the Sage's Tree of Life will blossom. The Dragon represents "Sexual Energy." They who attain Cosmic Consciousness have control over the Dragon and are pictured with two heads because they now live in the Divine realm as well as the Physical realm. They have returned to their original androgynous form.

In *"The Secret of The Golden Flower"*, a Chinese tantric meditation text, a similar formula is given for sexual sublimation. The text proceeds as follows:

"The water sign is the force of the kidneys. When instincts are aroused, the force runs down, it is then directed outward and creates offspring. If at the time of its release, the force is not allowed to go out, but is directed back in through will of thought, so that it is able to enter into the creative crucible and revitalizes the body, heart and mind, nourishing them, this is called the backward flowing method. Thus it is said: The Elixir of Life is dependant on the backward flowing method."

The same formula is found in the 17th statement or Sutra of the Raja Yoga Sutras of Sage Patanjali from India:

"In the state of Samadhi, with joyous and deliberate meditation on the self, the truth about absolute reality is revealed in all planes."

Samadhi is the state of meditation in which the soul disengages its identification with physical objects and the body and is able to behold the absolute reality which is itself. The soul is thus able to see that physical reality is nothing more than itself on various planes of existence. In this state, ordinary consciousness is transformed into super consciousness. This formula for self transformation reveals all truths and is available to all who pursue the course and practice of it with reflection, joyousness and one-pointed devotion.

In Indian Kundalini Yoga, the energy center at the level of the sexual organs is also under the water sign. It also reminds one of the Indian deity *"Ardhanari"* who wears an Ankh symbol in the area of the genitals which leads us to the understanding that the union of the sexual principles within one's self leads one to the realization of one's own androgynous nature. In the Egyptian Book of Coming forth By Day it is stated: *"In the spirit realm there is no sex."*

And again in the instruction of Aset to Heru:

"Son, sex is a thing of bodies, not of souls."

From the preceding passages, we are led to understand that the way to realize one's true nature lies in the transformation of sexual energy through a meditative life (practice of virtue, and reflection on one's acquired wisdom). Thus, in order to attain one's immortal androgynous all-encompassing nature, one must transform one's consciousness which identifies with the individual manifestation as a male or female, to a "sexless" (androgynous) state.

Tantra Yoga and the Magnetism of the Human Body

A close inspection of the statues and pictographs of Egyptian and Ethiopian deities (Neters) reveals that they had a keen understanding of the magnetism of the human body (see example on page 136). This was later expanded upon by the Indian Kundalini and Tantra Yoga systems as well as the Chinese Tantrists and Chi Kung practitioners. In addition, modern medical science now also corroborates the magnetic relationships of the earth, the body parts and the interrelation of these.

Horus and Set
$(+ -)$

As previously discussed, creation is composed of positive (electric) and negative (magnetic) forces. The human body is also composed of positive and negative forces, the interplay of which produces our physical form and more subtle bodies, health or illness, energy or weakness, etc. The left side of the body is magnetic (negative charge draws energy in) and the right side is electric (positive-charge, emits, gives energy). The top half of the body is negatively charged and the bottom half is positively charged. Thus, the human body has four poles which balance each other.

In general, the male human body is charged positive-electric, and in general the female body is charged negative-magnetic. The male sexual organs are electrically (positively) charged and the female sexual organs are magnetically (negatively) charged. In this manner, the male and female charges attract, balance and complement each other. Through higher expressions of sexual energy, LOVE, the body, mind and spirit interact with nature in increasing levels of consciousness leading to Universal Love and Hetep (ultimate sublimation, peace and satisfaction).

Horus (+) Heavens (cosmos, giver of energy).

Male +

Female –

Set (-) Earth (receiver of energy).

This predynastic statue of Min was originally 13 feet tall. This statue shows the idea of the power of sexual energy and the harnessing of that power. In addition, it will be noticed upon close inspection that the level at which the genitals are located is slightly above the groin. This area corresponds to the third energy center in which cosmic energy is processed for use throughout the entire body. In the Indian Kundalini Yoga system this center is called *"Manipura Chakra"*. This solar plexus is where Life Force, *Ra*, is most strongly manifested.

If properly sublimated (*Hetep*), through special meditations on this area, the body can develop immense physical power and health. In the Taoist systems of Yoga from China called Chi Kung* and Tai Chi, this area (solar plexus) is known as the lower Dan Tien where through mental will and concentration, spiritual energy is developed and then directed to the SHEN or immortal spirit (soul) whose seat is at the Upper Dan Tien located at the level of the eye brow (Egyptian Uraeus, Indian Anahata Chakra).

Above: diagram showing the poles of cosmic energy in nature and the human body. It is important to understand that cosmic (sexual) energy is one energy but with different poles. The different poles give rise to an interplay of molecules which then appear to give rise to separate objects. Indeed, all objects in nature and the human body are composed of the same material: energy, which is controlled by mental vibrations. This is the interplay of Heru and Set.

Once it is directed to the Shen, the spiritual energy begins a process of the expansion of consciousness, leading to the point where the individual Chi merges with the Universal Chi. Thus a vessel is prepared for the Spirit in which it can escape mortality. This vessel may be compared to the building of the *Sahu* or *Glorious Spiritual Body* of Egypt or the building of *"The Chariot"* in the Jewish Mystical Kabalistic system.

The Androgynous quality of the Human Body.

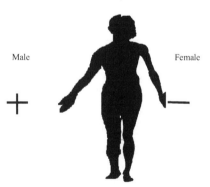

Male   Female

The Egyptian *"Sahu"* or Glorious Body is called *"Divya Deva"* or Divine Body by the Hindus of India. It is understood as a higher level of consciousness which develops out of the ordinary, every day ego-consciousness. Instead of believing oneself to be an individual having a dream, one knows oneself to be GOD, *acting* as an individual person in the waking, sleeping, and deep sleep states.

It is important to understand that each of us contains a male and female half. As we move toward universal understanding (Heruhood), we become "more androgynous" as we gradually allow the androgynous spirit within us, Heru, to have control of our being. It is only due to the identification with the ego that we believe we are members of a certain sex, race, country or planet.

Bottom left: The *"Microcosmic Orbit"* and the Chinese symbol of *The Tao*. Diagram showing the Chi energy circulation pattern around the body and the location of (A) the upper *"Dan Tien"* and (B) the lower *"Dan Tien"*. This system of macro-cosmic (universe) energy flow and micro-cosmic (individual human) energy flow constitutes the basis of acupuncture, the Chinese Yoga system of The Tao and Chi Kung*. The idea is to circulate one's psychic energy instead of allowing it to be wasted in the futile pursuit of worldly pleasures and attainments which as we have seen, are all always perishable and illusory in nature. Energy flows to the object of our mind's interest and attention so instead of placing one's attention on worldly pursuits, one "circulates" it by the force of mental will through the practice of meditation. Even while engaged in worldly duties, one who practices the conservation of spiritual energy through the maintenance of a balanced mind (Tao) can engage in any activity without losing spiritual energy or consciousness. Thus, he or she is said to be doing "nothing" even in the midst of performing heavy activity. Such a one is termed Sage. The task is then to integrate the two polarities (Ying and Yang) within one's own body, which are in reality two polarities of the same Life Force energy, in order to achieve this dynamic balance: *"The Tao".* By meditating on the circulating energy which begins at the lower Dan Tien, and concentrating it there, the meditator can store up energy and develop a psychic *embryo***. In time, the "child" becomes "old enough" to be mentally transferred to the upper Dan Tien where the child grows to form a glorious body for the spirit to inhabit after the death of the physical body.

ASAR AND SHIVA

Shiva or Siva is the one of the earliest representations of the Supreme Being: BRAHMAN. Like Asar, Siva has a companion, a co-creator. This is the female aspect of Creation: Shakti or Sakti. GOD is ALL that IS. When GOD creates, "He" creates out of "HIMSELF", his shadow then there is a "He" and a "She". There can be no "He" without his "She" and no "She" without her "He". Siva is consciousness, the cause of the universe and Sakti is it's power, the appearing universe. So Siva and Sakti are really one in the same being, two sides of the same whole. Like Asar, Shiva is is the lord of all forms of intoxication, music and dance. Like Asar, Shiva was dismembered and torn into pieces, and like Asar, Shiva was castrated by the deities representing evil.

The symbolism and occult meaning of CASTRATION in the ancient tantric teachings is the conservation of semen (male as well as female) or sexual energy and the transmutation of it into spiritual energy. In Tantric teaching, this is not accomplished through abstinence and meditation exercises but through sexual excitement and concentration-meditation after months or years of meditation practice with full understanding of the mysteries of the true nature of absolute reality (see section Who is GOD).

Below left: The God ASAR. The power symbolized by sexual energy is worshipped and cultivated in many of the cults whose philosophical system is based on Egyptian Mysticism. The cultivation and sublimation of sexual energy into spiritual energy was practiced in the Temples of Thebes, Karnak, and Heliopolis. Later these mysteries were merged with the Greek Tantric Mysteries of Dyonisius and Elucis. Asar is seen here in the form of Min with the Hawk (Heru) looking on while perched on a obelisk (Geb).

***Below right: The Trilinga.** This Nepali reproduction shows the different aspects of the Indian God Shiva. As in Egypt (see above), the Lingam (male phallus) in both the single and triune aspects and the Yoni (female vagina) were "worshipped".*

*Chi Kung means "Chi work" or "manipulation and development of Life Force energy." Chi Kung forms the basis of "Internal Kung Fu" or internal martial arts work.**The *"Embryo"* is to be understood as the union of breath energy or the soul (psychic-mental energy) and sexual energy with the spirit when thoughts are immobile and quiet. These energies are transformed into spiritual energy by concentration which forms a circuit in which the energy "stays" with the body instead of "flowing out" into the world. This new psychic component (embryo) of the mind grows through meditation, until <u>IT</u> becomes the focus of consciousness thereby eventually supplanting the ego-consciousness (everyday, waking consciousness).

For more on the Ancient Egyptian path of spiritual enlightenment through the path of sex sublimation and transcendental consciousness see the book: *EGYPTIAN TANTRA YOGA: The Art of Sex Sublimation and Universal Consciousness* by Dr. Muata Ashby.

CHAPTER 14: The Teachings For Reflection And Meditation.

TemT Tchaas
("Ancient Wisdom Teachings")

"Mastery of self consists not in abnormal dreams, visions and fantastic imaginings or living, but in using the higher FORCES against the lower, escaping the pains of the lower by vibrating on the higher."

Egyptian Mystical Wisdom

Essential Elements of a Spiritual Discipline

"Mastery of self consists not in abnormal dreams, visions and fantastic imaginings or living, but in using the higher FORCES against the lower, escaping the pains of the lower by vibrating on the higher."

Egyptian Proverb

1-Be virtuous at any cost- Virtue is the road to immortality.

2-Physical exercise- The body is the temple for the spirit. Keep it healthy through moderate exercise which balance the energies in the body, such as Indian Hatha Yoga, Chinese Chi Kung or Tai Chi.

3-Breathing exercise- Breathing properly produces health by proper distribution of Ra-Sekhem Life Force, Chi, Prana and develops spiritual vitality .

4-Silence- 2 hours daily- "The abomination of the soul: too much talking it is!"
The mind is fond of indulging in debates, argument and nonsense; curtail its opportunity to develop impure thoughts by keeping it quiet and thinking before you say anything. Examine the thoughts and decide if they are pure (spiritual), or if they are from your "mind beast" (your own personal wants and desires). Personal wants and desires must submit to the law of MAAT... "are they necessary or do I just want it?"; otherwise, the desires will rule your life, and you will never attain peace of mind.

5-Study teachings- Study the teachings and take time in silence or in a study group setting to think about them, and / or discuss them as they pertain to your life, the community, the world and the cosmos.

6-Listen- "Keep your ears open to the words of wisdom." Always be willing to listen to and accept the truth, even if it seems to contradict an old teaching you had accepted as truth. Until you attain Heruhood, you will not know the real, complete and -absolute truth because only when you become Heru are you able to see things with GOD's Eyes. The "TRUTH" can only be seen from the perspective of GOD.

7-Reflection- Think about the teachings every time you read or hear them, it sometimes takes a while for them to be fully understood and accepted by the mind.

8-Meditation- When you are able to stay still in a quiet room or other location, begin the practice of meditating even five minutes a day, building up to longer periods.

9-Right action- Perform selfless service at least once a day, expecting no reward. You are doing it for GOD. Always keep in mind that since everything in the universe is RA (universal consciousness of GOD), including you, you are doing service for yourself as you help others but remember, charity begins at home. Here too seek balance.

10- Hekau- Utter words of power in any language but with full understanding of the meaning repeatedly beginning with 5 minutes a day and gradually building up to an hour or more each day. Utter prayers in the morning upon waking up and in the evening before bed.

11- Vegetarian diet- Raw[4] (at least 50%-65% if possible), fruits, nuts and dairy products (natural-organic if possible) for the advanced. This diet should not be attempted when there is mental agitation from the environment

---

[4] Authors note: In all situations of life, the preferred method of making changes is gradual and steady. However, sometimes "mother nature" has his/her own wisdom about what is best for each individual and one may find themselves plummeted into a challenging situation. Where changes in diet, cleansings and fasts are concerned, the best procedure is to know as much as possible about one's body and its needs and proper cleansing procedures, then to seek competent help from a natural nutrition or herbal professional who can monitor your progress, especially during the initial cleansing period and during fasts. Due to a life of excess or simply by consuming a modern diet with reduced mineral and vitamin content (due to over-farming) and replete with preservatives and pesticide residues, the body may

or if one must carry out worldly duties which require a lot of physical strain. It should be looked upon as a ritual diet for those who can seclude themselves from the stresses of the world, preferably under the guidance of a spiritual preceptor. Otherwise a healthy vegetarian diet will be adequate for normal spiritual development. Heavy foods such as overly cooked foods and meats are poisonous to the body and produce aggressive, agitated mental tendencies. Overcooking tends to destroy the chemical constitution of the food in such a way that the body rejects it as a foreign substance (poison); toxic conditions may arise over a short time or over long periods. Change slowly, even if it's only to one vegetarian meal per week. The secret of success in the spiritual discipline lies in slow but incremental change in a set program. Also do not eat to excess (more than is required to sustain the body. If you normally overeat, change by eating one teaspoonful less per meal until you eat two thirds or three quarters of the normal serving. Never forget that since all beings are evolving at different levels, needs will vary according to the individual. Therefore, we must be the final judge of what is best for ourselves based on our own knowledge of nutrition and of our bodies. The latter comes from living a life style which allows one "listen" to the body so that one may be in tune with its needs. This requires a reflective, caring and honest way of being with respect to one's own life. It would not be worthwhile to change a diet to health foods only to increase the stress level and agitate the mind in other areas.   One must always practice MAAT, seeking the balance in all things. If foods or other ingested substances are not in line with mental balance, this may be a signal that they are against MAAT.

12- Wake up with the sun (RA)- The body is *"of the earth"* so it follows certain physical laws. Keep it in harmony with these to promote health and consistency.

13- Go to bed with the moon (Aset)- Same as above.

14- Do not use drugs or alcohol- The body is a machine through which the spirit energy (consciousness) flows, much like electricity through electrical wires. If the wires are damaged, the electricity (spirit) cannot operate properly. The desire for happiness and liberation of the spirit manifests as a desire of the spirit to expand beyond the confines of the body and life. Not knowing that this feeling can be accomplished through meditation, or not having enough will to apply themselves, some people seek the feeling of *"blissful freedom"* through drug use and abuse. Drug use causes the temporary disconnection of the spirit (consciousness) and the body but it also causes critical damage to the brain and nervous system and further, the drug induced experience is unpredictable and uncontrollable, thus causing more illusions and mental agitation in the mind along with physical dependence. The best way to achieve true bliss and ecstasy is to train one's own mind to reach those levels of consciousness. This process may be accomplished through the practice of virtuous living and meditation. In this manner the process may be accomplished at will and the process will be integrated into the psyche, therefore avoiding the mental or physical imbalances of drug abuse.

15- Cultivate contentment- You will be surprised at the number of things you can do without. Unnecessary wants and cravings agitate the mind.

16- Keep a diary- Stick to a spiritual routine. The diary will help you understand yourself better. Do not show it to those who are not initiated into the teachings.

17- Do not speak too much on spiritual matters- Too much debating causes mental agitation; also, those who are not ready to understand the teaching may consider you insane. *"Speak to those who understand you."*

18- If at all possible, keep company and study under a spiritual preceptor- Guru, Swami, Monk, Sage, etc. If this is not possible, develop the faculty of meditation and ask for intuitional assistance from your own BA (Spirit, Higher Self) or from Gods and Spirits (Neters, Angels); it is their function to help those who ask with sincerity and honesty.

---

develop toxic conditions and upon cleansing, may exhibit toxic reactions not unlike those of a drug addict in the state of withdrawal. In the short term, the body may become extremely ill during cleansing. This condition is usually a temporary phase and can be overcome through continued therapy and correct living. For further information consult the book Kemetic Diet..

19- Do work that is in keeping with your personality, goals and aspirations- When pursuing a career or job, pursue something you love to do, do it well and enjoy it passionately in a detached manner. By fulfilling one's worldly duties in a manner that is personally rewarding, other windows to expanded consciousness will open because one will live vibrantly, always searching to be better, always expanding, always growing. Statistics prove that the leading cause of death in the modern world is job and life dissatisfaction which leads to the hour of the week in which more people die of strokes and heart attacks than at any other time being: <u>Mondays at 9 A.M.</u> Be passionate but detached. Always be ready to let go and follow a higher calling since one's earthly activities are only a means to the end and not the end in themselves.

Selected Egyptian Proverbs and Teachings.

From: The Stele of Abu:

"Be chief of the mysteries at festivals (practice of Yoga), know your mouth, come in peace (Hetep), enjoy life on earth but do not become attached to it, it is transitory."

Attachment can be described as: any feeling which emotionally ties one to or causes desire for an object, including persons, places and things. The erroneous premise which manifests as attachment is the idea that happiness comes from something outside of oneself. Thus, we act in ways that we think will bring or hold objects close to us, which we think will bring us happiness, forgetting that WE are GOD and that GOD is everywhere and in all things. Therefore, in this World of constant gain and loss, we cannot own or hold anything, rather we must realize that we are supremely full, we are everything and since all is GOD, nothing is really being gained or lost. In situations of prosperity as well as in situations of adversity, we are ever full. Recall the teaching of Djehuti: *"As Above, So Below."*

Actions which are characterized by a feeling of attachment (described above) are detrimental to spiritual attainment and to the enjoyment of life because such actions invariably lead to disappointment, disillusionment and mental anguish (agitation). For example, if one engages in an act for the purpose of pleasing someone else or even to please oneself with the idea of deriving some benefit from the person or situation, be it material or psychological, one is leaving one's feeling of contentment and happiness open to the whims of others or to chance. In this example, one is <u>attached</u> to outside factors as determiners for one's mental state.

In this world of relativity, it is certain that every situation will not be pleasing or in keeping with our every expectation. Therefore, if one's intent is to achieve a state of equanimity (Maat), then one must strive to find the balance within one's own heart (mind) because this is the only factor which one can truly control: one's perceptions and reactions. One must understand that ultimately, one is the ruler of one's own self. That self is identical with all existence, and is supremely full and therefore, has no need for outside approval, validation or fulfillment. Our ignorance of this fact leads us to make our happiness dependent on factors outside of ourselves.

Through the incorporation of the teachings in our daily activities and by incorporating the practice of reflection and meditation, it is possible to intuitively discover this fact. One who understands this teaching would act because he or she wants to out of the "goodness" of their heart, not because they are looking for happiness by making others happy or by expecting something in return from them; these factors are always variable and therefore illusory. Since all is the Self, when one acts in the interest of others or the world, one is acting for oneself. In this manner, actions in the world may be undertaken with full responsibility for one's own actions. One's contentment with oneself and one's acceptance of one's actions as virtuous and the relinquishment of the outcomes, favorable or not, leave no room for mental agitation or anguish. Thus, full enjoyment of the world and happiness are best achieved with a mental attitude of detachment, living in a way which promotes purity of heart: decreasing mental disturbance (agitation) and increasing peace.

EGYPTIAN YOGA VOLUME 1

From The Stele of Djehuti-Nefer:

"Consume pure foods and pure thoughts with pure hands, adore celestial beings, become associated with wise ones: sages, saints and prophets; make offerings to GOD."

The association with sages (Good Association) is seen as a primary way to accelerate one's spiritual development. In India the process is known as *"Satsanga."*

On Ignorance

"The wickedness of the soul is ignorance; the virtue of the soul is knowledge."

"Who is it that affirms most boldly? Who is it that holds his opinion most obstinately? Ever they who hath most ignorance; for they also have most pride."

Ignorance is the root of all evil, pain and suffering, therefore, the end of ignorance is the main goal of the teachings.

On Pain

"As joy is not without its alloy of pain, so neither is sorrow without its portion of pleasure."

All high philosophical systems deal with the question of suffering. If viewed honestly, all facets of life are seen to be full of suffering; even those situations which appear to be joyous eventually lead one to the pain of disappointment when it is not possible to maintain them or to repeat them when one wishes to do so. Therefore, pleasurable situations, when not experienced with philosophical insight, lead to further mental agitation (pain). Egyptian philosophy states that the cause of pain and suffering is due to ignorance, ignorance of one's true self. In Indian Philosophy, the idea of pain is categorized into three causes and the chains of pain. In reality we are spirits but we suffer pain because:

Three causes of pain:

1- Pain caused from one's own body and mind (physical/mental diseases, one's own actions).
2- Pain caused by others.
3- Pain caused by acts of GOD (hurricanes, earthquakes).

The Chains of pain:

1-We come into a physical body.
2-We come into a body because there is mental agitation.
3-There is agitation because there is desire caused by attachments and hatred, you either want something or hate something else (never at peace).
4-There are attachments and hatred in the mind because the ego is in control (sense of duality). You do not see that everything is GOD so you like some things or hate others. This leads to mental agitation.

5- The ego is in control because you identify with it and you believe it is real and it has real desires for objects of the world as if they really exist.
6-The ego-personality exists because of ignorance. The soul ignorantly identifies with the ego-personality and its wants and desires and in so doing, suffers along with it. To remove pain from life it is necessary break the chain of pain which has ignorance at its root.

On Suffering

"Suffering in search of truth gives true meaning to the truth."

𓂋𓏤𓄿𓇋𓆓𓈖𓏏𓅓𓊪𓂝𓅓𓄿𓅱𓊪𓇳𓏤𓄿𓂋𓏭𓊪𓇯𓏏𓇳𓆓𓏤

"To suffer, is a necessity entailed upon your nature, would you prefer that miracles should protect you from its lessons or shalt you repine, because it happened unto you, when lo it happened unto all? Suffering is the golden cross upon which the rose of the Soul unfolds."

On Humility

"HUMILITY is a greater virtue than defying death; it triumphs over vanity and conceit; conquer them in yourself first!"

Cultivating humility is a way to control your ego; the Ba cannot dwell in a mind full of itself.

Law of Cause and Effect (Karma)

"Everything we do is sowing, and all of our experiences are harvests."

"Every cause has its Effect; every Effect has its Cause; everything happens according to Law; Chance is a name for Law unrecognized; there are many planes of causation, but nothing escapes the Law."

"O think not, bold man, because thy punishment is delayed, that the arm of God is weakened; neither flatter thyself with hopes that the Supreme winketh at thy doings; Its eye pierces the secrets of every heart, and remembered are they for ever..."

On Moodiness and Depression

"To change your mood or mental state, change your vibration."

"To destroy an undesirable rate of mental vibration, concentrate on the opposite vibration to the one to be suppressed."

"What is the source of sadness, but feebleness of the mind? What gives it power but the want of reason? Rouse yourself to the combat, and it quits the field before you strike."

Right Action Maat-Meskhenet Yoga (Karma Yoga)

"Be industrious, let thine eyes be open, lest thou become a beggar, for the man that is idle cometh not to honor."

"If Mind and Divine Speech are used as meant, you will not differ from the immortals in any way."

"The way to gain a good reputation is to endeavor to be what you desire to appear."

"Seek to perform your duties to your highest ability, this way your actions will be blameless."

"There is no life for the soul except in knowing, and no salvation but doing."

"Give thyself to GOD, keep thou thyself daily for God; and let tomorrow be as today."

On Listening

"The lips of Wisdom are closed, Except to the ears of Understanding."

"They who hear are beloved of GOD. Hearing creates good will. Hearing the voice of FATHER-MOTHER GOD requires silence of the body and of the mind."

"Hear the words of prudence, give heed unto her counsels, and store them in thine heart; her maxims are universal, and all the virtues lean upon her; she is the guide and the mistress of human life."

On Forgiveness

"If you are angered by a misdeed, then lean toward a man on account of his rightness. Pass over the misdeed and don't remember it, since GOD was silent to you on the first day of your misdeed."

"Why seeketh thou revenge, O man! With what purpose is it that thou pursuest it? Thinkest thou to pain thine adversary by it? Know that thou thyself feelest its greatest torments."

"Be always more ready to forgive, than to return an injury; they who watch for an opportunity for revenge, lieth in waste against themselves, and draweth down mischief on their own head."

"The root of revenge is in the weakness of the Soul; the most abject and timorous are the most addicted to it."

"One cannot force another to grow beyond their capacity."

Non-violence

"If you meet a disputant who is more powerful than you, fold your arms and bend your back. Confrontation will not make them agree with you. Disregard their evil speech. Your self control will match their evil utterances and people will call them ignoramuses."

On Change

"Change is Lord of the Universe."

"Nothing rests, everything moves; everything vibrates."

Readiness to Grow Spiritually

"When the ears of the student are ready to hear, then come the lips to fill them with wisdom."

"When the student is ready, the master will appear."

"Those who understand or believe will be persecuted and ridiculed."

"The lips of the wise are as the doors of a cabinet; no sooner are they opened, but treasures are poured out before you. Like unto trees of gold arranged in beds of silver, are wise sentences uttered in due season."

Double Nature of the Human Being

"Humankind is the sole animal that is twofold. One part is simple: the human "essential", as say the Greeks, but which we call "the form of the divine similitude". Humankind is also fourfold: that which the Greeks call "hylic", which we call "cosmic."

"Twain are the forms of food-for soul and body, of which all animals consist... Some are nourished with the twofold form, while others with a single... Their soul is nourished by the ever-restless motion of the Cosmos; their bodies have their growth from foods drawn up from the water and the earth of the inferior world."

"GOD hath made Humankind of soul and body-that is, of an eternal and a mortal nature; so that an animal thus blended can content the dual origin-admire and worship things in heaven, and cultivate and govern things on

earth... For it is plain that Humankind could not have sustained the strain of both, unless formed out of both natures, so as to be able to possess the powers of cultivating earthly things and loving Heaven."

Balance and Harmony

"Harmony is the union of opposites."

"In all thy undertaking, let a reasonable assurance animate thy endeavors; if thou despair of success, thou shalt not succeed."

"Everything flows out and in; everything has its tides; all things rise and fall; the pendulum-swing manifests in everything; the measure of the swing to the right is the measure to the left; rhythm compensates."

On Talking

"Speak not too much, for men are deaf to the man of many words; be silent rather, then shalt thou please, therefore speak not. Before all things guard thy speech, for a man's ruin lies in his tongue. The body is a storehouse, full of all manner of answers. Choose therefore the right one and speak well, and let the wrong answer remain imprisoned in thy body."

"Maligning others is abhorred by the KA."

"Words cannot give wisdom if they stray from the truth."

"Don't repeat slander nor should you even listen to it. It is the spouting of the hot bellied. Just report a thing that has been observed, not something that has been heard secondhand. If it is something negligible, don't even say anything. He who is standing before you will recognize your worth."

"If you are among the people, gain your supporters by building trust. The trusted are those who do not speak the first thing to come to mind; and they will become leaders. If people of means have a good name, and their face is benign, people will praise them even without their knowledge. Those whose hearts obey their bellies, however, ask for contempt instead of love. Their hearts are naked. Their bodies are unanointed. The great hearted are a gift from God. Those who are ruled by their appetites belong to the enemy."

"Proceed not to speak or to act before thou hast weighed thy words, and examined the tendency of every step thou shalt take; so shall disgrace fly far from you, and in thy house shall shame be a stranger; repentance shall not visit you, nor sorrow dwell upon thy cheek in this or many lives to come."

"Put a bridle on thy tongue; set a guard before thy lips, lest the words of thine own mouth destroy thy peace...On much speaking cometh repentance, but in silence is safety."

Opposites in Creation

"Man is separated into Soul and Body, and only when the two sides of his senses agree together, does utterance of its thought conceived by mind take place."

"Gender is in everything; everything has its Masculine and Feminine Principles; Gender manifests on all planes."

"Evil as well as good, both operate to advance the Great Plan."

"To have peace there must be strife; both are part of the structure of the world and requirements for the instruction of the children of GOD."

"Everything is dual; everything has poles; everything has its pair of opposites; like and unlike are the same; opposites are identical in nature, but different in degree; extremes meet; all truths are but half- truths; all paradoxes may be reconciled."

Will and Resolution

𓉈𓃀𓂋𓆑𓏏𓄿 𓈖𓄿𓂻 𓇋𓏤𓈖𓏏𓂀𓈖𓂝𓈖𓏌𓈖 𓈖𓆓𓂝𓈖𓄿 𓂝𓏏 𓈖𓏤

"Beware of irresolution in the intent of thy actions, beware of instability in the execution; so shalt thou triumph over two great failings of thy nature."

"Complacency, regret and sorrow are the discouragers from evil; know that ye are Gods with a divine destiny, discouragers are transient distractions leading away from the path of light."

"Be thou incapable of change in that which is right, and men will rely upon you. Establish unto thyself principles of action; and see that thou ever act according to them. First know that thy principles are just, and then be thou inflexible in the path of them."

"Those who gave you a body, furnished it with weakness; but The ALL who gave you Soul, armed you with resolution. Employ it, and thou art wise; be wise and thou art happy."

"The greatest bounties given to us are, judgment and will; happy are they who misapply them not."

Divine Nature of Man and Woman

𓏭𓏭𓏭 𓀭 𓁀𓁀 𓅆 𓀠 𓏭𓏭𓏭

"Gods are immortal men, and men are mortal Gods."

"Something is added to you unlike to what thou see; something animates thy clay higher than all that is the object of thy senses. Behold, what is it? Thy body remains STILL matter after IT is fled, therefore IT is no part of it; IT is immaterial, therefore IT is accountable for its actions."

On Learning

"They who grasps the truth of the Mental Nature of the Universe are well advanced on The Path to Self Mastery."

"Because the Begetter of all things consists of Life and Light, whereof Humankind is made. If, therefore, a Human shall learn and understand the nature of Life and Light, then shall the Human pass into the eternity of Life and Light."

"Learn that the advantage lieth not in possessing good things but in knowing the use of them."

"Every gesture, is a world to be mastered."

"Everything is a teacher."

"The self chooses the proper instruction for self."

"Beware of falsehoods from misunderstood teachings."

"The study of nature is the first rung on the ladder to greater understanding."

EGYPTIAN YOGA VOLUME 1

"Disregarding the absurd or unorthodox may mean a lost chance to understand the universal laws."
⯈—⎯‖▪◗⩑⟙▢◗◜◗⩑⬥➔‖▬⎯

On Sacrifice

⯈—⧄ ⧵ ▮⟜▬◜⠿⬤⎯◜ ▬⠿⠿ ⧵⬝⬝◟⯈◜⎯⧵◜◜▢◜⫶‖⧅⧵◗⬥◜‖ ■◜⧄⧵ ‖■▢◜

"Sacrifice protects the spirit from the pursuit of physical gratification."

"Sacrifice the first portions of the harvest, that your strength and faith to bring about what you desire may be increased; give the FIRST portion, to avoid danger of worldly indulgence; Give that you may receive. Fulfill the requirements of the universal law of equilibrium"

On Transcending the Ego

"Self sacrifice annihilates the personality."

"On the journey to the truth, one must stay on the path of love and enlightenment, the heart filled with greed and lust will be overcome by its selfishness."

On Temptation

"It is more difficult to be well with riches, than to be at ease under the want of them. Man governs himself much easier in poverty than in abundance."

On Simplicity

"The nature of the body is to take delight and pleasure in complexity; the way of truth is that of simplicity."

"Complexity is the decadence of society; simplicity is the path of reality and salvation."

On Past Lives

"The Race is never taught, but when God willeth it, its memory is restored by the Creator. You will see within yourself the Simple Vision brought to Birth by the compassion of God; no one can be saved before Rebirth."

On Knowledge and Wisdom

"They know themselves; they know the Cosmos as well."

"True knowledge comes from the upward path which leads to the eternal Fire; error, defeat and death result from following the lower path of worldly attachment."

On Dishonesty

"Do not conspire against others. GOD will punish accordingly. Schemes do not prevail; only the laws of GOD do. Live in peace, since what GOD gives comes by itself."

Honesty

"The blessings of thy eternal part are health, vigor, and proportion. The greatest of these is health. What health is to the body, even that is honesty to the Soul." ⚲⟟⌐

Argument and Confusion

"They who know self, good and pious are, and still while on earth, divine. They will not say much nor lend their ear to much. For those who spend time in arguing and hearing arguments, doth shadow fight. God is not to be obtained by speech or hearing."

Drugs

"Oh that thou did understand that wine is an abomination."

NETER

"NETER is in the self or nowhere else, if it is found in the self, it will be found EVERYWHERE."

Hatred, Envy, Hypocrisy, Deceit, Ambition

"The heart of the envious is gall and bitterness; his tongue spits venom; the success of his neighbor breaks his rest. He sits in his cell repining; and the good that happens to another, is to him an evil. Hatred and malice feed upon his heart, and there is no rest in him."

"An envious person wax lean with the fatness of their neighbors. Envy is the daughter of pride, the author of murder, the beginner of secret sedition, and the perpetual tormentor of virtue. Envy is the filthy slime of the soul; a venom, a poison, or quicksilver which consumes the flesh, and dries up the marrow of the bones."

"Attribute not the good actions of others to bad causes: thou cannot know their heart; but the world will know by this that thine is full of envy."

"The heart of the hypocrite is hid in his breast; he masks his words in the semblance of truth, while the business of his life is only to deceive."

"The ambitious will always be first in the crowd; pressing forward, looking not behind. More anguish is it to their mind to see one before them, than joy to leave thousands at a distance."

On Revenge

"Think not thou art revenged of thine enemies when thou slay them; thou put them beyond thy reach, thou give them quiet, and take from thyself all means of hurting them."

"There is nothing so easy as to revenge an offense; but nothing is so honorable as to pardon it."

On Contentment

"To be satisfied with little is the greatest wisdom; and they that increase their riches, increase their cares; but a contented mind is a hidden treasure, and trouble find it not."

"An immoderate desire of riches is a poison lodged in the mind. It contaminates and destroys everything that was good in it. It is no sooner rooted there, than all virtue, all honesty, all natural affection, fly before the face of it."

Contentment is a difficult feeling to develop because we mostly spend our time thinking about what we need to accomplish in the future or what we did or didn't do in the past. Other times we worry about what might happen in the future or regret what happened in the past. Sometimes we worry about what someone else is doing or not doing (why can't they just listen to me?, I know the best way! etc.), or what disastrous mistakes were made. Upon closer investigation, all attainments of a worldly nature occur in the realm of relative reality. Therefore, all worldly accomplishments, regardless of their far reaching or minute consequences, are bound to a sure end and will eventually be forgotten as the pages of history turn. Even those who appear to have had the greatest impact on the world have faded into the mist of history. Therefore, it must be clear that ALL worldly attainments are only pursuits of a mental illusion if they are pursued from an egotistical psychological outlook. More important than "what" we do is "how" we do it. Are we working to achieve *"purity of heart",* the virtue and mental peace which comes from *"washing the heart"* (see page 189).

The ego places importance on what it accomplished in the past or what "needs" to be accomplished in the future, not realizing the illusoriness of its desires. The person whose spirit identifies with the ego driven mind will believe that achievements in the realm of time and space (relative reality) are "really real", thus placing mental thinking time either into the future or the past. Consequently, a form of "automatic consciousness" develops in which the "present moment" is lost.

The present moment is where spiritual development best occurs. It is also where life may be lived most fully. Those who do not live in the present wake up one day after 10, 20, 30 or 40 years on a job, ready to retire, wondering "where did my life go?" Shortly thereafter they die, having spent their last few years regretting what they did not do or should have done with their lives.

A poor person worries about getting money and possessions whereas a rich person worries about losing them. Neither one has mental peace. Therefore, it is not one's circumstances that determines whether or not one has mental peace, but it is one's attitude in dealing with circumstances that is the crucial factor in achieving mental peace and contentment.

Contentment is only possible when the mind is freed from illusions about the past and the future. When the mind finally realizes that the "past" and the "future" really do not exist, then it will be possible for it to explore the "eternal present moment", for as modern physics concurs with ancient philosophy, time as well as space are dependent on the consciousness of the individual perceiver. Therefore, a minute for one person could be a year for another, depending on their conscious perception. Ancient philosophy states that time along with all other things in the realm of "time and space" are illusions created by our own consciousness. They are relative realities. What is normally called "time" or what seems to be the passage of time is nothing but an interval of eternity, a segment which the mind chooses to call an interval and therefore construct the idea of "the passing of time."

Wars, regardless of whether they are between the sexes, races or countries, are external reflections of the inability of those involved to sublimate their egos, to conquer their enemy (hate) within themselves. Thus, instead of doing battle with one's own fears and moral failings, the battle is externalized. Others are blamed for one's problems. One who is on the spiritual path must understand that the physical world is different for each person who is not enlightened because they use their mind instead of their heart to perceive reality. Therefore, a situation which may be pleasurable for one person may be painful for another. Thus, if the ego-personality dominates a persons perceptions of reality, that person will be living in their own world. In addition, it must be understood that our experiences in the physical world are based on our internal state of spiritual development (state of wisdom consciousness).

If we are currently unhappy with the state of the world (external) because of crime, war, pollution, hatred, etc., then we must search ourselves to be sure we are trying to eliminate those negatives within ourselves. We need to evaluate the purity of our thoughts (a form of spiritual food). As we purify our minds, our bodies will become purified as well. From there we will affect all that we come in contact with, thereby becoming a true point of light in the universe.

This transformation will be reflected in our mentations (thoughts, desires, feelings) and therefore, in our actions. Thus, having conquered the true enemies (ego-personality, selfishness, ignorance, etc.) within our minds, there will be no need or desire to conquer or hoard external objects or persons since we now know these to be nothing but our very selves.

All that truly exists is eternity. The best way to realize this is to reflect on the teachings just given and to promote "mindfulness" in every area of one's life, to live more and more in the present moment, and then to constantly meditate on this great truth. Contentment is for now and always, not for tomorrow or when "I accomplish this or that" or when "I get this or that." Contentment also means feeling satisfied with oneself and with what one is, what one has at the present moment with supreme thankfulness and peace, but it does not mean that achievements should not be pursued or plans made. Living in the present simply means being happy now, working now, enjoying now, having peace now and letting the future unfold. It means accepting the outcome of actions whatever they may be without resentment or remorse, realizing that one is always doing one's best and only one's best is expected and demanded by life. Thereafter, whether the project is successful or not is up to NETER.

On Wisdom

"Wisdom is a child of training; Truth is the child of Wisdom and Love."

"Death comes when the purpose of living is fulfilled; death shows what the reason for living was."

"Scorn also to depress thy competitor by any dishonest or unworthy method; strive to raise thyself above them by excelling them; so shall thy contest for superiority to be crowned with honor, if not with success."

"If the social order judges success by material gain, the most successful will be the most corruptible and selfish."

"Accurate reckoning (mathematics), the entrance into the knowledge of all existing things and all obscure secrets."

"If you meet a disputant who is not your equal or match, do not attack, they are weak. They will confound themselves. Do not answer the evil speech and give in to your animal passion for combat by venting your self against them. You will beat them through the reproof of the witnesses who will agree with you."
"What is the pay for titles, but flattery? How doth man purchase power but by being a slave to him who giveth it?"

"Magic is knowledge and strength; without strength, nothing worthwhile can be achieved, without knowledge, strength is uncontrolled."

"As above, so below; as below, so above."

"True wisdom is less presuming than folly. The wise person doubts often, and changes his mind; the fool is obstinate, and doubts not; knowing all but their own ignorance."

"The wise person feeds the KA with what endures, so that it is happy with that person on earth. The wise is known by his or her wisdom. The great are known by their wisdom."

"The wise wake up early to their lasting gain while the fool is hard pressed."

"All that exists on earth is an incarnation of the real essence from the non-material realm."

"Courage, will, knowledge and silence are essential qualities for those on the path of perfection."

"They who began to benefit from words of wisdom while they were children shall prosper in their affairs."

EGYPTIAN YOGA VOLUME 1

Controlling the Emotions and Senses

The Gods of the senses on the boat of Ra: At the Helm is Heru signifying that the soul who is in control of the senses will be the helmsman of the boat of his or her own destiny.

Setem	**Maa**	**Hu**	**Saa**
Hearing	Sight	Taste and	Understanding
		Godly food.	Knowledge
		Pure food.	Feeling/Touch

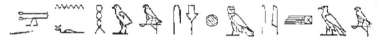

In the pyramid texts of Unas it is stated: *"Unas has taken possession of Saa and Hu".* **Saa protects us with mystical, magical powers bestowed by true understanding which lead to wisdom:** *"DJEHUTI"*
Wisdom bestows control over ones *Shai* **(Fortune) and** *Renenet* **(ability to reap one's fortune) and therefore one's** *Meskhenet* **(Destiny - Karma). One's destiny depends on one's** *WISDOM!*

Shai	*Renenet*	*Meskhenet*

The control of emotions must be understood as a practical as well as spiritual reality. As long as the physical form exists, there will be emotions and desires. The teaching of self control does not imply that emotions are not felt and experienced, even by a highly advanced Sage. However, it does imply that those feelings and emotions whose source is the physical form (body) are understood to be something separate from the innermost self. As an actor portrays a character and yet is separate from the character in reality, so too the Sage understands that the body and mind react to the environment. The soul of the Sage "acts" through the physical form. Therefore, emotions and responses are viewed with dispassion at all times. This is not to say that a highly advanced person who identifies with the spirit may not seek to fulfil certain desires of the body, i.e. eating, exercising or sleeping, since at this point these would be in accord with the higher self (divine will): taking care of the temple of the spirit (the body). If for some reason, the desire or pursuit does not fructify (come to fulfillment), it would be of no loss to the Sage. Whereas the ordinary person usually laments and engages in mental anxiety over the failure of a particular project or at the loss of an object of desire, the sage would view both positive and negative outcomes in the same way, with dispassion and contentment. This is possible because the Sage is supremely happy and fulfilled through the identification with the spirit instead of with the body (matter) and with the physical objects of desire which can never lead to supreme fulfillment. The Sage exists in the world for the sake of carrying out the divine will and therefore, experiences the world as a form of recreation. In Indian philosophy, the term "Leela" or divine sport is used to describe the Sage's attitude toward the world. For a Sage it is only at the time of death that the emotions and physical responses end. At the time of death, the person who has controlled the mind and reached the understanding of spiritual reality and identification with it (Sage, Saint) will not be led to experiences of hell or heaven which lead the soul back to earth in search of fulfillment of desires. The Sage will *"merge with the Sundisk"* and dissolve into the infinite and eternal ocean of existence: GOD.

"By keeping in subjection the belly, thou wilt be listened to. If thou hast eaten three loaves of bread, and hast drunk two vessels of beer, if you are not full contend against greediness."

"If you want to have perfect conduct, to be free from evil, then above all guard against the vice of greed. Greed is a grievous sickness that has no cure. There is no treatment for it. It embroils fathers, mothers and the brothers of the mother. It parts the wife from the husband. Greed is a compound of all the evils; a bundle of all hateful things. That person endures whose rule is rightness, who walks a straight line, for that person will leave a legacy by such behavior. On the other hand, the greedy has no tomb."

"Do not be greedy in the division of things. Do not covet more than your share. Don't be greedy toward your relatives. A mild person has a greater claim than a harsh one. Poor is the person who forgets their relatives; they are deprived of their company. Even a little bit of what is wanted will turn a quarreler into a friendly person."

"Things subject to birth abound in passions, birth in itself being passable. But where there's passion, nowhere is there Good; and where is Good, nowhere a single passion. For where is day, nowhere is night; and where is night, day is nowhere."

"When emotions are societies objective, tyranny will govern regardless of the ruling class."

"They who abandon the body's senses, know themselves to be Light and Life. The Joy from Knowledge allows room only for the Good; in them Righteousness and Bliss have their firm seat; unrighteousness and sorrow will flee away to them who give it room."

" Conceal your heart, control your mouth. Beware of releasing the restraints in you; Listen if you want to endure in the mouth of the hearers. Speak after you have mastered the craft."

"When you answer one who is fuming, turn your face and control yourself. The flame of the hot hearted sweeps across everything. But those who step gently, their path is a paved road. Those who are agitated all day have no happy moments, but those who amuse themselves all day can't keep their fortune."

The Cross, symbol of Time and Space

"As the whirlwind in its fury teareth up trees, and deforms the face of nature, or as an earthquake in its convulsions overturns whole cities, so the rage of an angry person throws mischief around them."

"Associate not with a passionate man, nor approach him in conversations; Leap not to cling to such a one, that t he terror carry you not away."

"Indulge not thyself in the passion of Anger; it is whetting a sword to wound thine own breast, or murder thy friend."

"Passions and irrational desires are ills exceedingly great; and over these GOD hath set up the Mind to play the part of judge and executioner."

"Feelings are good servants but poor masters."

"When ye have served your time, and have put off the world's restraint, and freed yourselves from deathly bonds, pray that GOD may restore you pure and holy to the nature of your higher self, that is of the Divine! Those who have lived in other fashion - impiously - both is return to Heaven denied, and there's appointed them migration into other bodies unworthy of a holy soul and base...souls in their life on earth run risk of losing hope of future immortality."

"There are two roads traveled by humankind, those who seek to live MAAT and those who seek to satisfy their animal passions."

"Mastery of the passions, allows divine thought and action."

"An infant's Soul is altogether a thing of beauty to see, not yet befouled by body's passions, still all but hanging from the Cosmic Soul! But when the body grows in bulk and draweth down the Soul into its mass, then doth the Soul cut off itself and bring upon itself forgetfulness, and no more shares in the Beautiful and Good (God); and this forgetfulness becomes vice."

"If a Soul on entering in the human body persists in its vice, it neither tastes deathlessness nor share in the Good; but speeding back again it turns into the path that leads to creeping things. This is the sentence of the vicious soul."

ıⳑ▬▬◢◳⊔𓏤▬⋀𓂝✺═𐦀▬❙❙◼️◠𓏠𓃾◢▬⋗𓍢▬◼️𓅓𓏏𓏤𓆱◢▬▬◢❙𓂝𓏤△𓇯⟶▦▬•𓉼🗆◠❙𓎡◉❙◼️

𓏤◢𓏏◼️𓃾◠𓎡𓏏𓏏◠❙❙◼️▬▬◼️𓏢

"The Soul that hath no knowledge of the things that are or knowledge of their nature, is blinded by the body's passions and tossed about. The wretched Soul, not knowing what it is, becomes the slave of bodies of strange form in sorry plight, bearing the body as a load; not as the ruler but as the ruled."

"I, GOD, am present with the holy and good, those who are pure and merciful, who live piously and give up their body unto its proper death. To them, my presence becomes an aid, straightaway they gain inner vision, knowledge of all things, and win the my love by their pure lives, and give thanks, invoking the my blessings and chanting hymns, intent on the me with ardent love. It is I, who will not let the operations that befall the body work to their natural end. I'll close all the entrances, and cut the mental actions off which base and evil energies induce. Mind-less ones, the wicked and depraved, the envious and covetous, and those who murder or do and love impiety, I am far off, yielding my place to the Avenging Demon, who rusheth on them through their senses."

"It is not possible to give one's Self to the body and the bodiless, things perishable and things divine. The one who has the will to choose is left the choice of one or other; for it can never be the two should meet. And in those Souls to whom the choice is left, the waning of the one causes the other's growth to show itself."

"Do not speak words of pride, even when thou art sitting with thyself."

"Do not be proud and arrogant with your knowledge. Consult with the ignorant and wise. Truth may be found among maids at the grindstones."

"Vain and inconstant if thou art, how canst thou but be weak? Is not inconstancy connected with frailty? Avoid the danger of the one, and thou shalt escape the mischief of the other."

"The senses give the meaning from a worldly point of view; see with the spirit and the true meaning will be revealed. This is the relationship between the object and its Creator, its true meaning."

"Knowledge derived from the senses is illusionary, true knowledge can only come from the understanding of the union of opposites."

"Before such wise and philosophic ones die, they learn to renounce their senses, knowing that these are the enemies of their immortal Souls."

"To free the spirit, control the senses; the reward will be a clear insight."

"Something is added to you unlike to what thou see; something animates thy clay higher than all that is the object of thy senses. Behold, what is it? Thy body remains STILL matter after IT is fled, therefore IT is no part of it; IT is immaterial, therefore IT is accountable for its actions."

EGYPTIAN YOGA VOLUME 1

On Evil

All things in creation (matter) came from the original "ONENESS", the original NETER. All things were ONE and undifferentiated (not divided into different objects with different names and forms). NETER has "created" matter but also lives in it as its soul. The soul (part of NETER) forgets it is NETER and sees itself as an individual among many individuals. In giving rise to matter, NETER has created the illusion of duality, separation from itself. The illusion of separation gives rise to feelings such as fear, greed, hatred, and anger, because the individual believes he / she must fight for his / her survival. Since the individual does not remember that he / she is immortal and a part of all other beings, he / she develops the idea of looking out for self and of having a good time since "you only live once". This imbalance develops due to ignorance about one's spiritual nature, therefore, ignorance is the root of all evils.

NETER is the Absolute Reality which lies beyond time and space. NETER is boundlessness, formlessness, timelessness, etc. We are *NETER.* Matter exists because NETER sustains it through the qualities of material existence. Matter is subject to existence within time and space, coldness, movement, and solidification into a physical form, tending to be drawn toward its original perfect state of equilibrium which existed before the apparent duality. As such, these are divine principles that affect every "physical" object including the human body. The primordial state of our true being is spirit because the very same "matter" that is given life, owes its existence to spiritual energy (soul). In order to have worldly experience, our spirit projects or clothes itself with matter. In so doing, the spirit forgets that it is spirit and "identifies" with the matter which composes the body. Looking for fulfillment and led by desires, the spirit, now clothed in matter, acts in ways which are in accordance with the laws of matter but because it remains ignorant of the underlying spiritual reality, the laws of matter, which originally were divine, become expressed as satanic or demoniac behaviors: fear, avarice, selfishness, vanity, hatred, passion, the endless (though unfulfilling) accumulation of objects or overindulgence in sexuality.

In and of themselves, time and space are not evil, however, when the spirit becomes identified with the limited concept of time and space, evil in the form of egotistical, self centered behavior emerges. The symbol for time and space, is the cross (+). The spirit is symbolically crucified on the cross of time and space when it enters into physical form. The passion of Jesus is a symbol of the passion experienced by every soul which comes into physical form. The task therefore, is to return to the primordial state of fulfillment by spiritualizing matter, one's own body and consciousness (mind), by identifying with our spiritual nature. Evil itself provides a road to realization of its own "wrongness" because evil actions create consequences of pain, suffering and death which allow the superficial mental consciousness to awaken to its deeper divine self, and eventually to discover the true equilibrium it cannot find in the world of time and space. The human form is the only one in which consciousness can "realize" itself to be both physical and spiritual at the same time. The way to "realize" one's spiritual nature is to hold the qualities of matter and spirit in the balance (MAAT) through virtuous actions such as selfless service, non-covetousness, etc. and by "crucifying" evil ideas, feelings or intentions when they arise in the mind.

Evil goads good (positivity) out of its complacency unto strength and higher wisdom through the struggle to overcome evil.

Therefore, there is really no such thing as good or evil. These are distinctions made by the ignorant who are unaware of the interconnectedness of everything and everyone in the Universe. Through the struggle of positive versus negative, Heru and Set, Ying and Yang, Giving and Receiving, the GREAT LAW of duality dictates positive or negative consequences according to our actions in handling circumstances.

Ignorance is the sure way to EVIL, SLAVERY, DISEASE and DEATH whereas knowledge and its correct application will lead to good physical and spiritual health on this earth and beyond. Therefore, armed with this understanding, one stops wishing that evil or negativity did not exist in the world. One understands firstly, that in labeling something evil or negative, we are making a judgment based on our individual perceptions and secondly, that they exist to show the way toward correctness, justice and righteousness; rather then, seek to learn from evil the true direction and destiny of thy divine Ba (self). One can then appreciate that the universe is set up in a system wherein everything that comes into being, becomes dual. In so doing, each side, positive and negative, works with the other to complement and urge the other unto greater and greater heights.

Since in the idea of a universal whole of creation, all is connected, good and evil do not really exist. They are only terms used to denote "opposites" in creation with no "good" or "bad" connotations. The idea of good and evil is only an illusion created by our own minds so that we may discern and differentiate, in effect, that we may judge between different courses of action to thereby interact in time and space and provide for our own well being. In our usual context, negative is used to denote a bad experience while positive is used to denote a wonderful experience.

In this context, positive describes: upward, forward movement, expansion of consciousness learning lessons of life, progress, life, health, etc. Negative then becomes the opposite: complacency, contraction of consciousness, not following the universal laws, illness, death and reincarnation.

Since we are spiritual beings, all situations we encounter which may be judged by our egos as "good" or "bad", may be viewed as positive since they provide us with the opportunity to perfect our practice of self-control, discipline and wisdom in dealing with situations which evoke passion, anger, hatred, lust or even elation and exuberance. This attitude towards life will lead us to attain purity of heart and enlightenment.

In Chapter 17 line 39-42 in the *Egyptian Book of Coming Forth By Day,* the idea of matter and its relationship to the spirit and the purification process through virtuous living are explained when the initiate speaks as follows:

"I have made an end of my failings, I have removed my defects. What then is it? The separation of the corruptible matter, it is the initiate, triumphant before the Gods all. Driven away are all of the defects which belong to him. What is this then? This is the purification on the day of his new birth."

The Devil

All evil is born out of the ignorance of the mind. Due to ignorance of our true nature, we forget we really are one with all other beings. We begin to think we are individuals (egoism) who must struggle against other individuals and we develop a fear of death. Due to ignorance, we hurt others by acting in evil ways. Thus, due to ignorance we commit crimes against others, the world and ourselves. Thus, we become "evil-doers", *Devils.*

It is therefore important to be careful not to become extreme in one's thoughts, to be understanding of others and to look at the worth of each individual since there are people who engage in devilish behavior on every continent of the world. From this understanding it is perhaps possible to see a larger and more beautiful view of the world and of creation as we expand our consciousness beyond the restrictions of any particular religious doctrine to understand that devilish behavior is a factor of our degree of separation from the ONENESS, separation which is caused by our own ignorance since the oneness is always there if we only purify our hearts (minds) in order that we may perceive it (oneness) through our inner vision (Eye of Heru).

On Steadfastness

"I am steadfast, son of steadfast, conceived and born in the region of steadfastness. "

In steadfastness their is harmony, because they who remain sturdy in the application of the wisdom they have gained through knowledge, study, experience and meditation will not be affected by the emotions or the worldly conditions.

The wise (Sages, Saints) are secure (steadfast) in the knowledge of their own connection to the universe and immortality; they know that worldly things are temporal and therefore, they live with thoughts which are elevated far above the worldly reality which so many think is important enough to die for or go crazy over. They know that GOD'S plan is perfect and that there are no coincidences. They understand that all circumstances (good or bad) are illusions, so they live beyond them, unaffected by the outcomes. Their sole mission is to live within the splendor of absolute reality and to assist others who wish to achieve the same joy, the joy that is not fleeting as are the earthly pleasures, but that which is transcendental and eternal (bliss).

It is in the steadfastness of wisdom that our true essence lies, and not in bodies subject to the changes of the world. As immortal and eternal soul-spirits, we can rise above the trials and tribulations which sway most people emotionally.

In steadfastness, happiness does not depend on the world but rather on one's own connection with the CREATOR and one's own spiritual development: remembering and reclaiming one's own original essence: HERUHOOD.

In the tradition of Vedanta Philosophy from India, Lord Krishna (see Heru and Krishna) explains steadfastness as follows:

*"Just as the embodied self enters childhood, youth and old age, so does it enter another body. This does not confound a STEADFAST man."**

*From the Bhagavad Gita

Steadfastness is knowing that since ALL that exists is GOD, ONE being, there is no world of multiple objects. An enlightened being knows that even though He or She does "things," performs various actions within the world, his or her true self deep within is not the body. The spirit (BA-Soul) is the true actor. The body is a perishable illusion. In effect, anything they do in the world is interacting with the "self." Therefore, from a philosophical point of view, they really are doing nothing; thus, there is inaction (peace) in action.

If we have a conversation with someone "else" we are really having a conversation with another piece of GOD, who is US (the same *"SELF"*).

One who is steadfast in this knowledge and acts accordingly, understands that the world is "created" for GOD to interact with GOD. We are all immortal "pieces of GOD" as it were. Therefore, GOD cannot hurt or kill GOD. There is no birth or death, only a mental illusion of these exists. Those who believe in this illusion will be subject to it. Just as a person who is emotionally upset when their new car is crashed, the person who is too attached to anything in the world, including their body, is emotionally devastated at the thought of its loss. As a car may be replaced, so too our bodies are replaced through reincarnation.

This wisdom allows us to be dispassionate and detached from the objects and temptations of the world. Detachment allows the mind to be free from agitation. A mind free from agitation can engage in introspection and peace. Introspection leads us to the discovery of our innermost self: our "Heruhood."

Through peace of mind, we are able to concentrate on our worldly endeavors and on the necessary VIRTUES and QUALITIES to attain HERUHOOD.

DISCIPLINE
The WILL to pursue our aspirations, and the strength to make them a reality.

EQUANIMITY

Emotional stability that comes from maintaining a balanced mind in situations of gain or loss. The serenity of knowing one's true self at all times, first through achieving intellectual knowledge and then through direct experience.

DISPASSION and DETACHMENT
(See Love and Joy)

CONTENTMENT
You are the universe. All is inside you. What else is needed?

FEARLESSNESS
You are all, therefore you cannot be afraid of your self.

The Sage knows that the _SPIRIT, SELF OR BA_, is immortal and eternal. NOTHING that happens in the world can destroy or change it. So THERE IS NO NEED to grieve for the loss of a loved one or the loss of an object. To live and act with this knowledge as the basis of one's every day consciousness is to maintain :
STEADFASTNESS.

On Fear

"Truth protects from fear."

Fear is a natural human tendency. It is a useful tool to let us know when we are in danger or how to avoid a potentially dangerous situation. The greatest fear by far is the fear of death. The fear of death, due to ignorance of the truth, is the root of all other fears. It translates into fear of the loss of one's possessions, fear of hunger, fear of rejection, and finally, fear of exploring the darkness of one's own mind, of self discovery.

"The expectation and the fear of death torture the multitude, who do not know True Reason."

Fear is overcome through the power of wisdom, gained through learning the teachings, meditating on them and applying them in every day situations of life.

As one explores the occult (hidden) world, through introspection and meditation, one will discover that what is commonly called "DEATH" is not death at all, but just a different form of consciousness which one will experience in another part of one's spirit. Self discovery is nothing more than the exploration of the realm usually referred to by the ignorant as death. The process of this experience is apprehensive at first, but as one gradually becomes used to the experiences of lights, sounds, apparitions, leaving the body, telepathy, etc., these impressions will become part of one's subconscious as well as one's conscious mind.

The goal is to be equally comfortable in all levels of experience and existence, to be one with the Universal Soul. This process may take days, weeks, months, years or lifetimes, depending on one's level of discipline, desire, love for all things, understanding, patience, devotion to GOD and fearlessness. One of the best ways to reduce fear is to develop Faith.

On Faith

Faith comes through understanding (indirect knowledge) developed from listening, reflecting, and practicing the teachings. The intellectual understanding transforms into intuitional understanding through meditation.

You may not yet understand your experiences but you know that they point to the fact that there is something beyond the ordinary states of consciousness:

EGYPTIAN YOGA VOLUME 1

WAKING, DREAM AND DEEP SLEEP.

On Patience, Perseverance and Forgiveness.

These three ideas are important since the road is long and only those who can endure will attain the coveted goal. In gauging the progress of your spiritual discipline, DO NOT judge yourself on the basis of if you have had a "good" meditation or if you are able to understand all of the teachings or if you have acted wrongly.

There will be ups and downs in your psychological journey. Sometimes you may stop and wonder if you are "doing the right thing and if the way you feel is normal." If at all, judgment of one's progress on the spiritual path should be based upon one's emotional detachment to worldly objects including people, which allows one to experience inner peace and the ability to control one's emotions, anger in particular. You will have to forgive yourself when you do not perform up to your expectation.

Emotional detachment is not to be confused with adopting a non-caring attitude, with alienation of others or physical separation from the world. One must try one's best to perform one's duties to perfection, while separating one's self from the actions.

Detachment and dispassion are mental disciplines. What good would it do to give up all your possessions only to be upset later because you were not ready to "give it all up" or "can't believe what you have done"? Rather, develop a feeling of "*I can take it or leave it*" or "*I will be the same with or without it*" or "*success or failure depends on the Neters; it is their will.*" The idea that: "*my body is just an instrument of GOD* **(the inner, higher self)**" should be cultivated. Understand that "*I am a servant of GOD and my ego is a changeable illusion.*" Further understand "*I am one with the NETER NETERU.*" In this manner, if the project fails or succeeds, you will remain as before, calm, at peace and in control, as is the observing BA, which is who you really are anyway.

Eventually, through sustained effort, it will require no "thinking" and one will develop strength of will to "do what is MAAT (truth, justice, righteousness)." One will begin to act consciously, aware of everything one does and every motivating thought that has come into one's mind. One will "know" which thoughts are righteous and which are not.

One will learn to "tell the difference between the real and the unreal." One will see the pettiness and ignorance of war, hate, greed, racism, sexism, attachment to possessions, and attachment to people (people who are variable, changeable and who at one time may love you and later may hurt you). One will now be able to attach yourself to GOD who is everything.

"Complacency, regret and sorrow are the discouragers from Set (evil); know that ye are Gods with a divine destiny; discouragers are but transient distractions leading away from the path of light."

On Love and Joy

TRUE love and joy cannot be found in the physical world. Upon reflection, one will see that the "pursuit of happiness" in the physical world, which one is taught to pursue from one's childhood, is a mistaken concept of reality: a relative reality, an illusion.

If there was an object or person that could provide true happiness, it would have universal appeal. It would make everyone happy all the time. Reflection on this point will reveal that there is no such object or person in the Universe. The mind is so constructed that it becomes bored with the objects of the world, with people and with the pleasures of the senses. It is the deep rooted need to experience complete bliss (searching for self), which makes us want to go back and pursue the same activity or object which provided short term gratification (mental serenity), again and again. Each time we return to the source of this illusory pleasure, we convince ourselves that the experience will be "better this time." If we are unable to return to the perceived source of pleasure we then become depressed and upset (disappointed).

Upsetness constitutes agitation of the mind. Agitation of the mind prevents peace of mind from occurring. This is the painful, suffering process of life as it is referred to by the Sages.

The emotional attachment is dispelled when one realizes the wisdom of the teaching. One will become more and more DETACHED and DISPASSIONATE towards the objects of the world and towards other personalities and egos. This will allow one to have more control over one's senses and passions. Peace of mind will now be possible. One will use objects and possessions but will not be attached to them, because one will know that nothing belongs to oneself. This is easily demonstrated when someone "dies" and have to leave all of their worldly possessions behind. Ownership is really an illusion.

Peace of mind is required for listening, reflection and understanding of the teachings and the development of true love and joy. True love and joy comes from discovering that GOD is within oneself and all creation; this is the coveted goal, the reason for existence on earth. The ULTIMATE "FUN": to live on all planes of existence (physical, astral, causal and absolute) at once, in balance (MAAT). One can love all people equally, understanding and forgiving their frailties since one now understands that their search for self is what is driving them; this however, is occurring in an unconscious (ignorant) way. One is able to see when one is "looking for love in all the wrong places." For those who ask, you can provide guidance based on your level of development. You will want to share your peace and wisdom with all, but you will also understand that others have their own lessons to learn, so they can only be helped to the extent that they are ready to grow. Growth is sometimes painful, giving up one way of thinking for another, and some may not be able to change a particular habit or trait in this life time.

Joy comes from expanding our consciousness because, since our true nature is that of spirit, the spirit finds joy in exploring the spiritual realm. Pain and sorrow come from experiences of disease, weakness, inability to control one's life, feeling like a victim of circumstances (a pawn), being unable to control one's emotions and moods, etc. Once one's mind is trained to understand and accept the reality of the spiritual world, it is free to explore that world, thereby making it possible for the soul to feel true joy at experiencing the realm beyond the physical body.

Through attainment of Heruhood, you can be of the greatest service. You will "KNOW" the right thing to do or say because you will be connected to the source of all things, the Universal consciousness.

"Those who through the error of attachment love their body, abide wandering in darkness, sensible and suffering the things of death, but those who realize that the body is but the tomb of the Soul, rise to immortality."

On Silence

"Be still and solemn silence keep; then shall GOD open the way for salvation. Withdraw into thyself and Father-Mother God will come. Throw away the work of the body's senses and thy divinity will come to birth; purge from thyself the animal torments, concerns with things of matter."

"The abomination of the sanctuary of GOD is: too much talking. Pray thou with a loving heart the petitions of which all are in secret. GOD will do thy business, hear that which thou say and will accept thine offerings."

"If you meet a disputant who is your equal, you will overcome them with silence while they speak evilly. Those who witness the encounter will remark on this and your name will be held in high esteem among the great."

"Those who knoweth GOD, being filled with all good things, think Godly thoughts and not thoughts like the many think; For this cause, they who Gnostic are, please not the many, nor the many them. They are thought mad and laughed at; they are hated and despised, and sometimes even put to death."

"It is better either to be silent, or to say things of more value than silence. Sooner throw a pearl at hazard than an idle or useless word; and do not say a little in many words, but a great deal in few."

"If you are a man of worth who sits at the council of a leader, concentrate on being excellent. Your silence is much better than boasting. Speak when you know that you have a solution. It is the skilled person who should speak when in council. Speaking is harder than all other work. The one who understands this makes speech a servant."

From: The Instruction to Merikare.

" LO THE MISERABLE ASIATIC"

DURING the ninth dynasty, 3000 B.C.E., before the first Eurasian invasion of Egypt by the Hyksos, a Pharaoh passed on to his heir the following wisdom:

"Lo the miserable Asiatic, he is wretched because of the place he's in, short of water, bare of wood. Its paths are many and painful because of mountains. He does not dwell in one place. Food propels his legs. He fights since the time of Heru."

Beware of your environment. Beware of your surroundings. Harshness in surroundings and general environment can cause negative stress which could lead to an unsettled mind.

An unsettled mind is difficult to control. A mind that is uncontrollable will have difficulty in concentrating. Poor concentration will not allow for reflection. Reflection is necessary to make sense of one's situation and to gain intellectual understanding. An non-reflective, confused or "Wrong thinking" mind will have difficulty meditating.

A non- meditating mind will have difficulty in transcending the world of apparent dualities. One will be endlessly pulled into the "world" and the apparent thoughts going on in the mind.

As the mind will be caught up in the endless waves of joys and sorrows, it will be unable to find peace. A mind filled with too much joy or too much sorrow due to its experiences in the world will be equally agitated and one will have difficulty concentrating and calming down. One extreme (ex. Joy) leads to another (ex. Pain).

The concept of the *"Miserable Asiatic"* became known in Egypt as the concept of *"The Land of Heru and the Land of Set"*. Since Set is the God of the desert, the Asiatics, who dwelt in the desert lands, became identified with Set and therefore, Setian behavior (impulsive, selfish, brute force, etc.).

WRONG THINKING

Wrong thinking implies misunderstanding the nature and purpose of life. Wisdom is gained from listening, study, experience, reflection (taking out quiet time to think about what has been learned) and meditation.

Wrong thinking is characterized by a mind that thinks in a way which promotes the lower animal nature thoughts of fighting, survival, sexual overindulgence, violence, deceit, anger and greed. In the uncontrolled mind, there is an endless pursuit of sensory and worldly pleasures which are never satiated. The mind is perpetually in pursuit of a fantasy, an illusion. Thus it never finds peace. The soul that identifies with this agitated mind will also think it is agitated and thus will also not find peace. This psyche is rendered incapable of higher intellectual achievement because the mind is ever occupied with worldly, physical (survival-related) concerns.

EGYPTIAN YOGA VOLUME 1

"Searching for one's self in the world is the pursuit of an illusion."
"As you think so shall you become."
"Virtues fail that are frustrated by passion at every turn."

"As a rock on the sea shore, stand firm, and let not the dashing of the waves disturb you. Raise your head like a tower on a hill, and the arrows of fortune drop at your feet. In the instant of danger, the courage of your heart will sustain you, and the steadiness of your mind beareth you through."

"The extension of the intellect which we possess for the survey of transcendent things, is very narrow; but most ample when it shall perceive with the felicity of self-consciousness."

"The all is mind; The Universe is Mental."

"Mind, as matter, may be transmuted, from state to state, degree to degree, condition to condition, pole to pole, vibration to vibration. Transmutation is a Mental Art."

"It takes a strong disciple to rule over the mountainous thoughts and constantly go to the essence of the meaning; as mental complexity increases, thus will the depth of your decadence and challenge both be revealed."

"The secrets of the universe cannot be discovered through study and research alone but the honest search for truth and the development of a incorruptible mind qualifies the seeker for higher instruction."

On Health

𓋹𓌉𓂋

The secret of physical health is a healthy mind. A healthy mind is a peaceful mind. A peaceful mind comes through wisdom, not only knowing the truth but experiencing it. From experience of the ULTIMATE TRUTH: *NETER NETERU* (GOD), no desires or mental agitations will arise because when one experiences GOD within one's BA (soul), there is complete fulfillment of all desires. Therefore, there is now the state of supreme mental balance, *HETEP* (supreme peace).

From the scriptures...

"The body becomes what the foods are, as the spirit becomes what the thoughts are."

"If you would preserve understanding and health to old age, avoid the allurements of Voluptuousness, and fly from its temptations.... For if thou hearken unto the words of the Adversary, thou art deceived and betrayed. The joy which it promises changes to madness, and its enjoyments lead on to diseases and death."

"The blessings of thy eternal part, are health, vigor, and proportion. The greatest of these is health. What health is to the body, even that is honesty to the Soul. Develop your spirit that it may gain strength to control the body and follow the natural Laws of nutrition and hygiene."

"Her name is Health: she is the daughter of Exercise, who begot her on Temperance. The rose blusheth on her cheeks, the sweetness of the morning breathes from her lips; joy, tempered with innocence and modesty, sparkles in her eyes and from the cheerfulness of her heart she sings as she walks."

"Yield not to emotion, for there are discarnate forces around us who desire emotional existence. In the heat of passion one surrenders to the influence of these, ill health and unwise living results. Through firm instruction one can master one's emotions and these forces; in this, make them serve one. Thus the slave becomes the master."

EGYPTIAN YOGA VOLUME 1

"If you would live in harmony with yourself and the Earth you must follow the laws of the Earth. For your body is of the Earth; lest it lead your SOUL to the path of disease, death and reincarnation. The Neters **(angels)** *of the divine will desert you, and those of evil will destroy your body and your spirit."*

"The source of evil is in your body. Evil entices the body through temptation of its weakest virtue. There can be no divinity in the unclean temple not made by hands where abomination rules."

"Your spirit is of God and the Body is of Earth."

"The source of illness is the food you ingest; to purge the dreadful UKHEDU which lurks in your bowels, for three consecutive days each month purge yourself with a cattle horn, its sharp end clipped off so as to create a small opening (for water to run through)."

The four Sons of Heru

The aim of all Teachings is to effect the *"Weaving of Heru"* inside of us, that is to say, to transform ourselves into a Heru (to achieve Heruhood). Heru is sustained by his four sons, who were represented by the four viscera which were removed from the body of the deceased at the time of embalment. In order to achieve Heruhood, these organs must be maintained in good health. Modern neuro-science has discovered that all cells in our body outside of the brain and central nervous system are capable of responding to thought by producing similar chemicals as are produced in the brain. Thus they can be called "thinking cells". Therefore, the body organs and limbs are an extension of the central nervous system. In this context, the human consciousness may be taken to any part of the body by simply concentrating on that part, to direct healing forces there, to insure proper mental energy distribution on a daily basis or to gain assistance with thought processes through using every available part of one's body. Thus, by proper diet and meditation on each organ, Life Force energy will be sent to each through the power of conscious will (meditation) and insure the proper distribution of creative energies to them. The sons of Heru are:

Imset (Liver, Man)
Imset (intelligence) is the one who *"Leads his brothers"*: *Hapi, Duamutef* and *Qebbsenuf,* (who represent the animal forces). The liver has an important role in cleansing the blood and is directly connected to the ego-personality and the brain. One glass of water with fresh squeezed lime juice first thing in the morning is an excellent liver cleanser.

Duamutef (Stomach, Jackal)
Decomposition and digestion transform organic matter to give life. Thus, life comes from death. This is the seat of the Sun (Ra) located at the solar plexus.

Hapi (Lungs, Baboon)
Through the lungs, Life Force is introduced to the body along with the air we breath. This air and Life Force then enters into the heart-lung circuit wherein it is exchanged with the impurities within. Breath is life.

Qebbsenuf (Small Intestine, Hawk)
Qebbsenuf means: *"He refreshes his brothers."* The small intestines provide refreshment by modifying food material in order that it may be assimilated.

Anpu, the Jackal God, is said to be the keeper of the "secret", the "Opener of the Way" to spiritual evolution. Like the Arc of the Covenant in the Christian Bible which housed the remains of the ten commandments, Anpu sits atop (guards) the Arc which contains the organs of Asar. The object of spiritual and physical health is to be in harmony with one's organs since they will be examined by Djehuti and the other 42 judges of MAAT for righteousness and truth. Taking care of the body and eating foods that will purify the physical atoms (sanctified food) are thus of paramount importance because these have an impact on the entire vibrational aspect of the mind. Lower vibrations are dense, therefore, favoring denser thoughts. Lighter foods such as fruits and vegetables favor higher vibrations thereby producing favorable conditions upon which to raise one's mental aspect to the higher spiritual levels.

In the *PEPI I Pyramid Texts it is stated:

> *"Command the Living One, The son of Sothis (Heru),*
> *To speak for this Pepi,*
> *To establish for Pepi a seat in the Sky!*
> *Commend this Pepi to the Great Nobel,*
> *The beloved of Ptah,*
> *To speak for this Pepi,*
> *To make flourish his jar-stands on earth,*
> *For Pepi is one with these four Gods:*
> *Imset, Hapi, Duamutef, Kebhsenuf,*
> *Who live by MAAT."*

*Pepi represents the King or Queen - a perfected human being.

On The Earth

From the Egyptian Book of Coming Forth By Day, the laws of Maat on protecting the ecology:

(15) "I HAVE NOT LAID WASTE THE PLOUGHED LANDS."
(36) "I HAVE NEVER BEFOULED THE WATER."

Establishing and honoring our connection to the earth is very important both symbolically and as a matter of absolute reality. As discussed in the section entitled "Modern Physics", all creation, the land, air, water, the heavens and all life forms are really one being. It is therefore important to preserve nature because in doing so, we are preserving ourselves. Existence in physical human form is not possible without a physical location in which to interact and evolve. Keeping a small garden from which one can establish a connection with the miracle of the growth of a seed into a life sustaining plant is an excellent way to provide a connection to the earth as well as sustenance for oneself. Other benefits are obvious, independence from artificial and destructive food sources (supermarkets and non-organic farms), and a connection to the energy in the earth. It is important for one to keep elevated (Godly) thoughts in one's mind from the tilling of the soil to the consumption of the food, to ensure that it will carry the highest vibrational quality (purity).

On Recreation

Recreation is a seldom discussed topic in philosophical treatises. It is usually seen as an "activity that is performed" in order to achieve some kind of regeneration of one's physical and psychological self. Also it is seen as a source of "fun" and excitement. From a deeper investigation, the understanding of commonly accepted forms of recreation becomes inadequate because "activity" based recreational activities have built into them, the elements of disappointment. Usually they are based on competition which pits individuals or teams against each other in a format that is designed to produce and promote conflict. Upon closer investigation and understanding, it becomes clear that the mind seeks to place itself in the most "pleasurable" environment or situations possible. However, the search leads it to believe that these situations will be found in "activities" therefore, whenever it experiences something pleasurable it seeks to repeat the activity. If the activity involves "winning" a game, it is bound for disappointment since that cannot occur each time the activity is undertaken. If the times of disappointment are used for introspection, it will become obvious that there is more to life on this earth besides that which can be seen, felt, touched, heard or smelled. A whole new world opens for exploration and true recreation.

True recreation is fully conscious, detached and peaceful. Only then is it possible to "feel" and appreciate the nature of one's being, of creation itself. The highest degree of recreation is therefore experienced at the point of enlightenment, when Heruhood is realized. Here, every activity in life becomes "play". Life itself becomes a *"divine sport"*. In Indian Vedanta philosophy this concept is called *"Leela".* There develops a continuous blissful feeling which does not pass from moment to moment as with those who move from activity to activity searching for a thrill to make them "feel alive," but existence becomes eternity, right in the very present moment. As modern physics shows, time is only a mental concept people put on intervals of eternity. The only reason why we believe time actually passes is because our minds are always concerned with the past or future events and rarely with the present moment. Raising one's spiritual awareness means becoming alive in the present, the here and now (see simple meditation). Recreation becomes a means to re-create one's consciousness at every moment instead of a means to forget oneself and to pass the time.

Life problems and situations become easy to deal with regardless of what happens because you understand that your existence does not depend on them, in fact they depend on you, and furthermore, as Ra rises each morning, there is a cycle set up by the Neters so that nothing lasts for ever in the cosmos. All things good and bad progress in an endless cycle. So negative situations will eventually give way to better ones and vice versa. Thus, armed with this higher understanding, life itself becomes play in the deepest sense of the meaning. Even though externally participating in life's victories and defeats, internally one becomes a witness to life rather than a participant who is bound to the apparent reality. Mere intellectual knowledge of this is far reaching but the intuitive realization of it within one's own consciousness is beyond words.

On Relationships[5]

It should be clear by now to the reader that he or she is not the body, the mind, the senses, nor the ego-personality. Further, it must be clear that the world as our senses perceive it is not what it appears to be. At least intellectually, you must by now understand that your true identity is the spirit which is neither male nor female. Therefore, what is the nature of relationships in the physical form and what is their purpose? One must understand that GOD (one's higher self) places one in situations and relationships based on one's own Meskhenet (karmic) identity and desires. Thus, it is one's very own consciousness that draws one's relationships to one. As that consciousness changes and evolves, so too will one's relationships and karmic destiny. Thus, our destiny is not pre-determined, rather, we create it at every moment.

In coming into the physical realm and vivifying matter (the physical body), the spirit gains experience through various situations in the process called living. The spirit is continuously striving (evolving) to return to its original state of oneness (Hetep) it lost when it became attached to a physical form. The problem arises when the mind "believes" itself to be a separate entity from others and develops an ego. In forgetting itself, the spirit searches for unity, oneness (Maat, The Tao), but in believing what the mind tells it through the senses, the spirit (soul) "identifies" with that information and thereby begins to search for unity and oneness in the way the limited senses and mind have convinced it to search. Childhood is an important period in developing one's sense of identity and correct understanding about the nature of reality. The ego-personality develops desires and conjures up ideas as to how to achieve the fulfillment of those desires. Desire fulfillment is of two types, ignorant and wise.

The ignorant form of desire fulfillment is based on an erroneous understanding of the nature of one's desires and the way to resolve them. All desires arise from the need to regain the feeling of infinite bliss which comes

---

[5] For more on the mystical teachings in reference to relationships and sexuality see the book Egyptian Tantra Yoga by Dr. Muata Ashby.

from achieving unity and supreme peace. Thus, the wise form of desire is the desire to attain enlightenment. Due to identification with the mind and body, we search for fulfillment (bliss) by trying to satisfy the desires which arise in the mind and body, not understanding that the mind and body are only instruments that are to be controlled. When the spirit based desire for unity becomes confused with the physical body-sense desires, it searches for unity by establishing intimate relationships with other individuals. We become happy because the performance of sense-based activities temporarily allows us to release tension in the mind. This temporary release of mental tension (agitation) is movement toward an illusion of peace, because once the tension has built back up, we must again seek situations which will provide the same release. Sometimes, this is attained through watching television, overeating, smoking, shopping, sexual activity and drugs. For some, when the frustration level builds beyond their ability to cope, they attempt suicide or if they perceive someone is a threat to their happiness or if they harbor deep resentment toward someone from the present lifetime or a previous one, they may become violent with that person, even to the point of murder. Since this type of activity is based on an erroneous understanding, the desires were never truly met and thereby resurfaced again and again causing an endless cycle based on ignorance. The peace (release of tension) we experience is only a glimpse of what is waiting for us in the enlightened state.

For these reasons, correct understanding of reality and of one's true identity is essential in conquering one's physical-sense desires in order to determine the true needs of the soul. The soul needs to expand beyond the confines of the physical body, family relationships and the physical world. From this position of freedom it experiences true peace and fulfillment from which it can then operate most effectively and peacefully in all realms. Therefore, all relationships including marriage and family are good to the extent that they assist one in achieving the lofty goal of self discovery. Every situation (good or bad) is a potential source of fulfillment. Dispassion, detachment, study, reflection and meditation along with a wisdom oriented participation in the practical world are the ways to achieve supreme fulfillment. One must cultivate dispassionate love, giving without expecting something in return. This provides the joy and peace that cannot come from possessive (ego based) loving which leaves one open for the pain of disappointment. One's own maturity and spiritual insight must guide one in deciding which relationships to engage in and to maintain. Maat and Djehuti are the best guides.

Although seemingly a selfish venture, the pursuit of enlightenment is the most selfless process which one can engage in because if a person develops the qualities necessary to achieve the coveted goal, all who come in contact with that person will benefit. Since all human beings are in reality expressions of the one Supreme Being, the best thing an individual can do is to free him / her self from Apopis and Set (feelings of selfishness, machismo, feminism, immorality, hate, sadness, sexism, racism, etc. which are all ego based mental conditions arising from ignorance). As each individual is saved, the world is thus one step closer to salvation. Therefore, doing one's best and then relinquishing the rest to NETER is the preferred course.

In relationships as any other area of life, the keys are honesty, patience, and dispassionate love. As one who aspires to achieve the greatest goal, one must realize that the road is full of obstacles and challenges.

Relationships need to be prioritized as follows:

1- Relationship with NETER comes first. One cannot have higher level interactions if one is spiritually unfulfilled. When one discovers one's connection to the Universal BA, one's purpose in life will become clear. From this point, all other relationships will occur in harmony with this paramount priority. Otherwise, life situations will always seem to be in contradiction with one's deeper feelings and lead to constant mental unrest.

2- Relationship to a partner.

3- Relationship to family members.

4- Relationship to other members of society.

Finally, for one's own peace, it must be realized that since most relationships occur in the area of personality-ego and all are karmically based, absolute honesty and truth is not always possible despite the best efforts of the individuals. Conflicts are bound to arise in all relationships. The most important factor is how those conflicts are handled. Achieving true unity and harmony in a relationship cannot occur if the consciousness of those involved remains at an egotistical level. A consciousness which is directed to the higher reality, absolute truth, MAAT, The TAO, NIRVANA, Christ Consciousness, etc. is required. Then, all the glory and beauty which exists above may be brought down and experienced below as well. Then, the souls and the matter which they vivify can commune as one.

Egyptian proverbs on Controlling and Sublimating the Sexual Life Force into Spiritual and Psychic Energy[6]

"Be circumspect in matters of sexual relations."

"Though all men suffer fated things, those led by reason (**guided by the HIGHER INTELLECT**), *do not endure suffering with the rest; but since they've freed themselves from viciousness, not being bad, they do not suffer bad. Though having thought fornication or murder but not having committed these, the Mind-led man will suffer just as though he had committed fornication, and though he be no murderer, as though he had committed murder because there was will to commit these things."*

"Beware of a woman or man from strange parts, whose city is not known. When they come, do not look at them nor know them. They are as the eddy in deep water, the depth of which is unknown. They whose spouse is far off writes to you every day. If no witness is near her they stand up and spread out their net: O! fearful crime to listen to them! Therefore, they who are wise avoid them and take to themselves a spouse in their youth; first, because one's own house is the best thing, and secondly, because an honest spouse will present you with a child like unto thyself."

"If you want friendship to endure in the house that you enter, the house of a master, of a brother or a friend, then in whatever place you enter beware of approaching the women there. Unhappy is the place where this is done. Unwelcome is he who intrudes on them. A thousand men are turned away from their good because of a short moment that is like a dream, and then that moment is followed by death that comes from having known that dream. Anyone who encourages you to take advantage of the situation gives you poor advice. When you go to do it your heart says no. If you are one who fails through the lust of women, then no affair of yours can prosper."

"When you prosper and establish your home, love your wife with ardor. Then fill her belly and clothe her back. Caress her. Give her ointments to soothe her body. Fulfill her wishes for as long as you live. She is a fertile field for her husband. Do not be brutal. Good manners will influence her better than force. Do not contend with her in the courts. Keep her from the need to resort to outside powers. Her eye is her storm when she gazes. It is by such treatment that she will be compelled to stay in your house."

"On the journey to the truth, one must stay on the path of love and enlightenment, the heart filled with greed and lust will be overcome by its selfishness."

From the "*Egyptian Book of Coming Forth by Day*," the virtuous must be able to say:

"I have not committed adultery."

"I have not lusted or committed fornication nor have I lain with others of my same sex."

---

[6] *See the book Egyptian Tantra Yoga by Dr. Muata Ashby.*

CHAPTER 15: THE PROCESS OF TRANSFORMATION

The Scarab is the symbol of Transformation from mortal consciousness to eternal consciousness, from animal to spiritual.

"Those who have learned to know themselves, have reached that state which does transcend any abundance of physical existence; but they who through a love that leads astray, expend their love upon their body, they stay in darkness, wandering and suffering through their senses, things of anxiety, unrest and Death."

Egyptian Mystical Wisdom

On The Spiritual Path

It is critical to understand that though the spiritual path takes place in the world of relative reality, it is essentially an individual journey whereby one is led to a level of consciousness that has no friends, no pain, no fun (in the ordinary sense), no family, no television, no sex, no illusions, etc., but wherein there is a fullness of all things, complete satisfaction and contentment within one's completeness, supreme peace. There is no need to want things since one now discovers that one IS ALL THINGS. There is nothing to want and also nothing to need. Those who consciously choose the spiritual path must know that they are choosing a more rigorous life of virtue. It is far easier to give into sensual pleasures and ego desires than to live in such a disciplined way.

3 LEVELS OF STUDENTS

The Egyptian System of Mystery (Yoga) Schools had 3 levels of students:

1- The Mortals
Students who were being instructed on a probationary status, but had not experienced inner vision.

2- The Intelligences
Students who had attained inner vision and have received a glimpse of cosmic consciousness.

3- The Creators or Beings of Light
Students who had become <u>IDENTIFIED</u> with or <u>UNITED</u> with the light (GOD).

The TEN Greater Virtues

"Salvation is the freeing of the soul from its bodily fetters; becoming a God through knowledge and wisdom; controlling the forces of the cosmos instead of being a slave to them; subduing the lower nature and through awakening the higher self, ending the cycle of rebirth and dwelling with the Neters who direct and control the Great Plan."

The *"fetters"* are what bind the soul to physical existence. These are: greed, lust, passion, avarice, covetousness, intemperance, and other such behaviors which are perpetuated by ignorance. Developing a virtuous character should be of paramount importance to the spiritual seeker since it is only through this attainment that is it possible to acquire the subtlety of mind-intellect needed to grasp the higher, deeper truths of one's own existence. For this reason, the focus of aspirants is first directed to the perfection of the higher virtues which are ten in number. These should be meditated upon and practiced at all times. Once these are mastered and peace of mind is achieved, the Seven Liberal Arts (Intellectual Yoga Philosophy) are taught in order for the aspirant to master the understanding of his / her personal existence as well as the existence of creation. Then the Greater Mysteries (Higher Yoga Philosophy) about the Self are taught. The purpose of this discipline is to remove the fetters which hold the soul involved (bound) to physical existence, thus freeing it from earthly suffering and the burden of reincarnation.

The 10 VIRTUES of the Initiates:

(1)"Control your thoughts," (2)"Control your actions," (3)"Have devotion of purpose," (4)"Have faith in your master's ability to lead you along the path of truth," (5)"Have faith in your own ability to accept the truth," (6)"Have faith in your ability to act with wisdom," (7)"Be free from resentment under the experience of persecution" (8)"Be free from resentment under experience of wrong," (9)"Learn how to distinguish between right and wrong," (10)"Learn to distinguish the real from the unreal."

ADMONITIONS FOR THOSE WHO WISH TO FOLLOW THE SPIRITUAL PATH

"Learn to see clearly, learn to wish for what is just, learn to dare what your conscience dictates, learn to keep your intentions a secret, and if, despite all your efforts, today brings no more than yesterday, do not lose courage, but continue steadfastly, keeping your goal before you with determination. Onward! The SEVEN COMPANIONS of the SOUL-the planetary spirits-guard the secret key which locks the past and opens the future. Let your efforts be aimed at the CROWN of the MASTER."

A Devotee of ASET is:

"One who ponders over sacred matters and seeks therein for hidden truth."

The Veil of Aset:

"I Aset, am all that has been, all that is, or shall be; and no mortal man hath ever unveiled me."

Unveiling Aset is unveiling our true self. One must go beyond the "mortal" waking consciousness to discover (unveil) one's true nature. Through the process of:

LISTENING - REFLECTION - MEDITATION.

These may be further clarified as follows:

Awakening of the spiritual self: Becoming conscious of the divine presence within one's self.

Purgation of the self: Purification of mind and body through a spiritual discipline. The aspirant tries to totally surrender "personal" identity or ego to the divine inner self which is the Universal Ba of all life. *Union* with the divine self. The divine marriage.

Illumination of the intellect: Experience and appreciation of the divine presence during reflection and meditation.

Mind Control though Wisdom:
"Thinking, understanding, reasoning, willing, call not these Soul! They are its actions, but they are not its essence."

STUDY, PATIENCE, DETACHMENT AND DISPASSION are the keys that open the way to control of the mind.

The teaching is not salvation. What you do with "it" determines your salvation or bondage to birth and death. Beyond the teaching lies salvation. It cannot be gained through thought alone, that is, it cannot be achieved by thinking. It must be known by intuition!

KNOW THYSELF: (The Supreme Good)

"The purpose of all human life is to achieve a state of consciousness apart from bodily concerns."
"Man is to become God-like through a life of virtue and the cultivation of the spirit through scientific knowledge, practice and bodily discipline."

"Salvation is the freeing of the soul from its bodily fetters; becoming a God through knowledge and wisdom; controlling the forces of the cosmos instead of being a slave to them; subduing the lower nature and through awakening the higher self, ending the cycle of rebirth and dwelling with the Neters who direct and control the Great Plan."

"Make your life the subject of intense inquiry, in this way you will discover its goal, direction, and destiny."

"To free the spirit, control the senses; the reward will be a clear insight."

EGYPTIAN YOGA VOLUME 1

THE WAY TO IMMORTALITY

☥

From the Ancient scriptures:

"To Know God, strive to grow in stature beyond all measure; conceive that there is nothing beyond thy capability. Know thyself deathless and able to know all things, all arts, sciences, the way of every life. Become higher than the highest height and lower than the lowest depth. Amass in thyself all senses of animals, fire, water, dryness and moistness. Think of thyself in all places at the same time, earth, sea, sky, not yet born, in the womb, young, old, dead, and in the after death state."

"Indeed they who are yonder (those who live righteously will join GOD after death), will be living Gods, punishing anyone who commits a sin. Indeed they who are yonder will stand in the boat (barque of RA) causing the choicest offerings in it to be given to the temples. Indeed he who is yonder will become a sage who will not be hindered from appealing to GOD whenever they speak."

"If you seek GOD, you seek for the Beautiful. One is the Path that leads unto GOD - Devotion joined with Gnosis."

"For the ill of ignorance doth pour over all the earth and overwhelm the soul that's battened down within the body, preventing it from finding Salvation."

"God sheds light on they who shake the clouds of Error from their soul, and sight the brilliancy of Truth, mingling themselves with the All-sense of the Divine Intelligence, through love of which they win their freedom from that part over which Death rules, and has the seed of the assurance of future Deathlessness implanted in him. This, then, is how the good will differ from the bad."

"The path of immortality is hard, and only a few find it. The rest await the Great Day when the wheels of the universe shall be stopped and the immortal sparks shall escape from the sheaths of substance. Woe unto those who wait, for they must return again, unconscious and unknowing, to the seed-ground of stars, and await a new beginning."

"Who has eaten the knowledge of every God, their existence is for all eternity and everlasting in their spirit body; what they willeth they doeth."

"If then thou learn that thou art thyself of Life and Light, and that thou only happen to be out of them, Thou shalt return again to Life."

"Unless thou first shalt hate thy Body, thou canst not love thy Self. But if thy love thy Self, thou shalt have INTELLECT, and having INTELLECT thou shalt share in the GNOSIS. GNOSIS will lead to love and love to salvation."

"The union of the Word and the Mind produces that mystery which is called Life... Learn deeply of the Mind and its mystery, for therein lies the secret of immortality."

"Anything built by humanity for its glorification will eventually fall; only that which is built according to the Great Law of the cosmos will transcend."

196

"A Soul, when from the body freed, if it has fought the fight of piety-to Know God and to do wrong to no one such a Soul becomes entirely pure. Whereas the impious Soul remains as it is, a slave to its passions, chastised through death, by its own self."

The Direct Path: Detachment and Dispassion, Wisdom and Virtue

From the scriptures:

"EMOTIONS ARE GOOD SERVANTS BUT POOR MASTERS".

"The body was created to be subservient to the Soul; while YOU afflict the Soul for the body's pain, behold YOU SET the body above it. As the wise afflict not their garment; so the patient grieve not their Soul because that which covers it is injured."

"Neither let prosperity put out the eyes of circumspection, nor abundance cut off the hands of frugality; they that too much indulge in the superfluities of life, shall live to lament the want of its necessaries."

"Glory, like a shadow, flieth from they who pursue it; but it follows at the heels of they who would fly from it; if thou courteth it without merit, thou shalt never attain unto it; if thou deservest it, though thou hidest thyself, it will never forsake you."

"See that prosperity elate not thine heart above measure; neither adversity depress thine mind unto the depths, because fortune beareth hard against you. Their smiles are not stable, therefore build not thy confidence upon them; their frowns endure not forever, therefore let hope teach you patience."

"Presume not in prosperity, neither despair in adversity; court not dangers, nor meanly fly from before them."

"When opulence and extravagance are a necessity instead of righteousness and truth, society will be governed by greed and injustice."

"Grief is natural to the mortal world, and is always about you; pleasure is a guest, and visiteth by thy invitation; use well thy mind, and sorrow shall be passed behind you; be prudent, and the visits of joy shall remain long with you."

"Ambition is to spiritual development what termites are to wood."

The wise person realizes that the universe is here for the experience of the divine self, the innermost spirit of all humans. Since this divine self cannot be killed or destroyed in any way by the occurrences of the world, there is really nothing to fear. Any ideas of pain, sorrow or pleasure are mental creations, the illusions based on relative reality. They who understand this teaching *FULLY* will attain salvation.

The Royal Path

The King (Pharaoh) is the symbol of the perfected human being, one who has achieved Heruhood. The following segment from the ancient Egyptian Pyramid Text of King Unas provides a description of the Royal Path (Yoga). The word *Unas* also means existence (consciousness).

"Purify yourself, Unas! Open thy mouth by means of the EYE of HERU. Invoke thy Ka, Asar (Asar), that he may protect you from all wrath of the Dead...

...they have seen Unas appearing as a soul (BA), as a Neter who lives upon (within, with) his fathers and feeds upon (within, with) his mothers.
It is Unas, Master of wisdom."

The KING, who has accumulated wisdom, is now seen as a Neter or Universal God Principle in nature. He has expanded his consciousness through virtue and wisdom.

> *"The Kas of Unas are behind him, his virtues are before him, his Neters are upon him; His Urei are on the crown of his head..."*

Unas' Kas or previous incarnations are "behind him", his Neters (Godly forces) are upon him. His virtues which he has lived and developed are with him. His Urei or third eye faculty has developed.

> *"(Unas) ...lives in (with) the becoming of every Neter, existing on their works (when) they come with their bodies full of magic through the action of (celestial) fire."*

Unas is in harmony with the Neters, so he is acquiring their supernatural powers. Unas is in communion with every Neter.

> *"It is Unas who will give Judgment together with He Whose Name Is Hidden, on that day of sacrificing the Elder One..."*

Unas will be conscious with GOD (*He Whose Name Is Hidden*, see NETER and Amun), within himself when he sacrifices his former self, the Elder One (lower self, ego sense, idea of himself as an individual personality). In order to achieve perfection, identification with the divine, Unas must cut (sacrifice) all his attachments so that the Ba will not be interested in joining once again with the earthly Ka for another incarnation.

"Unas, you have not gone as a dead person, you have gone as one living, to sit upon the throne of Osiris."

> *"Unas has appeared again in the heavens. He is crowned as Lord of the Horizon. He has reckoned up the dorsal vertebrae of the spinal cord. He seized possession of the "hatys" of the Neters. He has sustained Un (himself) on the Red Crown; he has swallowed the Green One. Unas feeds himself on the union, the conjunction that makes for the Sages. He is satisfied (htp) with living on the "hatys" and their magic power."*

Unas has developed his vital force (Sekhem, Kundalini, Serpentine Fire of Life, Chi) along the astral channels associated with his spine (see Judgment of the Heart). Unas acquired possession of the *"hatys"* or energy that is derived from the heart and lung complex by breathing rhythmically and deeply with concentration on the energy centers. Unas is now *"sustained"* (nourished) on human nature (Red Crown- Life Force) and he lives on the principles of the Neters (Green One - goodness, joy), thanks to which he will become a Sage, a Saint, Enlightened, Liberated, Born Again, Saved and he will return to his place of origin: GOD.

In conclusion:

> *"The "signatures" of Unas do not weaken in his hand for he has swallowed the wisdom of every Neter."*

Unas is in unwavering possession of his powers and as he has assimilated the knowledge of every Neter.

> *"Unas is liberated from the humanity that is in his limbs... Unas rises to heaven leaving the earth behind far from wife and rank... Unas has become one with GOD"*

Unas is now free from his human nature and worldly ideas about a job, marital status, social position; he is above all of these. Even if he continues to live among the living, discharging his duties as a king, he is not living in his ordinary mind, he is living in his eternal self; he is no longer in the mortal body even though he may continue to use the body as a practical reality in the world of time and space. Unas lives internally in eternity.

Unas is living, not unconsciously as most people are even when they are awake, but consciously established in his Godly nature. Unas has become Godlike while still alive, having acquired the "Knowledge of Every God" (wisdom and power).

The cosmic forces that are in the universe are also operating through us. To discover and master these is to study and "Know Thyself" through the process of YOGA.

The Osirian Path of life, death and resurrection (reincarnation), following the commandments (virtues) and judgment is the Path of Nature which works in accordance with the natural laws as set up by GOD through the Neters. The Direct Path of Unas is reserved for those whose calling it is to attain salvation while still alive, hence becoming a Sage, Saint, Buddha, Christ, Anointed one. Initiates are admonished: *"Turn away from the path of Asar,"* because it is full of pain and may require millions of years to grow in consciousness that way.

The formula from the hieroglyphs for achieving enlightenment is found in the *"Egyptian Book of Coming Forth By Day"* **and** *"The Pyramid Texts."* From the hieroglyphics on page 182 we receive the following instruction:

"GOD, the universal BA (spirit) gives humans their individual BA so they may experience and grow in consciousness (wisdom) and achieve immortality.

The Gods of the senses on the boat of Ra: At the Helm is Heru signifying that the soul who is in control of the senses will be the helmsman of the boat of his or her own destiny.

The hands of Djehuti (God of wisdom) are the God "SHAI" which means "destiny" and the Goddess "RENENET" which means "Fortune and Harvest." The implication is that we reap (harvest) the result of our actions (destiny) according to our level of wisdom.

They who achieve wisdom and order (Djehuti-Maat) will gain knowledge of the Amen-Ra (Neter Neteru, the hidden, ever-present one), the hidden world of GOD and our glorious eternal body (Sahu).

"DJEHUTI": Wisdom bestows control over one's Shai (Fortune) and Renenet (ability to reap one's fortune) and therefore one's Meskhenet (Destiny - Karma). One's destiny depends on one's WISDOM!

"DJEHUTI", the faculty of intuitive wisdom, experience of the divine, can be achieved by practice of MAAT and control of the senses."

The concept underlying the principles of *Shai* and *Renenet* is called: Goddess *"Meskhenet." Meskhenet* **is equal to the philosophy of** *"KARMA" of* the Indian Hindu, Samkhya, and Vedanta philosophies. The cultivation of an intuitive intellect which understands the nature of creation and the oneness of all things in the one Hidden GOD (has experience of virtue, has controlled the senses, and has upheld MAAT), will achieve *Saa-Amenti-Ra,* the intelligence or knowledge of the Amenti of Ra, the hidden world.

Our actions in life will determine our fate because the world is set up on the basis of cause and effect relationships. Everything that happens is "caused" to happen and the effect of the cause is the result. If one does not pay the light bill (cause), the lights will be cut off (effect). Similarly, one's deepest desires and aspirations (cause), will determine one's fate (effect), either in this current life or in a future one. If through ignorance one desires material riches as the main goal of existence, one's consciousness will be focused on that goal (cause) during life and the ideas that will come from one's consciousness will be centered around that goal, leading one to encounter people and situations related to that interest. This occurs in a mystical as well as practical way as one's mental vibrations attract others with similar mental vibrations. Thus, if one lives in fear, one will attract individuals and situations who will interact with one according to one's fears, also, without one knowing it, one will be drawn into situations because of one's fears. If, through ignorance, one longs for a certain object or position and is not able to attain that goal during one's life, then one's subconscious impressions will be carried in one's mind after death and will determine where one will go to fulfill those desires and aspirations in future incarnations. Thus, if one longs to be rich and to experience a life of luxury but was not able to attain it in the current life, one will be drawn back to earth or some other world system where those cravings can be further pursued.

Meskhenet is Karma[7]

Goddess (Neter) Meskhenet (Karma) is our own subconscious mind with its complex desires and cravings; these determine our fate. Thus, our fate is determined by the level of wisdom we have acquired because if we are very wise we will know the difference between truth and illusion (spirit needs and ego desires-illusions), and thereby control the ego, to discover our true self. Depending on one's spiritual background and evolution, one's conscience has developed impressions (ideas) about what the truth is. Subconscious impressions are the sum total of our experiences, knowledge and feelings built up over one's current lifetime or several previous ones. Changing these impressions takes sustained, constant and patient effort. Therefore, it would be very ignorant to think that one can live a life saying: "I will live my life any way I please and at the end I will change my personality." What one practices, one becomes. Having wisdom of the spirit world and of our true self as spirit, and having determined our own destiny, *"Meskhenet"* (Karma), our knowledge and wisdom will enable the emergence of divine powers within us to see through the greatest evil (ignorance) and achieve the highest good: to become Heru. We are now fit to assume a new eternal and immortal spiritual body, *"Sahu",* in which we will live with the Gods.

Meskhenet presides over the destiny of the individual during birth and death, thereby administering the disposition of the individual BA (soul) according to the actions of its conscience (AB) as weighed against the feather of MAAT (truth and righteousness).

Our present lives are a result of our past consciousness and present state of mind. Our present mental level of consciousness determines our actions and our actions determine the situations which we will create for ourselves in the future. In this way, at every moment, by our thoughts, we determine our own destiny. Thus a person who's consciousness is centered at the second energy center may find him or herself attracted to situations which involve sexual encounters. A person centered at the fourth energy-consciousness center may find him or herself in situations where love relationships will develop. Therefore, the culmination of Meskhenet (karma) is found at the energy consciousness center at the crown of the head (Uraeus-Buto) where one finds union with the Sundisk (NETER). In order to rise above the situations (pain) experienced at the lower levels, it is necessary to raise one's consciousness.

Thus, if one wants to attain Cosmic Consciousness, one must have that as one's first priority at all times. Therefore, one's goal in any endeavor must be first, to attain purity of heart (conscious and unconscious mind) and then to contribute to the world at large. Further, purity of heart means that one must practice out-stepping one's ego, thus, identifying with the universe instead of just a single minuscule personality among countless others.

It is the ego (one's concept of oneself as an individual personality) who takes the responsibility for actions and thoughts. Therefore, it is the ego that is tied to the outcome of a given situation. If the spirit forgets that it is a separate entity from the ego, that the ego is only its tool to have a "tangible" means to interact with the world, then the spirit will be bound along with the ego to whatever the effects of its actions are. Our level of wisdom depends on our ability to *"discern between the real and the unreal."* A confused, ignorant mind cannot easily determine the truth. Therefore, the ego and its desires are the cause of the bondage of the soul, mental confusion and mental distraction. Instead of being lead to higher achievement-evolution and bliss, the spirit will be led to worlds of mental illusion, and the cycle of aimless pleasure and pain in the worlds of time and space. Thus, it is understood that when one consciously practices yoga and succeeds in changing one's level of consciousness, one's Meskhenet (karmic entanglements) with the world begin to disintegrate.

---

[7] **Note: For more on the path of selfless service see the book** *The Wisdom of Maati* **by Dr. Muata Ashby**

Selfless Service

Selfless service, known as *"Ari Maat"* in Ancient Egyptian Philosophy or *"Karma Yoga"* in Indian Yoga Philosophy, is the performance of actions with the attitude of relinquishing the ego desires and allowing the spirit to dictate one's actions. In this manner contentment arises; one becomes mentally free of tension derived from conflicts between one's conscience and one's desires (ego) and at the same time free from Meskhenet (karma). Selfless service is serving oneself in the best possible way because one serves the higher self which is in everything, in oneself, in others, the sky, the ocean, everywhere. So from the highest perspective, perfect selfless service, working to bring true harmony and peace into one's life through the attainment of enlightenment, is also the most *selfish* way of life. This is the sanest way of life because fulfillment can only arise out of the satisfaction of the higher self (absolute reality). Insanity develops from the search for pleasure to satisfy the ego. The ego can never be satisfied because it is an illusion. Selfless service does not mean "service to your country" to promote patriotism, racism and sexism. These are only larger forms of egoism which in the end lead to society-wide feelings of envy, mistrust, hostility and selfishness.

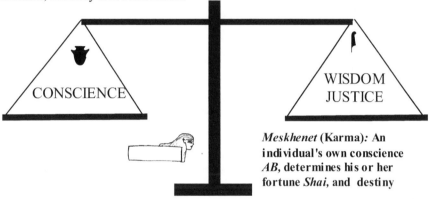

CONSCIENCE

WISDOM JUSTICE

Meskhenet (Karma): An individual's own conscience *AB*, determines his or her fortune *Shai*, and destiny

Meskhenet on the birthing block, presiding at the judgment, birth and death of the individual soul.

Below: Hieroglyphic symbols for the principal deities governing the process of karma in the individual.

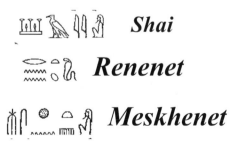

Shai

Renenet

Meskhenet

Distorted Vision of the World
due to Erroneous Subconscious Impressions of the Mind.

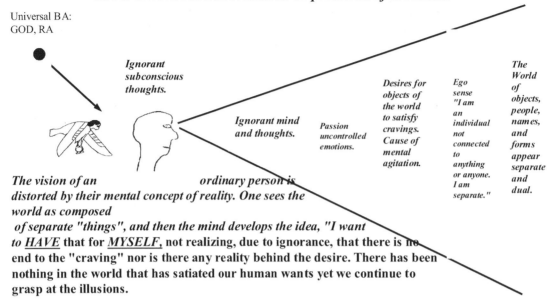

Universal BA:
GOD, RA

Ignorant subconscious thoughts.

Ignorant mind and thoughts.

Passion uncontrolled emotions.

Desires for objects of the world to satisfy cravings. Cause of mental agitation.

Ego sense "I am an individual not connected to anything or anyone. I am separate."

The World of objects, people, names, and forms appear separate and dual.

The vision of an ordinary person is distorted by their mental concept of reality. One sees the world as composed of separate "things", and then the mind develops the idea, "I want to _HAVE_ that for _MYSELF,_ not realizing, due to ignorance, that there is no end to the "craving" nor is there any reality behind the desire. There has been nothing in the world that has satiated our human wants yet we continue to grasp at the illusions.

- -

Corrected Vision of the World
due to Cleansed Subconscious Impressions.

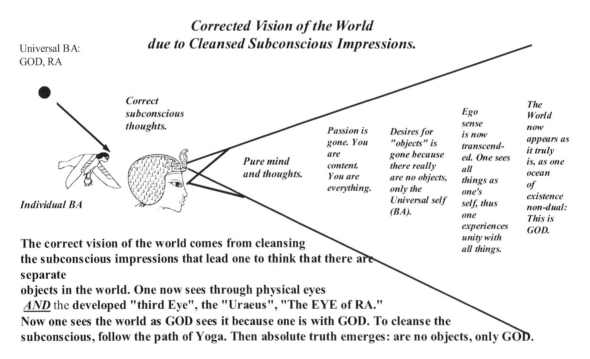

Universal BA:
GOD, RA

Correct subconscious thoughts.

Pure mind and thoughts.

Passion is gone. You are content. You are everything.

Desires for "objects" is gone because there really are no objects, only the Universal self (BA).

Ego sense is now transcended. One sees all things as one's self, thus one experiences unity with all things.

The World now appears as it truly is, as one ocean of existence non-dual: This is GOD.

Individual BA

The correct vision of the world comes from cleansing the subconscious impressions that lead one to think that there are separate objects in the world. One now sees through physical eyes _AND_ the developed "third Eye", the "Uraeus", "The EYE of RA." Now one sees the world as GOD sees it because one is with GOD. To cleanse the subconscious, follow the path of Yoga. Then absolute truth emerges: are no objects, only GOD.

The Meditative Mind

"Mind, as matter, may be transmuted from state to state, degree to degree, condition to condition, pole to pole and vibration to vibration.
Transmutation is a Mental Art."

Egyptian Proverb

The most important quality to develop is the meditative mind. This is not to be thought of as only the mind of a person that sits in a state of deep catatonic meditation but a person who, while he or she is involved in the affairs of the world, all the time KNOWS his or her true identity. This is the mind that interacts with every moment of existence unlike the previously discussed automatic mind. This quality represents the vision of Heru which is the vision to be regained. In a sense, people living in the ancient societies such as that of Egypt and India would not have needed to practice formalized forms of meditation as much as today. This is because then, knowledge of the existence of GOD and the Gods was not an object of speculation but it was inherent in the very fabric of the culture. Spirituality was an inseparable part of their practical life. Therefore, their minds would be constantly thinking about and accommodating divinity regardless of their activities. This attitude in itself constitutes a meditative state of mind. A similar technique of spiritual discipline enjoined by modern day spiritual preceptors is called *"mindfulness"*, wherein one maintains a sense of one's divine essence at every moment while performing one's daily tasks (breathing, walking, resting, or even while answering nature's call). Also known as the *"development of the witness"*, this technique aids the spiritual aspirant in developing an expanded awareness aside from the common waking consciousness. Through this practice, the soul separates itself from the ego-personality and obtains knowledge of itself through identification with itself instead of with the body, mind and sense perceptions.

"He who grasps the truth of the Mental Nature of the Universe is well advanced on the Path to Self mastery."
Egyptian Proverb

Foreigners who visited those countries (Egypt and India) were in awe of the spectacular forms of reverence to spiritual matters. Today, before most people are able to grasp deeper philosophical ideas such as those now being discovered by quantum physics, it is necessary for them to clear their mind of the erroneous notions of time and space and the desires that they have been indoctrinated into from the time of their birth into a materialistic society which incessantly promotes the idea of getting as much as one can for oneself at the expense of others. This dangerous notion of individuality is in direct contradiction with the essence of the soul thereby resulting in endless mental conflicts and agitation, the opposite of a meditative mind.

"Purification of the Heart (consciousness) *leads to the Highest Good: Eternal Life and Supreme Peace."*
Egyptian Proverb

The following instructions on meditation and reflection are given directly from the Egyptian scriptures:

"Contemplate thy powers, contemplate thy wants and thy connections; so shalt thou discover the duties of life, and be directed in all thy ways."

"When an idea exclusively occupies the mind, it is transformed into an actual physical state."

"Reason of Divinity may not be known except by a concentration of the senses like onto it."

"Wisdom that understands in silence; this is the matter and the womb from which humanity is born, and the True Good the seed."

"Get thyself ready and make the thought in you a stranger to the world-illusion."

"O praise the goodness of the Supreme Being with songs for thanksgiving, and meditate in silence on the wonders of HIS and HER love; let thy heart overflow with gratitude and acknowledgment, let the language of thy lips speak praise and adoration, let the actions of thy life show thy love to Universal Law."

"IF THOU WILT ATTENTIVELY DWELL (meditate) AND OBSERVE WITH THY HEART'S EYES, THOU WILL FIND THE PATH THAT LEADS ABOVE; NAY, THAT IMAGE SHALL BECOME THY GUIDE ITSELF, BECAUSE THE DIVINE SIGHT HATH THIS PECULIAR CHARM; IT HOLDETH FAST AND DRAWETH UNTO IT THOSE WHO SUCCEED IN OPENING THEIR EYES, JUST AS, THEY SAY, THE MAGNET THE IRON."

"Stand in a place uncovered to the sky, facing west to the sinking sun, and make your solemn worship, and the same way as he rises to the east in the morning. Now, make thy body still."

"Thou, alone can speak. Wonder at this glorious prerogative; and pay to the Supreme who gave to you the gift of life a rational and welcome praise, teaching your children wisdom, instructing the offspring of your loins in piety."

"Reflection is the business of Humankind; a sense of their state is the first duty: but who remembereth themselves in joy? Is it not in mercy then that sorrow is allotted unto us?"

Proper Breathing

Most people in the modern world do not know how to breathe properly. Most people (specially males) have learned to breathe by pushing out the chest in a "manly" or "macho" fashion. This mode of breathing is harmful for many reasons. The amount of air taken in is less and vital cosmic energy is reduced and becomes stagnant in the subtle vital energy channels, resulting in physical and / or mental disease. The stagnation of the flow of energy through the body has the effect of grounding one's consciousness to the physical realities rather than allowing the mind and body to operate with lightness and subtlety.

"Belly breathing" or abdominal breathing massages the internal organs and develops Life Force energy (Ra, Chi or Kundalini). It will be noticed that it is our natural breathing pattern when we lie down on our back. Instruction is as follows: A- Breathe in and push the stomach out. B- Breathe out and pull the stomach in. This form of breathing is to be practiced at all times, not just during meditation. It allows the natural Life Force in the air to be rhythmically supplied to the body and spiritual nervous system. This process is indispensable in the achievement of physical health and mental-spiritual power to control the mind (meditation).
Some important Egyptian Scriptures on breathing:

"Breath is life."

"I am the lotus pure coming forth from the god of light, the guardian of the nostril of Ra, the guardian of the nose of Hetheru; I make my journey; I run after him who is Heru. I am the pure one coming forth from the fields."

"Be as the Sun and Stars, that emanate the life giving essence; give life without asking for anything in return; to be a sun, breath rhythmically and deeply; then as RA shall you be."

Concentration

The practice of concentration leads to a state of mind wherein one's ego merges with the object being concentrated on. Since concentration on one object is psychologically equal to having "no thoughts" in the mind, the ego-consciousness is freed from the stimulation of the senses and of thinking of itself as an individual entity. Thus, one may concentrate on any *"one object"* or on *"no object"* and obtain the same results. Through concentration, the act of "focusing the psychic energy of the mind", the ego opens up and experiences expansion. Psychic energy of one's consciousness is therefore focused on the perception of itself instead of dissipating into the various thoughts and objects which attract the senses. In this manner, one's true identity is revealed, uncovered from the veil of the ego-consciousness. The expansion may feel as loss of body consciousness and identity. One may forget one's existence as an individual and may feel the sensations of floating or falling. Often fear is experienced at this point since one's ego-consciousness may have a strong grip on one's psyche, however, if this state is mastered and explored, one will reach the stage of expansion wherein one will experience *"Enlightenment Experiences"*. This stage is where meditation for the purpose of *"Liberation"* truly begins. This is the process of *"Knowing Oneself"*, where the meditator *"realizes"* that which is known (creation-GOD) is the same as the knower (one's ego-consciousness). The two become one. At this point all the symbols, ideas, fanciful notions and imaginations of our mind are left behind as the mind is emptied of its ego knowledge, for the time, so that the Universal spirit may fill that void with the knowledge of transcendental (Absolute) reality which is beyond mental ideations and rationalizations and thus, can only be understood by intuitive insight. All of the symbols, concepts, and deities, names and forms we have learned about were only tools to help the mind grasp the subtle teachings of existence and must now give way to one's own realization of one's own conscious existence.

Ordinarily, the correct practice of any concentration technique will lead to a meditative state (focused mind) which will carry over into the ordinary waking state. In Egyptian and Indian Kundalini (tantric) Yoga and Chinese Taoist meditation Yoga, one is said to be able to "enjoy" one's enlightenment because it focuses attention on and directs the natural sexual energies to promote one's evolution. These tantric techniques release vast amounts of energy and are touted to be the most powerful evolutionary mechanisms (requiring much training to understand and control). Thus, they are considered to be among the highest mysteries.

Above: The Egyptian Scarab God Khepera, rolling the black Sun (contracted ego - death), in order to transform it into the new life (expanded ego-enlightenment). Further insight into the symbol of the Scarab comes from "The Secret of the Golden Flower", an ancient Chinese meditation text:

"The scarab rolls his ball and in the ball develops life as the result of the undivided effort of his spiritual concentration (of mental and sexual energy). If now an embryo can grow in manure, and shed it's shells, why should not the dwelling place of our heavenly heart (conscience-mind) also be able to create a body if we concentrate (energy) the spirit upon it?"

Concentration On The Energy Centers Of The Body Along With Breath Control: The SHU (breath control) Meditation

<u>To Begin:</u> Be seated or lie down in a relaxed pose. See the diagram at left for the location of the energy centers. VISUALIZE yourself gaining cosmic energy. See it accumulating in the body. Place your concentration on the first energy center at the base of the spine as you inhale. See the energy tapping that spot, then see it rising through the other energy centers going up to the sixth center where the pineal gland is situated (The Uraeus). Exhale and see the energy go back down to the first center. Inhale and repeat the exercise. Feel the increasing levels of PEACE *(htp)* develop.

You are increasing your psychic energy levels which will enable you to control your emotions, passions, and desires and thereby have a peaceful mind to allow the universal spirit inside of you to reveal itself. This technique in particular is beneficial in sublimating *(htp)* sexual energy into spiritual - psychic energy. By visualizing the energy flowing up toward the head, to the sixth and seventh energy centers, it is possible to "SUBLIMATE" *(Hetep)* the energy and transform it into spiritual energy. One may practice this visualization when aroused.

Don't see yourself as the "body" but as the eternal and immortal BA. See yourself as the BA (soul, piece of GOD) who is connected to RA, the Universe. See yourself in this manner during ALL activities. In this relative world, you are interacting with other divinities (as aspects of your supreme self) who have bodies just as you do. Eventually you will move above and beyond your individual consciousness, and you will see yourself as the Universe without trying. You will live in eternity right now, every second.

Concentration and meditation tips

Begin by meditating for 5 minutes each day, gradually building up the time. The key is consistency. It is better to practice for 5 minutes each day than 20 minutes one day and 0 minutes the next. Do a formal sit down meditation whenever the feeling comes to you but try to do it at least once a day. Do not eat for at least 2 hours before meditation. It is even more preferable to not eat 12 hours before. For example: eat nothing (except only water or tea) after 6 p.m. until after meditation at 6 a.m. the following morning. Do not meditate within 24 hours of having sexual intercourse. Meditate alone in a quiet area, in a dimly lit room (candle light is adequate). Do light exercise (example: Tai Chi, Chi Kung or Hatha Yoga) before meditating, then say Hekau (affirmations, prayers, mantras, etc.) for a few minutes to set up positive vibrations in the mind. Burning your favorite incense is a good way to set the mood. Keep a ritualistic procedure about the meditation time. Do things in a slow, deliberate manner.

When ready, try to focus the mind on one object, symbol or idea such as the Ab (heart) or Hetep (Supreme Peace). If the mind strays, bring it back gently. Patience, self-love, self-forgiveness and tenacity are the keys here. Gradually, the mind will not drift towards thoughts or objects of the world. It will move toward subtler levels of consciousness until it reaches and communes with the source of the thoughts and objects, NETER, GOD. This is the desired positive movement of the practice of meditation because it is from NETER that all inspiration, creativity and altruistic feelings of love come. NETER is the source of *Hetep Mer* (peace and love). NETER is the source of all things. NETER is who you really are.

Transcendental Self

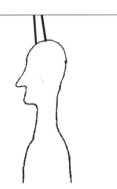

Transcendental Self

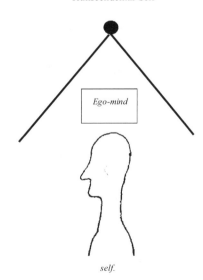

Ego-mind

self.

The Ego-mind-self *"cleansed"*, through concentration or other spiritual disciplines. Consciousness expands allowing the perception of the all encompassing *Transcendental Self* as well as

MEDITATION AND ENLIGHTENMENT ACCORDING TO THE EGYPTIAN BOOK OF COMING FORTH BY DAY

In the Egyptian *Book of Coming Forth By Day*, the process which leads to the state of super consciousness is described in the form of separate utterances contained within various individual spells or chapters to be spoken by those who wish to "fashion their hearts" (minds) into eternal forms. In chapter 1, utterances 18-20 where the initiate speaks as follows:

"I am one with Heru on this day of clothing, opening the storehouses of washing the still of heart, unbolting the door of concealed things in Restau, I am one with Heru."

The day of clothing refers to receiving one's glorious spiritual body. Opening the storehouses refers to the releasing of the stored up potential within oneself. Washing of the still heart refers to the cleansing of the mind through virtuous living (MAAT) which leads to mental peace and through meditation wherein the heart (mind) is cleared of subconscious impressions of passion, desire and illusions and sexual energy is accumulated and transformed into spiritual energy. When the endless stream of thoughts in the mind is controlled or made still, the unbolting of the door of concealed things *Restau* (realm of Ra) occurs; this is the subconscious spirit world of GOD (Re) within us. The result of this practice is to become one with Heru (GOD).

In chapter 21 the initiate pleads that his mouth (memory - consciousness) be restored:

"Hail to you lord of Light... may you restore to me my mouth (memory) and may my heart (mind) assist me at the time of destroying the night (ignorance)."

In chapter 23, utterance 6, the initiate describes his / her resolve in seeking liberation from the *"Pool of Double Fire"* (world, physical existence, state of duality). Through the force of will manifested in the ability to accomplish the *"wish of the heart"*, the initiate has *"quenched"* the heart which was agitated with desires, passions, etc. from involvement with the world of duality. Through force of will and a disciplined mind (heart), the initiate directs him / herself to identification with Asar (physical manifestation of the nameless GOD) and thus becomes one with *"That Being Who Is At The Top Of The Steps"*.

"I am Asar, Lord of Restau, I (initiate) *share with That Being Who Is At The Top Of The Steps. Due to the wish of my heart I have come here from the Pool of Double Fire, I have quenched these fires in myself."*

In chapter 97 the initiate seeks to attain a frame of mind of equanimity (definition on page 160) which will prepare him / her to *"plunge into the divine pool"* of *"heaven and earth"* to unite them within him/herself:

"May I be purified in the lake of propitiation and equipoise. Then let me plunge into the divine pool beneath the two divine sycamores of heaven and earth"

In chapter 23 the initiate is assisted and affirms that the bonds (fetters) which were placed on his mouth by Set (egoism, desires, individuality, selfishness, etc.) have been removed by Ptah, Djehuti, Atum and Shu:

"My mouth has been opened by Ptah, Djehuti (wisdom) comes with magic, and the fetters of Set which obstructed my mouth are destroyed."

Chapter 26, utterances 7-9: Once the initiates know they have gained control (power) over their heart (mind), when they *know their heart*, then they will *not lose consciousness* as an ordinary person will at the time of death of the physical body but will retain the power to go in and out of the spirit world according to the desire of the spirit. Also, an initiate will not suffer through reincarnation but will live on in *BKA* (spirit-soul) form as an initiate is well established (enlightened) in the spirit rather than the body consciousness:

"I know my Heart, I have achieved power over it, I have achieved the power to do what pleases my Ka (spirit), I will remain aware in my Ab (heart), my Ba (soul) will not be fettered or restrained at the entrance of the West, I will be able to come and go as I please."

"ab"
cleansed,
purified,

The importance of purifying or *"washing the heart"* appears throughout the entire book. Washing the heart means that the heart is relieved of feelings, be they feelings of joy, happiness, anger or sorrow. Developing dispassion is also a classic tenet of Indian Vedanta and Buddhist philosophies. In Egyptian mythology and philosophy, the symbol for cleansing or purifying the heart (mind) is composed of a leg and / or human figure (sometimes beside the symbol for water) over which a jug of water is poured. Washing the heart is called *"ab"*. This symbol is used to continuously remind the aspirant to practice Djehuti and Maat (wisdom and good judgment based on that wisdom), thus attaining stability:

"I am the ab (cleansed-washed one) *in Tettetu"* (stability; see Djed pillar) chapter 1- utterance-24 and again in chapter 81- utterance 1, the initiate states: *"I am the ab* (pure-washed one) *coming forth from the fields."*

"Stilling the Heart (mind)" appears in Chapter 63a, utterances 4-5, where the initiate has *"made him / herself to live"* by stilling his heart:

"I am the mighty one, the still of Heart... that I may make myself to live..."

The following lines taken from various statements throughout the book show the gradual realization of the initiate that the Gods are in reality aspects of him / herself. Further, the initiate understands *(Saa)* his / her true nature and its power:

"I am The Great God, the self created one, Nun...I am Ra...I am Geb...I am Atum...I am Asar...I am Min...I am Shu...I am Anpu...I am Aset...I am Hetheru...I am Sekhmet...I am Orion...I am Saa...I am the Lion... I am the young Bull...I am Hapi who comes forth as the river Nile..."

The state of enlightenment is further described in chapter 83 and 85 where the initiate realizes that the seven Uraeus deities or bodies (immortal parts of the spirit) have been reconstituted:

"The seven Uraeuses are my body... my image is now eternal."

These seven Uraeuses are also described as the *"seven souls of Ra"* and *"the seven arms of the balance (Maat)"*. Thus, we are to understand that the seven primordial powers (Uraeuses) are our true essence (see parts of the spirit). Further, the same seven are GOD. Thus, GOD'S soul and our souls are identical. It is this same soul which will judge us in the balance. Therefore, we came into existence of our own free will, and we are the supreme masters (judges) of our own destiny. We may put together our divine form by attaining a purified heart or live in ignorance, ruled by passion and mortality. In chapter 30, the initiate affirms that his / her vertebrae, back, and neck bones are firm (see Djed pillar):

"The four fastenings of the hinder part of my head and back are now firm."

In chapter 17, utterances 5-6 and 14-17, the initiate realizes that he or she is not an individual human personality but the universal primordial spirit (Tmu) which created creation in the beginning. The initiate further realizes that he or she is *"the only one"* who exists. The initiate has reached the state of all consciousness where past (Asar), present (Initiate) and future (Ra) meet in one absolute reality (Heru):

"I am Tmu in rising up. I am the only one. I came into existence in Nu. I am Ra in his rising in the beginning of time." "I am Yesterday, Today and I know Tomorrow. Who then is he? Now Yesterday is Asar, now Tomorrow is Ra, on the day of the destruction of his enemies and the appointment of his son Heru."

For those who have succeeded in achieving the state of Cosmic Consciousness and the state of oneness which lies beyond, the experience is thus described:

Above: "Heru in the Phase of Resurrection." The Eye of Heru is "at the top" of the pyramid where he was symbolically resurrected. The "CAPSTONE" (top of the pyramid) represents the Eye which has reached full power (enlightenment). The pyramid form has many symbolic meanings. In this symbolic format it speaks of the meditation practitioner who, as an "un-enlightened" individual, is considered as a mortal. When the practitioner is successful however, he or she is able to leave the "House of Fire" (ancient name of the pyramid form). In this context, the human body is the house of fire in which the "elixir of life" (sexual energy) is churned and sublimated so that the meditator can develop an expanded consciousness to attain freedom (immortality). See section: "The Secret of the Philosopher's Stone." The pyramid form is known to harness cosmic energy. If a practitioner meditates inside a pyramid or with his/her body in the position of a pyramid (cross-legged with arms outstretched to the knees-Lotus Pose), it is said that he or she is able to harness Life Force energy. The eye and the triangle were later used in Christian Iconography to symbolize the all seeing eye and the Trinity, Father, Son and Holy Ghost

"Every part of my body is divine...I am Yesterday, Today and Tomorrow... I am All things...Behold, I am the heir of all eternity, to me has been given everlastingness...I am the heir, the Exalted One, the Mighty One, Still of Heart...GOD is I and I am He... I Am That I Am... I can come or go between this world and the next as I please and in any form I choose...I am the great GOD who came into existence and made all things to exist, I am the only One..."

Thus, when the ultimate intuitive discovery dawns on us, we realize that each one of us is one with all things, that each one of us is *all* that exists, that each one of us, each tree, each star is *One being*: US. We are the Supreme Monarchs of creation; all the stories about Sages, Gods and philosophies speak about none other than us in all of our glory. We have now arrived at the exalted state of consciousness. While alive, and then after the death of the body, we can explore the vast regions of our unconscious wherein time, space, and thought are manifested according to our will. This is the *"Astral Afterlife"* to be experienced in the eternal *"Realm of Light"*, the philosophy which predates even the pyramid texts (see Realm of Light).

Egyptian Magic

"To change your mood or mental state, change your vibration."

EGYPTIAN YOGA VOLUME 1

*"To destroy an undesirable rate of mental vibration, concentrate on the opposite
vibration to the one to be suppressed."*

It is appropriate here to discuss the essence of Egyptian Magic in a way which may help us to understand the purpose of rituals, hekau and mind control (meditation) from a spiritual perspective.

The two previous quotes from the *Kybalion*[8] are considered to be the basis of the art of mental transformation (see spiritual alchemy). They express in simple terms, the essential process by which the mind may be cleansed (washed) of undesirable elements and thereby purified in order to attain enlightenment.

As human beings, we are used to making statements such as "I am hungry" or "I am sad." These statements and the feelings which they evoke constitute powerful vibrations which affect the mind. So by repeating them with conviction, we may truly believe that we are hungry, sad, angry, happy, etc. As discussed in Chapter lll, Egyptian Physics, matter, including our bodies, is only energy in a particular state of vibration. Therefore, through a purified and trained mind, we may control our vibrational state. Western psychology is only now discovering the power of affirmations to create new moods and feelings, and thus, new realities. The mind can either make itself feel "good" or "bad" according to its disposition. This in turn can affect the physical body, causing it to be healthy or ill.

There are other more subtle mental changes which we produce on a daily basis, many of which we are unaware. When we buy a new car or put on a special garment and makeup to go to a party for instance, we are really dressing for a ritual, not only physically, but mentally as well. As we slip into the car or into the garment, we may subconsciously feel "powerful", "beautiful", "sexy", etc. This "identification" with the objects and the costume helps us feel and act in certain ways. The rituals and utterances in the *"Pert em Hru"* or Egyptian *"Book of Coming forth by Day"* are designed for the purpose of assisting the initiate to change his or her "identity" from the perishable ego which upon the death of the body will be dispersed or *"annihilated in the Abyss"* to that of a spiritual being equipped with a spiritual body. A being with full awareness of itself and with the power to control its own destiny has the power to be born again at a time and place of its own choosing, to exist as a being of light (God / Goddess), or to dissolve into the ocean of existence from whence it came (NETER, GOD).

Thus, through the practice of meditation and having gained the ability to achieve out of body experiences, the practitioner is able to direct the mind to control subtle matter. When practiced at the highest levels, the mind creates a new "reality" using etheric energy according to its will and strength, just as it created the physical body and ego-personality on earth. By *"knowing one's heart"* (attaining control over the mind), subtle etheric matter and energy is controlled in such a way that is "becomes" whatever the mind directs it to. In this manner, at the utterances: *"I am fully conscious"* and *"I am Goddess Aset"* for instance, the memory which would normally have been lost in the ordinary process of death (equal to the memory loss of one's ego upon falling asleep) will remain and ethereal matter will coalesce into an etheric (subtle) form in the likeness of Aset, in accordance with the mental conception of the initiate.

In this context, the term *"Magic"* is a misnomer for what truly constitutes a most sublime practice of spiritual evolution. It must be well understood that even the creation of a spiritual body is performed in the realm of time and space with materials that are themselves emanations of the cosmic mind (GOD) and therefore, even though the adept may, through this process be able to live on for eons, there will be an inevitable end since: ALL proceeds from the ALL and eventually ALL returns to the ALL. Therefore, the practitioner of spiritual development should not get caught even in this higher form of illusory existence, remembering always that the highest identification is with the ALL and not with any personality, be it human or Godlike. This practice is very much similar to the mantras and rituals contained in the Indian scriptures, the Indian Siddha philosophy and Tibetan Buddhist philosophy.

---

[8] The *Kybalion* is an ancient text attributed to the God Hermes Trismegistus (Egyptian Djehuti), which contains essential teachings of Egyptian wisdom concerning the nature of the mind and creation.

ALTERED STATES OF CONSCIOUSNESS

Through constant and consistent practice of meditation, new physical sensations and mental states may be experienced. These may range from simple tingling sensations to major vibrations in which the physical or subtle bodies will be churned with such force that the meditator may feel as though something physical or mental is wrong. As the process of any form of growth is sometimes easy or hard depending on the attitude and disposition of the learner and the material to be learned, so too the process of Yoga will range from "difficult" and "painful" to "easy" and "painless" (blissful). The process of spiritual evolution, which is sped up by the practice of meditation, may cause the release of mental and physical energy blockages in proportion to the level of force exercised by the meditator and the level of cleansing needed by the meditator. The meditative experiences may occur with such unpredictable force and speed as to range from tranquil movements to transcendent states of consciousness or may include physically violent and disorienting psychic effects which may challenge the physical health and sanity of the practitioner. The physical and subtle bodies may even perform "spontaneous yogic postures" or **Kriyas** (purifications) without the assistance of the conscious mind. When this level of introspection is reached, seeking the assistance of a competent meditation instructor would be most advisable, preferably someone who can council the meditator as to the various aspects of the psychic planes wherein higher ego psychological states of bliss and ecstasy are experienced, and who has knowledge of the realm in which the *"Unitive"* state of consciousness (Enlightenment), is experienced beyond the state of meditation itself. For more information on meditation experiences, altered states and the effect of different meditation techniques on the brain, consult the suggested reading list, especially note the books marked with two asterisks (**).

NOTE: If you are interested in the path of meditation and the Yoga of Meditation, the books *Meditation: The Ancient Egyptian Path to Enlightenment, Initiation Into Egyptian Yoga, The Egyptian Yoga Movements of the Gods and Goddesses* and *The Path of Divine Love* by Dr. Muata Ashby will be your emphasis in the study and practice of the teachings.

CHAPTER 6: ESSENTIAL KEMETIC YOGA EXERCISES AND POSTURES FOR MENTAL AND PHYSICAL HEALTH

"Her name is Health: she is the daughter of Exercise, who begot her on temperance. The rose blushes on her cheeks, the sweetness of the morning breathes from her lips; joy, tempered with innocence and modesty, sparkles in her eyes and from the cheerfulness of her heart she sings as she walks."

Egyptian Mystical Wisdom

EGYPTIAN YOGA VOLUME 1

The main purpose of physical exercise is to maintain the body in good enough condition to allow the soul to have entry into the world and to have the opportunity to experience through interaction with the world. Through interaction with the outer-world (universe), the inner-world (soul) becomes aware of itself as a living entity and thereby has the opportunity to achieve the highest possible goal, to achieve all that is achievable, to become "Godlike", to "know itself." Even though there is much knowledge, wisdom and experience to be gained from pain, disease and suffering, in the task of achieving supreme self knowledge, a healthy body is indispensable.

To this end, exercises which will assist the proper distribution of vital energies (sexual energies) and mental peace should be practiced. Preferably, the following exercises should be practiced under the supervision of a qualified instructor to insure that they are performed properly so as to avoid injury.

On a subtler level, certain physical exercises have the effect of stimulating the subtle energy centers where sexual energy (Ra, Chi, Prana, Kundalini) is developed and stored.

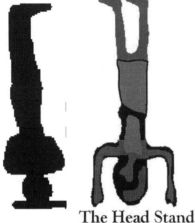

The following poses may be followed by the meditation exercises presented in the meditation section.

Above left: The ancient Egyptian *Head Stand*. One of the most beneficial poses for promoting the distribution of vital energies by reversing the flow of blood to the brain and upper psychic energy centers. It requires supreme control of mind and

The Head Stand

body and is not recommended for novices or the untrained. The modern head stand pose (right center) is suited for beginners and others who which to gain the same benefit with less concentration and effort. Above center: Tripod Headstand. Above right: Modern Yoga head stand can be easily performed by making a V shape with the arms to form a triangle with the head, thus achieving a tripod effect. Hold this position only as long as comfortable.

Above: The Ancient Egyptian god Geb in the Plough Pose.

A   B

Above right: *A- Jubilating Was scepter from the relief of Djoser.*
B- Jubilating Rekhyt bird. Scene from the relief of Amenemhet I. The Rekhyt bird symbolizes "The People of Egypt".

In the *HENU* exercise (Figures A and B above right and on following page), prayers are offered to GOD. Henu symbolizes "praise", "rejoicing" and "jubilation". There are many hieroglyphic reliefs showing Gods as well as initiates performing the Henu exercise. First one kneels on one knee and extends one arm with palm open while at the same time holding the other arm closer to the body with closed fist. Then the extended arm is drawn back and the hand is closed as it touches the chest. The performance is repeated several times and ends with the final position where one arm is raised behind the head with closed fist and the other arm touches the chest with closed fist.

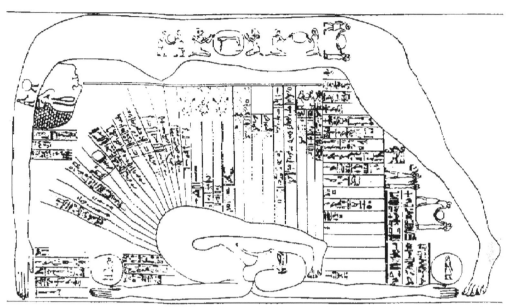

Above: The Egyptian God and Goddess Geb and Nut perform Yogic poses in the process of their separation. The result of their separation creates "Heaven and Earth", i.e. *creation.* Creation is composed of a mixture of two basic principles called *"The Pairs of Opposites"*, also known as Ying and Yang principles in the Taoist System.

A

Figure A: Ramses I performing the Henu w Anubis. From the Pha tomb at Thebes..

"I am the lotus pure coming forth from the god of light, the guardian of the nostril of Ra, the guardian of the nose of Hathor; I make my journey; I run after him who is Horus. I am the pure one coming forth from the field."‡

B- Female figures from the old empire.

Figures B and C. The Egyptian religious reliefs at right are reminiscent of Chinese Chi Kung, Tai Chi, the dances of the ! Kung people of Afrika and the Whirling Dervishes. In Chi Kung, Tai Chi and the dancing of the Dervishes, these movements serve to harmonize the spiritual energies of the body and to produce a trance state of mental consciousness in the performer. When practiced with conscious emphasis on the movements, slowness and concentration, they are an effective form of meditation as well as physical exercise.

C- Male figures from the tomb of Baqti III, Beni Hasan.

The Wheel. A backward stretch, good for promoting spinal flexibility and redirecting vital energies to the head.

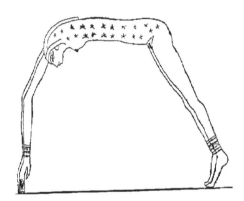

Above: Goddess Nut in the forward stretch. The reverse position to the backward stretch.

At right: The God Shu in the pose as separator of his children (Nut-heaven and Geb-earth). This pose is very similar to a Chi Kung pose which depicts the Happy Buddha with up stretched arms. The arms are raised and lowered while breathing rhythmically.

Above: The God Geb in the spinal twist position. This posture promotes flexibility of the spine. Should be practiced by facing both directions and twisting the head back as far as possible.

In the proverb (lower right), the initiate affirms his / her control over the nostril of Ra-Hetheru which comes forth from the **"God of Light"**. This form of yogic breathing called *"solar breathing"* is known as the stimulating, exciting, energizing breath wherein the left nostril is held closed while breathing in and exhaling through the right nostril. In the Indian yoga this exercise is called ***"SURYABHEDA"*** or "Sun-piercing" exercise. It is one of the eight types of breath control *pranayama†*. In this passage the initiate assumes the role guardian of the nostril of Goddess Hetheru, who is identified with Buto or Uraeus, the life giving serpent, and the Eye of Ra (right eye), the solar energy force which destroys mental illness (ignorance) and physical illness. Thus, through the perfection of this exercise, it is possible to awaken the life-force energy (serpent-power or Kundalini-Shakti*) and develop the energy centers of the body.

The exercise is performed by sitting in the cross-legged position, closing the eyes and closing off the left nostril while inhaling. The subject inhales and holds the breath for as long as comfortable and then exhales, gradually lengthening the time that the breath is held. This practice may be aided by pressing the chin against the chest while holding the breath. While inhaling, the subject visualizes the life-force energy rising as a serpent, through the energy centers. Exhalation should be performed slowly. This exercise is repeated again and again until the practitioner becomes pure, ready to make the journey from the field (earth).

†Pranayama is the Indian name for all forms of breath control exercises.
*Kundalini-Shakti is the Indian name for the Life-Force energy in the human body coiled up as a Serpent (Kundali)- Shakti (Power).
‡From the Egyptian Book of Coming Forth By Day, C-31, line 1.

NOTE: For more on the Ancient Egyptian Art of health and physical exercise see the book: EGYPTIAN YOGA *The Movement of The Gods and Goddesses* by Dr. Muata Ashby.

Appendix A: A Chronology of World Religious, Mythological and Philosophical Systems.

c. >36,766 B.C.E-10,858 B.C.E. Egyptian Pre-dynastic history

c. 10,000 B.C.E.   The Sphinx: Heru in the Horizon.

c. 10,500 - 5,700 B.C.E. Egyptian Pre-dynastic history

c. 5,700 - 342 B.C.E.   Egyptian Dynastic History

c. 5,500 B.C.E. (Yoga), pyramid   Egyptian Philosophy

texts, Egypt.

c. 2,500 B.C.E Religion -Yoga,   Pre-Aryan Dravidian

India.

c. 1,700 B.C.E. Persia and India   Invasion of Egypt, Europe,

by the Indo-Europeans

(Aryans).

c. 1,400-900 B.C.E   Aryan Vedas, India.

c. 1,350 B.C.E.   Cannaanite Religion.

c. 1,200-500 B.C.E. Egypt.   Old Testament- Moses,

c. 1,200 B.C.E.   Olmecs. Central America.

c. 1,200 B.C.E.   Jainism, India.

c. 1,030 B.C.E.   Druids.

c. 800 B.C.E. Indian Vedanta-   Upanishads-Classical

Yoga, India.

c. 800 - 500 B.C.E.   Vasudeva - Krishna, India

c. 700 B.C.E. philosophy, India.   Samkhya-Yoga

c. 700 B.C.E.-500 C.E.Greek mythology and Mystery religions,

Greece-Egypt.*

c. 600 B.C.E.   Zoroaster, Persia.

c. 600 B.C.E. India.   Buddhism (Theravada),

c. 550 B.C.E.   Confucianism, China.

c. 500 B.C.E.   Taoism- Lao Tsu, China.

c. 500-51 B.C.E.   Celtic Religion.

c. 500-100 B.C.E. Bhagavad Gita,   Hinduism- Mahabharata,

Patanjali- India.

c. 324 B.C.E. and India by   Invasion of Egypt, Persia

Alexander the Great.

c. 300 B.C.E.-300 C. E Gnosticism, Jewish Essene and Therapeut

Palestine,   cults throughout: Egypt,

Buddhists send   Greece and Rome.

Persia, China   missionaries to Egypt,

Greece and Rome.

c. 200 B.C.E. Mystery   Roman composite and

India.*   religions, Greece-Egypt-

c. 100 B.C.E -100 C.E. Mahayana Buddhism develops becomes

dominant religion in India.
Missionaries sent to Egypt,

Persia,   China Greece and Rome.

c. 200 C. E. Agamas, Hindu   Shaivism- Puranas and

scriptures, India.

c. 300 C. E. decedents of   Mayas (central America-

the Olmecs).

c. 325 C. E.   Christianity, Rome.

c. 400 C. E.   Theodocius of Rome decrees that
Orthodox Christianity is the only form of
Christianity allowed in the Roman Empire. All
other forms of Christianity and all other religions
and cults are outlawed. Dark ages of Europe begin.
An exodus of religious leaders, artists, scientists
out of Europe and into Asia begins, leading to the
flowering of culture in the Middle East, West and
Central Africa.

c. 450 C. E.   Fall of Roman Empire.
Legends of
                         Arthur as King and God
derived from
                         Greek Gods become popular
in British
                         Isles.

c. 600 C. E.   Islam- Muhammad, Egypt-
Arabia.

c. 700 C. E.   Sufism-Mystical Islam,
Arabia,
                         Turkey, Egypt.

c. 712 C. E.   Shintoism, Japan.

c.1,095 - 1,270 C. E. Crusades of Europe against
the Muslims

the Orient   led to increased contact with

                         and the European
renaissance.

c. 1,000-1,500 C. E.   Invasion of India by
Muslims.

c. 1,200 C. E.   Kabbalism, Jewish.

c. 1,300 C. E.   European Renaissance.
c. 1,450 C. E.   Sikhism (Muslim-Hindu),
India.

c. 1611 C.E.   King James Version of Old
and New
                         Testament.

The preceding dates are approximations. They
represent the approximate date in which the
religious precepts were first codified.
Archeological and sociological history suggest that
all of these systems
undoubtedly existed for a long time before actually
being "written down".

*Mystery religions based on the Egyptian
mysteries of Aset and Asar and those of Buddha
and Krishna (India).

CLOSING NOTE from the author and the editor.

The Egyptian mysteries (higher spiritual teachings), as with most ancient sciences and mythological systems, were developed for the enlightenment of all, according to the individual's level of spirit-soul development. It was, as it is today, up to the individual to seek beyond the outer expressions of religions and philosophies and to find their own way to freedom.

We begin life as helpless individuals and then take on the virtues, failings and errors of our first teachers. If as we mature we do not realize their errors, we will continue on the path of instability and unhappiness, believing that "this is life."

SALVATION IS THE HIGHEST GOAL in a world of illusory and transitory pleasures that end in "death". If you concentrate or focus your mind and ponder the ancient philosophies of the world, this becomes readily apparent. For even the pleasures and happy moments of the world lead to more let downs and the endless search for the next "happy" moment. Is there no better way to achieve an everlasting, ever present happiness, regardless of the circumstance that one may find oneself in?

Our ignorance causes us to look outside ourselves to someone else, a country, a group of people, a doctrine or a possession for happiness and pleasure, when we already have all the tools necessary for our own salvation and the power to provide for our own health and happiness.

We are obliged to do our own research, and then, we must put into practice what we have learned, otherwise, it will be worthless. These studies led us to the conclusion that all of the world religions have a basis of commonality in their origin and basic philosophy; differences would seem to be due to individual interpretations and the personality of the original exponents and the religious leaders who followed them throughout history.

The right time?

When the mind asks questions like: Who am "I" really?, Why am "I" not truly happy? Is this all that "I" am?, What is "my" purpose?, Who is "me"?, and Is there more to life than this?, then it is time to seek answers. One may seek information from many sources such as self help groups, books or religious organizations, but what does it all mean? Who will help you sort it out? WHO will guide "you" on your search?

There is only one person that can manage your growth as an individual: *YOU.* Otherwise you risk wasting your most valuable resource, yourself, by trusting in others to do your job. Do not be lazy. Prove things for yourself, and when a real master appears, either in physical form or otherwise, you will *KNOW,* and not just think you know. You will trust that person implicitly and you will progress quickly. Even if there is no master in the physical form, trust your intuition. Intuition can be a form of inspiration from the invisible world for all who ask with sincerity and virtue.

"When the student is ready the master will appear."

The search for self is a science, an initiatic science for those who wish to be all they truly can be. It is open to all who wish to achieve the greatest freedom, regardless of race, sex, or country of origin. Get all the book knowledge you can and then put it into practice.

Don't let others who are ignorant discourage you with their ignorance, and most importantly, don't let your own conditioning and closed-mindedness stand in your way. These are only obstacles to test your determination.

If you make truth your only objective, you will arrive at what only you can discover: the truth. Search for a Master who has as his or her goal, the upliftment of humanity or pray for divine assistance; it will come.

The only limitation is in ignorance. Practice the teachings. Discover the higher self within.

"Ignorance is slavery", whether to food, to pleasures outside of the body, to others, to our emotions and erroneous beliefs, or to cosmic forces that exist in the universe.

> *"Ask and it shall be given, seek and ye shall find, knock and it shall be opened."*

This teaching provides a formula for the seekers of truth. Never be satisfied with what you are told, only with what you know in your heart.

The search for answers begins with one's own dissatisfaction with life, the deep rooted feeling that something isn't right, that this is not how life is supposed to be. Book learning must continue with a spiritual preceptor, as well as teaching from within, using one's intuition. Look into meditation and physical purification, i.e. natural diet.

Explore the effects of diet on the mind and body. Note the changes in your ability to control your mind. Discover the changes that a chemical free (organic) and meat free (vegetarian) diet will "*ALLOW*" you to make. Find out why ancient sages warned against food additives and the effect of meat eating on your ability to control your emotions and bodily functions.

Physically, in dreams or otherwise, you will KNOW. Original Sages such as Ptahotep (Egyptian Sage), Jesus, Mohammed, Buddha, etc., said their teachings were to help us become like them: Masters of Love.

Strive to realize that good and evil, male and female, black and white, Ying and Yang, life and death, etc. are but two sides of the same reality.

The path from slavery to self mastery may be viewed as follows: First, one must believe that one's deepest being (self) is divine. Then, rising above earthly thinking, *Geb,* and with the help of their *Aset,* the mothering, loving principle and *Anpu,* the faculty of discerning friend and foe, the task is to practice *MAAT.* We must develop the intuitive and understanding faculty, *Saa,* so that we may understand the wisdom of the teachings which will allow us to control the senses, Hu.

Armed with the nurturing faculty, *Aset,* discrimination, *Anpu,* the Law, *MAAT,* understanding and intelligence, *Saa and Hu,* having purified ourselves, we become *Min,* full of sublimated sexual fire. We can now marry *Hetheru.* She is the love, fertility, sensuality and beauty faculty of our deepest self. Now we are ready to do battle with our own ignorance and evil tendencies, our lower nature, *Set.*

Having vanquished Set, we are now ready to "know", to experience the truth *(Djehuti),* and not just have information and be intelligent about it. We have sublimated the *Eye of Ra,* the Life Force. We will experience the Absolute Divinity inside us.

The direct path of Yoga is a mental discipline and involves the renunciation of all things in the world as individual objects with names and forms. Your wisdom now allows you to understand that ALL the objects of the world are only appearing as they do because of an illusion created by relative reality. In order to transcend this illusory condition, it is necessary to engage oneself in a constant discipline of mental detachment, dispassion and renunciation of all objects, including possessions, the body, the mind, and most importantly, the ego sense. You are not a limited personality. You are the Universal immortal and eternal spirit who operates through the use of a body and thinking mind.

<u>IMPORTANT:</u> This discipline is MENTAL and does not require you to give up your "possessions", nor does it require that you retire to a secluded mountain top location. A higher understanding will reveal that matter, that is to say, the objects of the world that are treated as possessions, are not in themselves evil, rather, evil thoughts, behaviors, feelings arise out of an immature understanding of what matter is and what should be the proper attitude that one should cultivate towards it. Peace can be found in the noisiest city if the techniques of wisdom are understood and applied properly. Therefore, it would not be necessary to make a pilgrimage to Egypt since after all, the trip <u>must</u> ultimately be a mental one and further, Egypt represented a reflection of heaven, not heaven itself. Therefore, if a trip is possible, that would be fine to the extent that it helps one to move closer to the divine, but the main goal must be to reach and touch the divine, which is the underlying reality behind every physical thing in existence, including the land called Egypt. This task can be accomplished anywhere in the world where it may be possible to grow in wisdom and which provides the opportunity to perform inward movement and exploration (meditation).

Ultimately, Yoga is a mental discipline, supported by physical health, which requires: *"COMPLETE UNDERSTANDING OF REALITY AS IT TRULY IS."* Exercises are performed to condition the body and nervous system to a form that will promote sufficient health and physical purity to produce an internal environment in which spiritual attainment may be possible.

We must clean out our subconscious mind which has impressions of a world of multiplicity and replace them with impressions of the ABSOLUTE REALITY, the truth, which indicates that all things are ONE.

This is done through acquiring wisdom and "DWELLING" (meditating) on it constantly until it becomes the reality. It is also important to understand that this is an integral path. That is to say, nothing needs to be given up except erroneous notions of who you are and what the world is. In doing so, you will continue to perform your worldly duties and interact with people but internally, mentally, you will always remain steadfast in the knowledge of what is to most people occult (hidden) truth. Through detachment from that which is illusory, we can join with and love the only reality there is: GOD. In this realization alone lies eternal salvation.

Simple but not necessarily easy!

The main doctrines of attaining self mastery and expansion in consciousness are said to be simple, but simple does not necessarily mean easy. Many people find them hard to believe and understand despite their simplicity.

Now you have very high intellectual knowledge, but this is not enough. GOD cannot be known by thinking. It is necessary to go beyond the thinking process to the wisdom-knowing state of being. This is the state wherein the human attains the "Godlike" state of consciousness. This can be accomplished through listening, reflection, and meditation on the teachings.

No one sees a problem when a basketball, football or tennis player practices 8-10 hours a day to become "perfect." But when someone tries to institute a rigorous spiritual discipline, they are called fanatics, insane, etc. Yet how can we expect to become good at spirituality if we do not practice? Practice must be continuous. This point cannot be stressed more strongly. Spiritual discipline must be maintained until one becomes "Godlike" in consciousness. This is the highest good.

Now you must concentrate your life in this direction, regardless of the activity you engage in: sitting, standing, walking, on the phone, driving, while making love.

While you carry out the normal duties, be detached from them, always KNOWING it is all GOD, until you don't have to make any effort to remember WHO you are.

"If you travel on a road made by your own hands each day, you will arrive at the place where you would want to be."

Egyptian Proverb

You will know who you are all the time and you will live in this peace, never getting caught up in the illusory desires for worldly things. Even when your body sleeps, you will remain always conscious, knowing you are dreaming. You will be the master in the waking everyday state and during sleep. To become enlightened requires a one pointed unwavering desire to put GOD (your higher self) first in your life, that is, before all other egotistical desires. Endurance, patience and discipline are required as this (for most) cannot be achieved overnight, and perhaps not even in this lifetime. However, this should not discourage one because enlightenment is not really something to seek; it is what we already are, enlightened beings, however because of our ignorance, we are unable to experience this true nature.

Therefore, one should always have a sense of eternity about its attainment, "I have all the time in the world to accomplish this goal", yet at the same time maintain a sense of the present moment, the only true time we (as bodies) really have, "I will achieve enlightenment in this very lifetime."

There is a tendency to become overwhelmed by a sense of urgency or overly enthusiastic when one first gains understanding into the mysteries of enlightenment. This fire is fueled by a tremendous release of energy due to the removal of energy blocks caused by ignorance.

Caution must be exercised and one must adhere to the philosophy of MAAT (balance) as one proceeds.

Do not apply undue pressure and criticism on oneself, and do not feel regretful if you feel the need to "take a break" from thinking about the teaching and hang out with those you have now termed "negative". This is the process of integration. Trust your spirit to guide you. Change is a process; it takes time and requires the utmost patience, with oneself and with others (who are really oneself, having come from the same father-mother GOD).

Eventually one will realize that these "negative" people are nothing more than other souls, who, like you, are searching for that ultimate bliss, albeit in all the wrong ways and places, much in the same way as you once did. Thus, one realizes that there are really no negative people, just various degrees of ignorance. With this insight, one can convert anger and frustration into feelings of compassion and understanding for others. *"let he who is without sin cast the first stone."*

Explore the power of positive affirmation which restructures the subconscious impressions. Even though trying to better one's actions and behaviors, there may be times when one feels that they are making no progress or are even regressing, however, with continued striving (effort) towards the goal and affirmation of the goal, whether it is waking up earlier in the morning to do spiritual exercises or stop smoking, it will be achieved.

Once we experience the power that positive affirmation can have in our lives, we will develop faith in the process. As this faith becomes rooted deeply in one's heart, one will KNOW that they will also realize the goal of enlightenment, and regardless of the outer realities of one's life, inwardly, one will steadfastly continue to affirm that goal.

The problem is, we judge and criticize ourselves much too harshly, and we give up too easily, telling ourselves, we are too weak or we have no willpower. So what if it takes 1000 tries of stopping smoking before one is able to stop. Isn't it better to quit at the age of 50 or 60 than not at all in this lifetime.

It's a good thing our parents did not give up on us when we were first learning to walk and kept falling down or that we did not know how to have self defeatist attitudes, otherwise we would still be crawling our hands and knees today. So, no matter if we are falling on our faces or behinds with our efforts, we must still continue to strive forth, because we know: *"The truth shall set us free".*

Engage in activities that help you remember the teaching. The music you play, the places you go, the people you live and associate with, make sure these are not dragging you into negative thoughts, acts or feelings. If they are, always take your time away. Read elevating texts, contact someone who is ahead of you in spiritual development (preferably a Sage, Guru, or other Enlightened person).

The technique of maintaining "Good Association" is called "Satsang" in Indian Yoga discipline. The admonition given by Egyptian texts is *"Keep company of the Sages and Wise Ones."* The main goal is to keep the mind full of elevated thoughts and gradually purify the subconscious until any ideas of a world of "many" objects is gone. Also, the "subtle desires" which cause you to desire worldly objects will be cleaned out. It is the desire for worldly objects that is keeping you from controlling the senses to calm the mind. A calm mind is essential to attaining the "Beatific Vision" of GOD.

𓀀 𓀁 𓏺 𓊼 𓈖 𓏏 𓊖 𓈖 𓃀 𓈖

"𓀀 𓀁 *man and woman achieve the highest good* 𓏺 *(Godhood) and eternal life* 𓊼 𓈖 *through stability* 𓊽 *(Djed) of the vital life force* 𓊼 *(Buto), mental equanimity and good judgment* 𓆄 *(Maat), Wisdom* 𓊖 *(Djehuti), Love for self and others* 𓃀, *and Devotion* 𓂓 *(Ka) to the Self!"*

ADMONITIONS FOR THE SPIRITUAL SEEKER

FROM ANCIENT EGYPT:

"When the ears of the student are ready to hear, then come the lips to fill them with wisdom."

"The lips of Wisdom are closed, except to the ears of Understanding."

"When the student is ready the master will appear."

"Those who understand or believe will be persecuted and ridiculed."

"Of all marvels, that which most wins our wonder is that man has been able to find out the nature of the Gods and bring it into play. Since then, our earliest progenitors were in great error-seeing they had no rational faith about the Gods, and that they paid no heed unto their cult and holy worship-they chanced upon an art whereby they made Gods. To this invention they conjoined a power that suited it derived from cosmic nature; and blending these together, since souls they could not make, they evoked daemon's souls or those of angels; and attached them to their sacred images and holy mysteries, so that the statues should, by means of these, possess the powers of doing good and the reverse."

"Such words as these have few to give them ear; nay, probably they will not even have the few. They have, moreover, some strange force peculiar to themselves, for they provoke evil unto even more evil."

"And now that thou hast learnt these lessons, make promise to keep silence on thy virtue, and to no soul, make known the handling on to you the manner of Rebirth, that we may not be thought to be calumniators."

"Keep this sermon from translation in order that such mighty Mysteries might not come to the Greeks and to the disdainful speech of Greece, with all its looseness and its surface beauty, taking all the strength out of the solemn and the strong - the energetic speech of Names."

"Unto those who come across these words, their composition will seem most simple and clear; but on the contrary, as this is unclear, and has the true meaning of its words concealed, it will be still unclear, when, afterwards, the Greeks will want to turn our tongue into their own - for this will be a very great distorting and obscuring of even what has heretofore been written. Turned into our own native tongue, the teachings keepeth clear the meaning of the words. For that its very quality of sound, the very power of Egyptian names, have in themselves the bringing into act of what is said."

"Avoid conversing with the many on your knowledge; not to keep it selfishly but to not seem ridiculous unto the multitude. The like's acceptable to the like; the unlike's never friend to the unlike."

"Let these words rest in the casket of thy belly, that they may act as a peg on thy tongue."

"The truth shall set you free"

"The spirit is life and the body is for living."

FROM INDIA:

"In the same way as the unwise act with attachment, so should the wise act without attachment for the guidance of the world... and let not the wise unsettle the understanding of the ignorant, attached to action and worldly objects, but acting himself with equipoise should engage them in action also."

From the Bhagavad-Gita 3.25-26

FROM CHINA:

"They who speak do not know; they who know do not speak."

From the Tao Te Ching

Reading List

EGYPTIAN PYRAMID TEXTS
EGYPTIAN COFFIN TEXTS
EGYPTIAN BOOK OF COMING FORTH BY DAY OF UNAS
EGYPTIAN BOOK OF COMING FORTH BY DAY OF ANHAI
EGYPTIAN BOOK OF COMING FORTH BY DAY OF ANI
EGYPTIAN BOOK OF COMING FORTH BY DAY OF KENNA
EGYPTIAN BOOK OF COMING FORTH BY DAY OF ANKHWAHIBRE
PYRAMID TEXTS OF THE PYRAMID OF UNAS
STELE OF TEHUTI-NEFER
STELE OF ABU
THE GREENFIELD PAPYRUS
THE EBERS PAPYRUS
THE TURIN PAPYRUS
VARIOUS PAPYRI
"Rig Veda" by Aryan and Indian Sages
"TemTTchaas: Egyptian Proverbs" by Muata Ashby
"The Bible" by ancient Essene priest (original Christians)
"Gnostic Gospels" by ancient Essene priest (original Christians)
"The Mystery of the Sphinx" on video by John Anthony West
"The Ancient Egyptian" by Sir J. Gardner Wilkinson
"Health Secrets from The Ancient World" by John Heiinerman
"Ancient Egypt the Light of the World " by Gerald Massey
"The Gods of the Egyptians Vol. I,II" by E. Wallis Budge
"Hindu Myths" by Wendy O'Flaherty
"The Great Book of Tantra" by Indra Sinha
"SADHANA" By Swami Sivananda
"The Kybalion" by Hermes Trismegistos
 "Vivekacudamani" by Shankaracarya
"African Presence in Early Asia" edited by Ivan Van Sertima and Runoko Rashidi
"Jnana Yoga" by Swami Jyotirmayananda
"Serpent in the Sky" by John Anthony West
"The fruits of The Tree of Life" by O. M. Aivanhov
"Sports and Games of Ancient Egypt" by Wolfgang Decker
"Civilization or Barbarism" by Cheikh Anta Diop
"Smithsonian Magazine" June 1993
"Echoes of the Old Darkland" by Dr. Charles Finch
"The Bhagavad Gita" translated by Antonio DE Nicolas
"The Opening of the Way" by Isha Schwaller DE Lubicz
"Sacred Science" by R.A. Schwaller DE Lubicz
"The Goddess Sekmet" by Robert Masters
"Life Force" by Leo Ludzia
"Recovering the Soul" by Dr. Larry Dossey
"Know Thyself: Jnana Yoga" by Omram Mikhael Aivanov
"Mind- It's Mysteries and Control" By Swami Sivananda
"Stolen Legacy" by George G.M. James
"Egyptian Book of the Dead" by E. Wallis Budge
"Egyptian Book of the Dead" by R.O. Faulkner
"The Upanishads" by Swami Prabhavananda
"African Presence in Early Asia" by Dr. Ivan Van Sertima
"Hero of a Thousand Faces" by Dr. Joseph Campbel
"Creative Work: Karma Yoga" by Edmond Bordeaux Szekely
"Origin and Evolution of Religion" by Albert Churchward
"The Tantric Way" by Ajit Mookerjee and Madhu Khanna
"Kundalini" by Gopi Krishna
"Myths and Symbol in Ancient Egypt" by R.T. Rundle Clark
"The Secret of The Golden Flower: A Chinese Book of Life" Translation by Richard Wilhelm

INDEX

Other Books From C. M. Books

P.O.Box 570459
Miami, Florida, 33257
(305) 378-6253 Fax: (305) 378-6253

THE YOGA AND MYSTICAL SPIRITUALITY BOOK
SERIES

This book is part of a series on the study and practice of Ancient Egyptian Yoga and Mystical Spirituality based on the writings of Dr. Muata Abhaya Ashby. They are also part of the Egyptian Yoga Course provided by the Sema Institute of Yoga. Below you will find a listing of the other books in this series. For more information send for the Egyptian Yoga Book-Audio-Video Catalog or the Egyptian Yoga Course Catalog.

Now you can study the teachings of Egyptian and Indian Yoga wisdom and Spirituality with the Egyptian Yoga Mystical Spirituality Series. The Egyptian Yoga Series takes you through the Initiation process and lead you to understand the mysteries of the soul and the Divine and to attain the highest goal of life: ENLIGHTENMENT. The Egyptian Yoga Series, takes you on an in depth study of Ancient Egyptian mythology and their inner mystical meaning. Each Book is prepared for the serious student of the mystical sciences and provides a study of the teachings along with exercises, assignments and projects to make the teachings understood and effective in real life. The Series is part of the Egyptian Yoga course but may be purchased even if you are not taking the course. The series is ideal for study groups.

Prices subject to change.

1. EGYPTIAN YOGA: THE PHILOSOPHY OF ENLIGHTENMENT An original, fully illustrated work, including hieroglyphs, detailing the meaning of the Egyptian mysteries, tantric yoga, psycho-spiritual and physical exercises. Egyptian Yoga is a guide to the practice of the highest spiritual philosophy which leads to absolute freedom from human misery and to immortality. It is well known by scholars that Egyptian philosophy is the basis of Western and Middle Eastern religious philosophies such as *Christianity, Islam, Judaism,* the *Kabala,* and Greek philosophy, but what about Indian philosophy, Yoga and Taoism? What were the original teachings? How can they be practiced today? What is the source of pain and suffering in the world and what is the solution? Discover the deepest mysteries of the mind and universe within and outside of your self. 8.5" X 11" ISBN: 1-884564-01-1 Soft $19.95

2. EGYPTIAN YOGA II: The Supreme Wisdom of Enlightenment by Dr. Muata Ashby ISBN 1-884564-39-9 $23.95 U.S. In this long awaited sequel to *Egyptian Yoga: The Philosophy of Enlightenment* you will take a fascinating and enlightening journey back in time and discover the teachings which constituted the epitome of Ancient Egyptian spiritual wisdom. What are the disciplines which lead to the fulfillment of all desires? Delve into the three states of consciousness (waking, dream and deep sleep)

and the fourth state which transcends them all, Neberdjer, "The Absolute." These teachings of the city of Waset (Thebes) were the crowning achievement of the Sages of Ancient Egypt. They establish the standard mystical keys for understanding the profound mystical symbolism of the Triad of human consciousness.

3.   THE KAMITAN DIET GUIDE TO HEALTH, DIET AND FASTING Health issues have always been important to human beings since the beginning of time. The earliest records of history show that the art of healing was held in high esteem since the time of Ancient Egypt. In the early 20th century, medical doctors had almost attained the status of sainthood by the promotion of the idea that they alone were "scientists" while other healing modalities and traditional healers who did not follow the "scientific method' were nothing but superstitious, ignorant charlatans who at best would take the money of their clients and at worst kill them with the unscientific "snake oils" and "irrational theories". In the late 20th century, the failure of the modern medical establishment's ability to lead the general public to good health, promoted the move by many in society towards "alternative medicine". Alternative medicine disciplines are those healing modalities which do not adhere to the philosophy of allopathic medicine. Allopathic medicine is what medical doctors practice by an large. It is the theory that disease is caused by agencies outside the body such as bacteria, viruses or physical means which affect the body. These can therefore be treated by medicines and therapies The natural healing method began in the absence of extensive technologies with the idea that all the answers for health may be found in nature or rather, the deviation from nature. Therefore, the health of the body can be restored by correcting the aberration and thereby restoring balance. This is the area that will be covered in this volume. Allopathic techniques have their place in the art of healing. However, we should not forget that the body is a grand achievement of the spirit and built into it is the capacity to maintain itself and heal itself. Ashby, Muata ISBN: 1-884564-49-6 $24.95

4.   INITIATION INTO EGYPTIAN YOGA Shedy: Spiritual discipline or program, to go deeply into the mysteries, to study the mystery teachings and literature profoundly, to penetrate the mysteries. You will learn about the mysteries of initiation into the teachings and practice of Yoga and how to become an Initiate of the mystical sciences. This insightful manual is the first in a series which introduces you to the goals of daily spiritual and yoga practices: Meditation, Diet, Words of Power and the ancient wisdom teachings. 8.5" X 11" ISBN 1-884564-02-X   Soft Cover $24.95 U.S.

5.   *THE AFRICAN ORIGINS OF CIVILIZATION, MYSTICAL RELIGION AND YOGA PHILOSOPHY* HARD COVER EDITION ISBN: 1-884564-50-X $80.00 U.S.   81/2" X 11"   Part 1, Part 2, Part 3 in one volume 683 Pages Hard Cover First Edition Three volumes in one. Over the past several years I have been asked to put together in one volume the most important evidences showing the correlations and common teachings between Kamitan (Ancient Egyptian) culture and religion and that of India. The questions of the history of Ancient Egypt, and the latest archeological evidences showing civilization and culture in Ancient Egypt and its spread to other countries, has intrigued many scholars as well as mystics over the years. Also, the possibility that Ancient Egyptian Priests and Priestesses migrated to Greece, India and other countries to carry on the traditions of the Ancient Egyptian Mysteries, has been speculated over the years as well. In chapter 1 of the book *Egyptian Yoga The Philosophy of Enlightenment,* 1995, I first introduced the deepest comparison between Ancient Egypt and India that had been brought forth up to that time. Now, in the year 2001 this new book, *THE AFRICAN ORIGINS OF CIVILIZATION, MYSTICAL RELIGION AND YOGA PHILOSOPHY,* more fully explores the motifs, symbols and philosophical correlations between Ancient Egyptian and Indian mysticism and clearly shows not only that Ancient Egypt and India were connected culturally but also spiritually. How does this knowledge help the spiritual aspirant? This discovery has great importance for the Yogis and mystics who follow the philosophy of Ancient Egypt and the mysticism of India. It means that India has a longer history and heritage than was previously understood. It shows that the mysteries of Ancient Egypt were essentially a yoga tradition which did not die but rather developed into the modern day systems of Yoga technology of India. It

further shows that African culture developed Yoga Mysticism earlier than any other civilization in history. All of this expands our understanding of the unity of culture and the deep legacy of Yoga, which stretches into the distant past, beyond the Indus Valley civilization, the earliest known high culture in India as well as the Vedic tradition of Aryan culture. Therefore, Yoga culture and mysticism is the oldest known tradition of spiritual development and Indian mysticism is an extension of the Ancient Egyptian mysticism. By understanding the legacy which Ancient Egypt gave to India the mysticism of India is better understood and by comprehending the heritage of Indian Yoga, which is rooted in Ancient Egypt the Mysticism of Ancient Egypt is also better understood. This expanded understanding allows us to prove the underlying kinship of humanity, through the common symbols, motifs and philosophies which are not disparate and confusing teachings but in reality expressions of the same study of truth through metaphysics and mystical realization of Self. (HARD COVER)

6. AFRICAN ORIGINS BOOK 1 PART 1 African Origins of African Civilization, Religion, Yoga Mysticism and Ethics Philosophy-Soft Cover $24.95 ISBN: 1-884564-55-0

7. AFRICAN ORIGINS BOOK 2 PART 2 African Origins of Western Civilization, Religion and Philosophy(Soft) -Soft Cover $24.95 ISBN: 1-884564-56-9

8. EGYPT AND INDIA (AFRICAN ORIGINS BOOK 3 PART 3) African Origins of Eastern Civilization, Religion, Yoga Mysticism and Philosophy-Soft Cover $29.95 (Soft) ISBN: 1-884564-57-7

9. THE MYSTERIES OF ASET: The Path of Wisdom, Immortality and Enlightenment   Through the study of ancient myth and the illumination of initiatic understanding the idea of God is expanded from the mythological comprehension to the metaphysical. Then this metaphysical understanding is related to you, the student, so as to begin understanding your true divine nature. ISBN 1-884564-24-0 $24.99

10. EGYPTIAN PROVERBS: TEMT TCHAAS *Temt Tchaas* means: collection of ——Ancient Egyptian Proverbs How to live according to MAAT Philosophy. Beginning Meditation. All proverbs are indexed for easy searches. For the first time in one volume, ——Ancient Egyptian Proverbs, wisdom teachings and meditations, fully illustrated with hieroglyphic text and symbols. EGYPTIAN PROVERBS is a unique collection of knowledge and wisdom which you can put into practice today and transform your life. 5.5"x 8.5" $14.95 U.S   ISBN: 1-884564-00-3

11. THE PATH OF DIVINE LOVE The Process of Mystical Transformation and The Path of Divine Love This Volume will focus on the ancient wisdom teachings and how to use them in a scientific process for self-transformation. Also, this volume will detail the process of transformation from ordinary consciousness to cosmic consciousness through the integrated practice of the teachings and the path of Devotional Love toward the Divine. 5.5"x 8.5" ISBN 1-884564-11-9 $22.99

12. INTRODUCTION TO MAAT PHILOSOPHY: Spiritual Enlightenment Through the Path of Virtue Known as Karma Yoga in India, the teachings of MAAT for living virtuously and with orderly wisdom are explained and the student is to begin practicing the precepts of Maat in daily life so as to promote the process of purification of the heart in preparation for the judgment of the soul. This judgment will be understood not as an event that will occur at the time of death but as an event that occurs continuously, at every moment in the life of the individual. The student will learn how to become allied with the forces of the Higher Self and to thereby begin cleansing the mind (heart) of impurities so as to attain a higher vision of reality. ISBN 1-884564-20-8 $22.99

13. MEDITATION The Ancient Egyptian Path to Enlightenment   Many people do not know about the rich history of meditation practice in Ancient Egypt. This volume outlines the theory of meditation and presents the Ancient Egyptian Hieroglyphic text which give instruction as to the nature of the mind and

its three modes of expression. It also presents the texts which give instruction on the practice of meditation for spiritual Enlightenment and unity with the Divine. This volume allows the reader to begin practicing meditation by explaining, in easy to understand terms, the simplest form of meditation and working up to the most advanced form which was practiced in ancient times and which is still practiced by yogis around the world in modern times. ISBN 1-884564-27-7 $24.99

14. THE GLORIOUS LIGHT MEDITATION TECHNIQUE OF ANCIENT EGYPT ISBN: 1-884564-15-1$14.95 (PB) New for the year 2000. This volume is based on the earliest known instruction in history given for the practice of formal meditation. Discovered by Dr. Muata Ashby, it is inscribed on the walls of the Tomb of Seti I in Thebes Egypt. This volume details the philosophy and practice of this unique system of meditation originated in Ancient Egypt and the earliest practice of meditation known in the world which occurred in the most advanced African Culture.

15. THE SERPENT POWER: The Ancient Egyptian Mystical Wisdom of the Inner Life Force.   This Volume specifically deals with the latent life Force energy of the universe and in the human body, its control and sublimation. How to develop the Life Force energy of the subtle body. This Volume will introduce the esoteric wisdom of the science of how virtuous living acts in a subtle and mysterious way to cleanse the latent psychic energy conduits and vortices of the spiritual body. ISBN 1-884564-19-4 $22.95

16. EGYPTIAN YOGA MEDITATION IN MOTION Thef Neteru: *The Movement of The Gods and Goddesses* Discover the physical postures and exercises practiced thousands of years ago in Ancient Egypt which are today known as Yoga exercises. This work is based on the pictures and teachings from the Creation story of Ra, The Asarian Resurrection Myth and the carvings and reliefs from various Temples in Ancient Egypt 8.5" X 11" ISBN 1-884564-10-0 Soft Cover $18.99   Exercise video $21.99

17. EGYPTIAN TANTRA YOGA: The Art of Sex Sublimation and Universal Consciousness This Volume will expand on the male and female principles within the human body and in the universe and further detail the sublimation of sexual energy into spiritual energy. The student will study the deities Min and Hetheru, Asar and Aset, Geb and Nut and discover the mystical implications for a practical spiritual discipline. This Volume will also focus on the Tantric aspects of Ancient Egyptian and Indian mysticism, the purpose of sex and the mystical teachings of sexual sublimation which lead to self-knowledge and Enlightenment. 5.5"x 8.5" ISBN 1-884564-03-8 $24.95

18. ASARIAN RELIGION: RESURRECTING ASAR The path of Mystical Awakening and the Keys to Immortality NEW REVISED AND EXPANDED EDITION! The Ancient Sages created stories based on human and superhuman beings whose struggles, aspirations, needs and desires ultimately lead them to discover their true Self. The myth of Aset, Asar and Heru is no exception in this area. While there is no one source where the entire story may be found, pieces of it are inscribed in various ancient Temples walls, tombs, steles and papyri. For the first time available, the complete myth of Asar, Aset and Heru has been compiled from original Ancient Egyptian, Greek and Coptic Texts. This epic myth has been richly illustrated with reliefs from the Temple of Heru at Edfu, the Temple of Aset at Philae, the Temple of Asar at Abydos, the Temple of Hetheru at Denderah and various papyri, inscriptions and reliefs. Discover the myth which inspired the teachings of the *Shetaut Neter* (Egyptian Mystery System - Egyptian Yoga) and the Egyptian Book of Coming Forth By Day. Also, discover the three levels of Ancient Egyptian Religion, how to understand the mysteries of the Duat or Astral World and how to discover the abode of the Supreme in the Amenta, *The Other World*   The ancient religion of Asar, Aset and Heru, if properly understood, contains all of the elements necessary to lead the sincere aspirant to attain immortality through inner self-discovery. This volume presents the entire myth and explores the main mystical themes and rituals associated with the myth for understating human existence, creation and the way to achieve spiritual emancipation - *Resurrection.* The Asarian myth is so powerful that it influenced

and is still having an effect on the major world religions. Discover the origins and mystical meaning of the Christian Trinity, the Eucharist ritual and the ancient origin of the birthday of Jesus Christ. Soft Cover ISBN: 1-884564-27-5 $24.95

19. THE EGYPTIAN BOOK OF THE DEAD MYSTICISM OF THE PERT EM HERU $26.95 ISBN# 1-884564-28-3 Size: 8½" X 11" I Know myself, I know myself, I am One With God!–From the Pert Em Heru "The Ru Pert em Heru" or "Ancient Egyptian Book of The Dead," or "Book of Coming Forth By Day" as it is more popularly known, has fascinated the world since the successful translation of Ancient Egyptian hieroglyphic scripture over 150 years ago. The astonishing writings in it reveal that the Ancient Egyptians believed in life after death and in an ultimate destiny to discover the Divine. The elegance and aesthetic beauty of the hieroglyphic text itself has inspired many see it as an art form in and of itself. But is there more to it than that? Did the Ancient Egyptian wisdom contain more than just aphorisms and hopes of eternal life beyond death? In this volume Dr. Muata Ashby, the author of over 25 books on Ancient Egyptian Yoga Philosophy has produced a new translation of the original texts which uncovers a mystical teaching underlying the sayings and rituals instituted by the Ancient Egyptian Sages and Saints. "Once the philosophy of Ancient Egypt is understood as a mystical tradition instead of as a religion or primitive mythology, it reveals its secrets which if practiced today will lead anyone to discover the glory of spiritual self-discovery. The Pert em Heru is in every way comparable to the Indian Upanishads or the Tibetan Book of the Dead." Muata Abhaya Ashby

20. ANUNIAN THEOLOGY THE MYSTERIES OF RA The Philosophy of Anu and The Mystical Teachings of The Ancient Egyptian Creation Myth Discover the mystical teachings contained in the Creation Myth and the gods and goddesses who brought creation and human beings into existence. The Creation Myth holds the key to understanding the universe and for attaining spiritual Enlightenment. ISBN: 1-884564-38-0 40 pages $14.95

21. MYSTERIES OF MIND AND MEMPHITE THEOLOGY Mysticism of Ptah, Egyptian Physics and Yoga Metaphysics and the Hidden properties of Matter This Volume will go deeper into the philosophy of God as creation and will explore the concepts of modern science and how they correlate with ancient teachings. This Volume will lay the ground work for the understanding of the philosophy of universal consciousness and the initiatic/yogic insight into who or what is God? ISBN 1-884564-07-0 $21.95

22. THE GODDESS AND THE EGYPTIAN MYSTERIESTHE PATH OF THE GODDESS THE GODDESS PATH The Secret Forms of the Goddess and the Rituals of Resurrection The Supreme Being may be worshiped as father or as mother. *Ushet Rekhat* or *Mother Worship*, is the spiritual process of worshipping the Divine in the form of the Divine Goddess. It celebrates the most important forms of the Goddess including *Nathor, Maat, Aset, Arat, Amentet and Hetheru* and explores their mystical meaning as well as the rising of *Sirius,* the star of Aset (Aset) and the new birth of Hor (Heru). The end of the year is a time of reckoning, reflection and engendering a new or renewed positive movement toward attaining spiritual Enlightenment. The Mother Worship devotional meditation ritual, performed on five days during the month of December and on New Year's Eve, is based on the Ushet Rekhit. During the ceremony, the cosmic forces, symbolized by Sirius - and the constellation of Orion ---, are harnessed through the understanding and devotional attitude of the participant. This propitiation draws the light of wisdom and health to all those who share in the ritual, leading to prosperity and wisdom. $14.95 ISBN 1-884564-18-6

23. *THE MYSTICAL JOURNEY FROM JESUS TO CHRIST* $24.95 ISBN# 1-884564-05-4 size: 8½" X 11" Discover the ancient Egyptian origins of Christianity before the Catholic Church and learn the mystical teachings given by Jesus to assist all humanity in becoming Christlike. Discover the secret meaning of the Gospels that were discovered in Egypt. Also discover how and why so many Christian churches came into being. Discover that the Bible still holds the keys to mystical realization even though its original

writings were changed by the church. Discover how to practice the original teachings of Christianity which leads to the Kingdom of Heaven.

24.   THE STORY OF ASAR, ASET AND HERU: An Ancient Egyptian Legend (For Children)   Now for the first time, the most ancient myth of Ancient Egypt comes alive for children. Inspired by the books *The Asarian Resurrection: The Ancient Egyptian Bible* and *The Mystical Teachings of The Asarian Resurrection, The Story of Asar, Aset and Heru* is an easy to understand and thrilling tale which inspired the children of Ancient Egypt to aspire to greatness and righteousness.   If you and your child have enjoyed stories like *The Lion King* and *Star Wars you will love The Story of Asar, Aset and Heru.* Also, if you know the story of Jesus and Krishna you will discover than Ancient Egypt had a similar myth and that this myth carries important spiritual teachings for living a fruitful and fulfilling life. This book may be used along with *The Parents Guide To The Asarian Resurrection Myth: How to Teach Yourself and Your Child the Principles of Universal Mystical Religion.* The guide provides some background to the Asarian Resurrection myth and it also gives insight into the mystical teachings contained in it which you may introduce to your child. It is designed for parents who wish to grow spiritually with their children and it serves as an introduction for those who would like to study the Asarian Resurrection Myth in depth and to practice its teachings. 41 pages 8.5" X 11"   ISBN: 1-884564-31-3 $12.95

25.   THE PARENTS GUIDE TO THE AUSARIAN RESURRECTION MYTH: How to Teach Yourself and Your Child the Principles of Universal Mystical Religion.   This insightful manual brings for the timeless wisdom of the ancient through the Ancient Egyptian myth of Asar, Aset and Heru and the mystical teachings contained in it for parents who want to guide their children to understand and practice the teachings of mystical spirituality. This manual may be used with the children's storybook *The Story of Asar, Aset and Heru* by Dr. Muata Abhaya Ashby. 5.5"x 8.5"   ISBN: 1-884564-30-5 $14.95

26.   HEALING THE CRIMINAL HEART BOOK 1 Introduction to Maat Philosophy, Yoga and Spiritual Redemption Through the Path of Virtue   Who is a criminal? Is there such a thing as a criminal heart? What is the source of evil and sinfulness and is there any way to rise above it? Is there redemption for those who have committed sins, even the worst crimes?   Ancient Egyptian mystical psychology holds important answers to these questions. Over ten thousand years ago mystical psychologists, the Sages of Ancient Egypt, studied and charted the human mind and spirit and laid out a path which will lead to spiritual redemption, prosperity and Enlightenment.   This introductory volume brings forth the teachings of the Asarian Resurrection, the most important myth of Ancient Egypt, with relation to the faults of human existence: anger, hatred, greed, lust, animosity, discontent, ignorance, egoism jealousy, bitterness, and a myriad of psycho-spiritual ailments which keep a human being in a state of negativity and adversity. 5.5"x 8.5"   ISBN: 1-884564-17-8 $15.95

27.   THEATER & DRAMA OF THE ANCIENT EGYPTIAN MYSTERIES: Featuring the Ancient Egyptian stage play-"The Enlightenment of Hetheru' Based on an Ancient Egyptian Drama, The original Theater - Mysticism of the Temple of Hetheru $14.95 By Dr. Muata Ashby

28.   GUIDE TO PRINT ON DEMAND: SELF-PUBLISH FOR PROFIT, SPIRITUAL FULFILLMENT AND SERVICE TO HUMANITY Everyone asks us how we produced so many books in such a short time. Here are the secrets to writing and producing books that uplift humanity and how to get them printed for a fraction of the regular cost. Anyone can become an author even if they have limited funds. All that is necessary is the willingness to learn how the printing and book business work and the desire to follow the special instructions given here for preparing your manuscript format. Then you take your work directly to the non-traditional companies who can produce your books for less than the traditional book printer can. ISBN: 1-884564-40-2 $16.95 U. S.

29.   Egyptian Mysteries: Vol. 1, Shetaut Neter ISBN: 1-884564-41-0 $19.99 What are the Mysteries? For thousands of years the spiritual tradition of Ancient Egypt, S*hetaut Neter,* "The Egyptian Mysteries," "The Secret Teachings," have fascinated, tantalized and amazed the world. At one time exalted and recognized as the highest culture of the world, by Africans, Europeans, Asiatics, Hindus, Buddhists and other cultures of the ancient world, in time it was shunned by the emerging orthodox world religions. Its temples desecrated, its philosophy maligned, its tradition spurned, its philosophy dormant in the mystical *Medu Neter*, the mysterious hieroglyphic texts which hold the secret symbolic meaning that has scarcely been discerned up to now.   What are the secrets of *Nehast* {spiritual awakening and emancipation, resurrection}. More than just a literal translation, this volume is for awakening to the secret code *Shetitu* of the teaching which was not deciphered by Egyptologists, nor could be understood by ordinary spiritualists. This book is a reinstatement of the original science made available for our times, to the reincarnated followers of Ancient Egyptian culture and the prospect of spiritual freedom to break the bonds of *Khemn,* "ignorance," and slavery to evil forces: *Såaa* .

30.   EGYPTIAN MYSTERIES VOL 2: Dictionary of Gods and Goddesses ISBN: 1-884564-23-2 $19.99 This book is about the mystery of neteru, the gods and goddesses of Ancient Egypt (Kamit, Kemet). Neteru means "Gods and Goddesses." But the Neterian teaching of Neteru represents more than the usual limited modern day concept of "divinities" or "spirits." The Neteru of Kamit are also metaphors, cosmic principles and vehicles for the enlightening teachings of Shetaut Neter (Ancient Egyptian-African Religion). Actually they are the elements for one of the most advanced systems of spirituality ever conceived in human history. Understanding the concept of neteru provides a firm basis for spiritual evolution and the pathway for viable culture, peace on earth and a healthy human society.   Why is it important to have gods and goddesses in our lives? In order for spiritual evolution to be possible, once a human being has accepted that there is existence after death and there is a transcendental being who exists beyond time and space knowledge, human beings need a connection to that which transcends the ordinary experience of human life in time and space and a means to understand the transcendental reality beyond the mundane reality.

31.   EGYPTIAN MYSTERIES VOL. 3 The Priests and Priestesses of Ancient Egypt ISBN: 1-884564-53-4 $22.95 This volume details the path of Neterian priesthood, the joys, challenges and rewards of advanced Neterian life, the teachings that allowed the priests and priestesses to manage the most long lived civilization in human history and how that path can be adopted today; for those who want to tread the path of the Clergy of Shetaut Neter.

32.   THE KING OF EGYPT: The Struggle of Good and Evil for Control of the World and The Human Soul ISBN 1-8840564-44-5 $18.95   Have you seen movies like The Lion King, Hamlet, The Odyssey, or The Little Buddha? These have been some of the most popular movies in modern times. The Sema Institute of Yoga is dedicated to researching and presenting the wisdom and culture of ancient Africa. The Script is designed to be produced as a motion picture but may be addapted for the theater as well. 160 pages bound or unbound (specify with your order) $19.95   copyright 1998 By Dr. Muata Ashby

33.   FROM EGYPT TO GREECE: The Kamitan Origins of Greek Culture and Religion ISBN: 1-884564-47-X $22.95 U.S. FROM EGYPT TO GREECE This insightful manual is a quick reference to Ancient Egyptian mythology and philosophy and its correlation to what later became known as Greek and Rome mythology and philosophy. It outlines the basic tenets of the mythologies and shoes the ancient origins of Greek culture in Ancient Egypt. This volume also acts as a resource for Colleges students who would like to set up fraternities and sororities based on the original Ancient Egyptian principles of Sheti and Maat philosophy. ISBN: 1-884564-47-X $22.95 U.S.

34. THE FORTY TWO PRECEPTS OF MAAT, THE PHILOSOPHY OF RIGHTEOUS ACTION AND THE **ANCIENT EGYPTIAN WISDOM TEXTS <u>ADVANCED STUDIES</u>** This manual is designed for use with the 1998 Maat Philosophy Class conducted by Dr. Muata Ashby. This is a detailed study of Maat Philosophy. It contains a compilation of the 42 laws or precepts of Maat and the corresponding principles which they represent along with the teachings of the ancient Egyptian Sages relating to each. Maat philosophy was the basis of Ancient Egyptian society and government as well as the heart of Ancient Egyptian myth and spirituality. Maat is at once a goddess, a cosmic force and a living social doctrine, which promotes social harmony and thereby paves the way for spiritual evolution in all levels of society. ISBN: 1-884564-48-8 **$1895 U.S**.

Music Based on the Prt M Hru and other Kemetic Texts

Divinity

Music of Ancient Egypt

Muata Ashby

Available on Compact Disc $14.99

Sung with original Ancient Egyptian language and musical instruments

WHAT IS KEMETIC (Ancient Egyptian Spiritual) MUSIC?

From the Ancient Sounds the *Music of Ancient Egypt* Collection is an exploration of Ancient Egyptian musical forms and mystical teachings using Ancient Egyptian musical instrument reproductions to discover the mysteries of Kemetic (Ancient Egyptian) devotional musical feeling. Music that fuses Ancient Egyptian feeling with modern rhythms of the world including West African, Middle Eastern, Soul, Jazz, and East Indian styles. Using authentic the Ancient Egyptian words derived from inscriptions and hymns.

MERIT'S INSPIRATION
NEW Egyptian Yoga Music CD
by Sehu Maa
Ancient Egyptian Music CD
Instrumental Music played on
reproductions of Ancient Egyptian Instruments– Ideal
for <u>meditation</u> and
reflection on the Divine and for the practice of spiritual
programs and <u>Yoga exercise sessions.</u>
©1999 By
Muata Ashby
CD $14.99 –UPC# 761527100429

ANORATIONS TO RA AND HETHERU
NEW Egyptian Yoga Music CD
By Sehu Maa (Muata Ashby)
Based on the Words of Power of Ra and Hetheru
played on reproductions of Ancient Egyptian
Instruments **Ancient Egyptian Instruments used:**
Voice, Clapping, Nefer Lute, Tar Drum, Sistrums,
Cymbals – The Chants, Devotions, Rhythms and
Festive Songs Of the Neteru – Ideal for meditation, and
devotional singing and dancing.
©1999 By Muata Ashby
CD $14.99 –
UPC# 761527100221

SONGS TO ASAR ASET AND HERU (HERU)
NEW
Egyptian Yoga Music CD
By Sehu Maa
played on reproductions of Ancient Egyptian Instruments– The Chants, Devotions, Rhythms and Festive Songs Of the Neteru - Ideal for meditation, and devotional singing and dancing.
Based on the Words of Power of Asar (Asar), Aset (Aset) and Heru (Heru (Heru)) Om Asar Aset Heru is the third in a series of musical explorations of the Kemetic (Ancient Egyptian) tradition of music. Its ideas are based on the Ancient Egyptian Religion of Asar, Aset and Heru (Heru) and it is designed for listening, meditation and worship. ©1999 By Muata Ashby
CD $14.99 –UPC# 761527100122

HAARI OM: ANCIENT EGYPT MEETS INDIA IN MUSIC
NEW Music CD
By Sehu Maa

The Chants, Devotions, Rhythms and
Festive Songs Of the Ancient Egypt and India, harmonized and played on reproductions of ancient instruments along with modern instruments and beats. Ideal for meditation, and devotional singing and dancing.
Haari Om is the fourth in a series of musical explorations of the Kemetic (Ancient Egyptian) and Indian traditions of music, chanting and devotional spiritual practice. Its ideas are based on the Ancient Egyptian Yoga spirituality and Indian Yoga spirituality.
©1999 By Muata Ashby

CD $14.99 –
UPC# 761527100528

RA AKHU: THE GLORIOUS LIGHT
NEW
Egyptian Yoga Music CD
By Sehu Maa
The fifth collection of original music compositions based on the Teachings and Words of The Trinity, the God Asar and the Goddess Nebethet, the Divinity Aten, the God Heru, and the Special Meditation Hekau or Words of Power of Ra from the Ancient Egyptian Tomb of Seti I and more...
played on reproductions of Ancient Egyptian Instruments and modern instruments - **Ancient Egyptian Instruments used: Voice, Clapping, Nefer Lute, Tar Drum, Sistrums, Cymbals**
– The Chants, Devotions, Rhythms and Festive Songs Of the Neteru – Ideal for meditation, and devotional singing and dancing.
©1999 By Muata Ashby
CD $14.99 –
UPC# 761527100825

GLORIES OF THE DIVINE MOTHER
Based on the hieroglyphic text of the worship of Goddess Net.
The Glories of The Great Mother
©2000 Muata Ashby
CD $14.99 UPC# 761527101129

Order Form

Telephone orders: Call Toll Free: 1(305) 378-6253AMEX, Optima, Discover, Visa or MasterCard ready.Fax orders: 1(305) 378-6253

Please send the following books. I understand that I may return any books for a full refund-for any reason, no questions asked.

ITEMS   Cost

_____   _____

_____   _____

_____   _____

_____   _____

_____   _____

_____   _____

                                                    Sub-total   _____

Shipping-Book Rate: Air Mail: $6.50per book and $.50 for each additional

                                                    Shipping   _____

Name:_____

Address:_____

City:_____ State:_____ Zip:_____

Sales tax: Please add 6.5% for books shipped to Florida addresses

_____Payment:_____

_____Check_____

_____Credit card: _____ Visa, _____ MasterCard, _____ Optima, _____ AMEX,
_____ Discover

Card number:_____

Name on card:_____

Exp. date:_____/_____

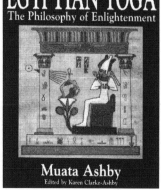

Copyright 1995-2005 r. R. Muata Abhaya Ashby
Sema Institute of Yoga
P.O.Box 570459, Miami Fl. 3327

www.Egyptianyoga.com

Made in the USA
Monee, IL
16 February 2024

53636803R00136